International Trade

INTERNATIONAL TRADE

An Introduction
to Method and Theory

A.Myrick Freeman III

BOWDOIN COLLEGE

HARPER & ROW, PUBLISHERS
New York, Evanston, and London

INTERNATIONAL TRADE: An Introduction to Method and Theory
Copyright © 1971 by A. Myrick Freeman III

Contents

Preface

In writing this book, I tried to accomplish four things which I felt were not done adequately, if at all, in the other books currently on the market. The first was to provide a continuing emphasis on the method of economics as a science throughout the book. I wanted to do this for two reasons. I think that students of economics should come away from their courses with some understanding of why we say that economics is a science rather than a funny branch of geometry (or business management). The introductory textbooks as a rule make some attempts in the first chapter or two to deal with methodological questions; but this is generally ineffective because the student has no frame of reference for what he reads and typically there is no follow-up in the rest of the course. Here I have tried to provide a frame of reference by making the core of the book an exposition of the development and *testing* of alternative hypotheses about the determinants of trade. My second reason is the impression that by learning how the knowledge came into being the student will come away with a firmer grip on the knowledge itself.

Related to the emphasis on methodology is an attempt to help the student discover how we stand right now in terms of our understanding of how the real world works. The chapter on empirical relevance not only states results, both positive and negative, but also attempts to describe the problems faced by empirical investigators and the interaction between empirical work and further theoretical developments. I also felt that some of the new approaches such as the work of Posner and Hufbauer and Kenen should be discussed and related to the conventional analysis by describing it as attempting to make up for the weaknesses of the Heckscher-Ohlin analysis.

Lastly I wanted to make clear the inability of the analyst to make unambiguous statements about the gains from trade or welfare changes without making explicit value judgments about income distribution. For this reason I eschewed the use of community indifference curves in the body of the text. If they are used without a full and careful qualification, the student is likely to overlook the fundamental welfare question. Realizing the popularity of the community indifference curve device in undergraduate teaching, I have included two appendixes in which they are developed and used to discuss the gains from trade and optimum tariffs. For those who wish to use them, they are available; but the text can be used without reference to the appendixes.

I have operated on the assumption that the typical student using this book has had only the introductory course in economics and has forgotten part of what he learned there. Isoquants, production possibilities curves, etc., are developed from scratch. This may be tedious to a few but will probably be appreciated by many. I have kept the exposition nonmathematical.

I would like to express my appreciation to two classes at Bowdoin College who used earlier versions of this material and in various ways helped me to discover where the hard spots were. Professors Phillip Sorensen and Richard Cooper read parts of earlier versions of the manuscript and made helpful suggestions. Carlie Cline typed the manuscript and maintained her usual cheerful outlook all the while.

A. MYRICK FREEMAN III

International Trade

Chapter

The Study
of International Trade

OBJECTIVES

All too often in the academic study of subjects students lose sight of
the general objectives and the significance of their course of study.
In the introductory chapter I try to convey to the reader my notion of
what this book is trying to accomplish and what it all means. Occasional rereadings of the first chapter may help the student to put
the pieces of his day-to-day reading into the larger framework of the
course as a whole.

The objective of this book is to explain the flows of goods and
services among nations engaging in international trade. We seek to
answer the question, "Why do nations trade?" The answer to this
question should take the form of a fully developed theory of international trade. This theory should be capable of developing predictions about the impact of trade and changes in trade on such
economic variables as relative product and factor prices, real incomes,
and economic welfare. In addition the theory should provide a basis
for evaluating alternative steps a nation might take in the realm of
trade policy. We will find that no single theory can yet claim to have
these capabilities. Rather we have several theories, each of which
aids in our understanding of certain aspects of trade, but each of
which is incomplete in some respect.

The second objective of the book is to illustrate the process of
theory building and testing in economics. If none of the theories of
international trade is completely adequate, how are they tested
and evaluated? If a theory is inadequate, how is it improved, or how
is a new theory built which might be better? And what do we mean

by better? Careful study of the development and testing of theories should provide a better understanding of economics as a science, and what it is that economists do.

The second objective may be far more important in the long run than the first. The one thing that the twentieth century, with its rapid pace of discovery and scientific advancement, has taught us is that most of what we learn is more or less wrong. New discovery makes it so. Therefore it is important to understand how old knowledge is tested and verified, or rejected, and new knowledge is added. My hope in this book is to involve the student to a much greater extent than usual in this process.

WHY DO NATIONS TRADE?

The flows of goods and services which we seek to explain are not inconsequential. For example, flows of goods and services from abroad into the United States (imports) in 1968 totaled over $33 billion. Exports from the United States in 1968 were almost $37 billion or 4 percent of our Gross National Product (GNP). For other countries the amounts are smaller, but the percentages and the importance of trade are frequently greater. British imports in 1968 were about £7.9 billion, or about $19 billion. This was about 22 percent of the United Kingdom's total economic output. In the Netherlands, exports and imports each amount to over one-third of GNP in that country. In 1968 the aggregate value of all exports from non-Communist nations was over $212 billion, with the six largest trading nations, the United States, Germany, the United Kingdom, France, Canada, and Japan, accounting for a little over half of the total. Although the United States is the largest trading nation in the world, the nations of Western Europe, including Britian, account for about half of all trade among non-Communist nations.

In view of the busy commerce among nations which lies behind these data, one might be tempted to state that Western Europe, for example, could not survive without trade. Such a statement would be at best misleading, and strictly speaking it is wrong. Could Europe feed itself, for example, in the absence of imports of agricultural products? Given the quantities of resources presently devoted to agriculture, the answer is clearly no. Given present levels of consumption of sugar, fruits, chocolate, or vegetable oils, again the answer is no. But if Europe were willing to accept drastically less satisfying but nutritious diets or to devote vastly greater quantities of resources to agriculture, or some combination of the two, it could feed itself. It is even technically possible to grow bananas in Norway. But at what cost?

The point of all this is that trading and the specialization in production that goes with it permit higher standards of living or levels of real income than would otherwise be possible. Without trade, standards of living would be lower, and for any country the more so, the greater the current importance of trade in that nation's economy. Although this proposition may seem obvious, it will be carefully demonstrated in a later chapter. The proposition is logically equivalent to that better known proposition that if each individual specializes in performing that productive task which he can do best, his productivity and the output of the farm or factory where he works will be greater than in the absence of any specialization and division of labor.

Students in economics are taught very early that the existence of markets and the opportunity for exchange is a prerequisite for the kind of specialization and division of labor which would allow a nation to make the best use of its endowment of resources.[1] This establishes a presumption in favor of free markets as a way of organizing the economic activity of a society. Of course there are problems with the free market economy: markets are poorly suited for the provision of public goods such as national defense; external effects such as water pollution and the benefits of on-the-job training are not reflected in market prices; the resulting income distribution may not be considered desirable; and finally because of monopoly power, markets may not be free and competitive.

Similarly in international economics there is a presumptive case for the free flow of goods and services and factors of production in international trade. Trade should be free of such restrictions as quotas, import and export controls, and tariffs. Recognition of this has been the main force behind the Kennedy Round of tariff reduction negotiations recently completed. Yet while political leaders and economists laud the progress made toward free trade at the Kennedy Round, steel producers in the United States are calling for increased tariffs on steel products, and cattlemen and dairymen are asking for lower quotas on beef and cheese imports into the United States. And one might ask why, if free trade is so desirable, did the Kennedy Round come so close to failure? The answer can be found in the study of international markets and trade. As in the case of free markets within a country, the results of free trade may not be satisfactory to all in terms of the distribution of the gains from trade within and between countries. Also monopoly elements and external effects may cause a divergence from the optimum.

[1] In the absence of markets, elaborate systems of control and detailed and exhaustive sets of calculations are required to produce equivalent results. And the controls and calculations themselves are not without cost. See Heinz Köhler, *Welfare and Planning*, New York, Wiley, 1966, for a good elementary discussion of the effectiveness of markets and alternative systems of control in achieving an efficient use of available resources.

4   We have not yet directly answered the implied question in the heading of this section, why do nations trade? But the answer has emerged from our discussion of the possibility of self-sufficiency and the benefits of specialization. Nations trade because it is beneficial to do so, beneficial in the sense that it permits economic units (firms, households, governments) to exhange goods and services they can produce relatively more cheaply for those goods and services that they desire but could only produce for themselves at a higher cost. Free trade would permit the highest level of benefits, but these benefits are not evenly distributed and not everyone is happy with the way they are distributed. Herein lies the cause of most problems in trade policy.

WHAT IS DIFFERENT ABOUT INTERNATIONAL ECONOMICS?

International economics might be called a derivative branch of economic theory. It draws very heavily on three basic branches of economic theory: price theory or microeconomics; the theory of income determination or macroeconomics; and monetary theory. International economics is distinguished by the institutional setting in which transactions take place. Trade between nations is different from trade within nations for three reasons.

First, two different monies are involved. An individual normally finds that one form of money is more useful to him in his particular circumstances than another. The resident of the United States finds that dollars are more useful than British pounds. This means that when goods and services are exchanged, arrangements must also be made for exchanging currencies. This exchange is complicated by the possibility that the two currencies may change in relative value. If the relative value or purchasing powers of two currencies were forever fixed, and they were equally useful to the residents of both countries, the currencies would be as different as nickels and dimes. There would be no monetary problems of interest to students of international economies.

The second difference is that in the international economy there are barriers to the movement of goods and services and, more important, factors of production between nations. The least important of these barriers is distance and the cost of transportation. Transportation costs are less important in the international trade in diamonds than they are in the trade in oranges between California and New York. There are frequently barriers to the flows of goods and services in the form of customs officials, tariffs, and quotas. But the most important class of barriers consists of those which impede the movement of factors of production, capital and labor, among nations.

Of course land and natural resources are by definition immobile. The flows of labor are impeded partly by law and administrative barriers such as immigration quotas, and more importantly by differences among countries in custom, language, and political systems and by the usual preference for familiarity and certainty over the hazards of the strange and unknown. Capital typically has more international mobility than labor; but similar legal and intangible barriers make capital less mobile between nations than it is within a nation. Since only by accident would two nations have the same or similar endowments of the several factors of production, factor immobility can allow differences in the prices of factors (wages, interest rates, and land rents) to persist over time. Differences in factor prices lead to differences in cost which in turn make trade between nations profitable.

The third major distinction between international and national trade is really a catchall for the influence of all other economic differences which can be traced to different cultural and political units. Included here are differences in economic policies which might affect relative price and employment levels, rates of growth, interest rates, income distributions, or degrees of competitiveness in domestic markets. Also differences in tastes and preferences among nations can be economically important.

We have been simultaneously working toward an economic definition of a nation and a list of the characteristics of economic relations between nations. For our purposes a nation is defined as an area within which there is a unified, cohesive system of markets, a single set of economic policies, and a single currency system. The latter two characteristics imply a single central government for each nation. A strictly economic definition would focus on the first characteristic. Cohesive markets mean a high degree of mobility of capital and labor between markets within the nation. A nation's economic boundaries mark an area beyond which capital and labor are much less mobile than they are within the nation. The boundary is indicated by a break or discontinuity in the geographic mobility of factors of production. By this definition the boundary between the United States and Canada is very weak, and all boundaries are getting weaker.

Although international economics has borrowed heavily from basic economic theory, it has also made important contributions to the understanding of some aspects of economic activity within a nation. In a nation as large as the United States it misrepresents reality to speak of a single cohesive system of markets. Labor is cheap in the South. Appalachia is poor and underdeveloped. The economy of Florida is vastly different from that of Colorado. The list of differences among regions within the United States is quite long and sounds remarkably similar to the list of possible differences among nations. International economic theory has much to say about economic relations among regions. Regions have different economic characteristics because of the uneven distribution of natural resources, the quantity and quality of land, and the less than perfect interregional mobility of labor. This, of course, corresponds to the second "distinction" noted between international and national trade.

Theories of international trade which are used to explain the flows of goods and services among nations can also be used to explain the flows among regions. In one way the theoretical problems are simpler because the complications of different currency systems and national policies are not present in the study of regional and interregional economics. However, nothing is free; this simplification is not gained without cost. Before international economic theory can be applied to regional problems, conceptually satisfying and operational or useful definitions of regions must be established. In the case of nations, definitions and well-marked boundaries are ready made. Statistics are gathered on a national basis and this makes national boundaries useful. But suppose one were to study the South as a region. Where does he draw the line? Does he include Texas? Maryland? And although much economic data are gathered and arranged by state, states are not always very good approximations to the economic regions under study.

THE ROLE OF THEORY IN THE
STUDY OF ECONOMIC PROBLEMS

One of the objectives of this text is to show how scientific method can be used in the study of international economic problems. Method refers to the set of rules and procedures a scientist adopts when he starts out to investigate or study something. These rules should tell him something about what he is trying to accomplish by his work, in a very general sense how to go about it, and finally how to evaluate his results when he is finished. Although textbooks often refer to "The Scientific Method," there is by no means complete agreement among scientists on all aspects of appropriate method. In fact controversies over methodological issues are often among the most long-lasting and bitter of scholarly debates. The purpose here is neither to start nor end such a debate, but rather to state in as simple a form as possible those methodological principles which have guided the development, testing, and application of those parts of international economic theory to be discussed in this text.

The first step in understanding method in economics is to distinguish between positive and normative analysis. Positive analysis is concerned with what is, with explanation and prediction of observable phenomena; normative analysis is concerned with what ought to be. Statements about what ought to be are based on value judgments which have no scientific basis; they are not verifiable. For example the theory of consumer demand provides an explanation of consumer response to a fall in the price of a commodity, other things being equal. It yields the prediction that a fall in the product's price will lead to an increase in the quantity purchased. This is positive analysis. To shift to another example, the statement that the rate of price increase is too high is a normative statement involving a value judgment about what constitutes an acceptable rate of inflation of prices. A third statement to the effect that the government should raise taxes to reduce inflationary pressures involves both positive and normative analysis. First there is the normative judgment or choice concerning inflation and other things such as income distribution, level of unemployment, and growth rates. Then there is the prediction that raising taxes will have the desired effect. This prediction is based on an implicit piece of theorizing or positive analysis of the determinants of national income and price levels.

In normative analysis alternative states of the world are compared and ranked. In international economics, for example, we will wish to compare the state of no trade or autarky with free trade, or the state of free trade with that of tariffs on imports. Comparisons can be completely objective; but if evaluations and choices are to be made, a criterion must be established and the relevant characteristics of the alternative states examined in the light of this criterion. Formally a criterion is a rule, perhaps a functional relationship, by which different states can be (at least) ordinally ranked.

One such criterion is efficiency in resource use. Alternative states of an economy can be compared on the basis of the size of output or net national product. By this criterion full employment is preferred to unemployment; competitive markets are preferred to monopolies. There are other possible economic criteria, too. One is the distribution of income. Efficiency looks at the size of the economic pie; distribution looks at the way in which it is sliced. Efficiency and distribution are the two alternative criteria which play the largest role in normative analysis in international economics as well as in other branches of the discipline. This does not rule out the selection of other standards such as the growth of the economy (how fast?), the degree of stability of national income (boom or bust?), or the quality of life and the quality of the environment. Many of the most bitter debates concerning economic policies have their foundations in the conflicting interests of different groups and in differences in value judgments concerning objectives.

Normative analysis and the making of economic policy are obviously closely linked; but they are not exactly the same thing. As the example above concerning inflation and taxes showed, to choose among two alternative policy actions (to raise taxes or not) one must predict the consequences of each action; and this requires theory. Since this book is about theories in international economics, it will be necessary to understand the process of developing a theory. Here positive analysis or theorizing is explained step by step.

The first step, naturally, is the selection of a problem, a phenomenon that has not been fully or adequately explained, or a policy problem where one of the issues is the impact of one of the proposed actions. In one sense this is easy because there is so much still to learn. But in another way it is hard because the way that the problem is defined influences all the subsequent steps. In some formulations the problem may turn out to be impossible to solve, while other forms of statements of the problem might be trivially easy. Becoming a good theorist is partly a matter of developing the necessary judgment and experience in asking the right questions.

The second step is the construction of a model, and this is an apt term. Models of ships do not include tiny replicas of each fastening and fitting; rather they include only enough detail to convey the essential elements of the ship. What is considered essential by the model builder depends on the purposes of the model. Models for testing the hydrodynamic properties of the hull concentrate on reproducing the external hull shape and the weight distribution characteristics to the exclusion of all other detail. And so it is with economic models. The irrelevant (or, rather, what is thought to be the unimportant for the purpose at hand) is excluded.

The process of model building begins with the adoption (or the development, if necessary) of a language, a set of definitions and concepts which are as unambiguous as possible. In economics much of the language is in existence, and this step is implicit rather than explicit. For beginning students in economics, learning this language is one of the main problems. This language is used to build by assumption and postulation a set of relationships between concepts or between variables. To draw an example from macroeconomics, the economist's language includes definitions for national income, consumption, and investment. The simplest model of income determination consists of a set of relationships between these variables which has been postulated, namely that consumption is an increasing function of income, and investment is invariant to income.

In economics models are not made to be set on the mantelpiece; they are meant to be used. Models can be manipulated verbally, graphically, or mathematically to produce conclusions. This manipulation is a logical process of deduction. Therefore any conclusions can only be accepted as true within the context of the model and the language used. The more comprehensive the model, the more conclusions can be wrung from it. From the income determination model, one can deduce that there may be an equilibrium value for income, under what conditions this is true, and what determines that equilibrium value. One can also conclude that the effect of an increase in investment will be to increase national income by a larger amount. Some of these conclusions are of interest in their own right, such as the equilibrium conditions. Such statements are called the properties of the model. Other conclusions may be stated as hypotheses which are subject to testing. Hypotheses are "true" in the sense that they follow logically from the model, but they are highly tentative in the sense that they may or may not be consistent with observation. It is this comparison of hypothesis and reality which is the purpose of scientific investigation.

Hypotheses are statements derived from models which are in principle subject to refutation. After gathering appropriate data by observation and measurement, one may find that what the models say is true "just ain't so." In this case the hypothesis must be rejected as a description of reality, and the model must be discarded or rebuilt in the light of this new information. At this point the process of theorizing can become iterative. Hypothesis testing is a source of information about the problem being investigated. This information can be used to redefine the problem or to alter the structure of assumptions and postulates in the model itself. Successful tests may suggest new aspects of a model or may provide building blocks out of which more comprehensive models can be constructed.

Hypothesis testing is usually a statistical process carried out in accordance with rules derived mathematically. There are important points to remember. First, hypothesis testing requires more than a superficial search for a few historical cases which are consistent with the hypothesis. Rather, statistical testing of hypotheses can be described as a search of all known cases or a random sample of known cases to determine, if possible, whether the hypothesized result occurred more often than can be attributed to pure chance. Second, on the basis of statistical tests hypotheses can be rejected, but they can never be accepted. The best that can be said is "not rejected." The nature of the tests is such that other better and undiscovered hypotheses cannot be ruled out as possibilities; and there is always that slim chance that the apparent successful test of the hypothesis was due to pure chance.

Models which produce hypotheses which have not been refuted by observation gain the status of theories. Theories are in a simplified manner descriptive of real world processes which are producing observable phenomena. Theories are useful as building blocks. A comprehensive theory of income determination must be based on theories of investment behavior and consumption. Rational macroeconomic policy is impossible without a theory of income determination. Normative economic analysis and rational policy formulation rest on the results of positive economic analysis which has produced a body of theory capable of explaining economic reality.

All too often one hears, "That sounds fine in theory but it won't work in practice." Statements such as this are probably the result of two things: first, a misunderstanding of the term *theory* and the process of theorizing, and second, a reaction to those who place too much faith in the predictive and explanatory power of existing theory. On the second point, the economic world is changing as fast as it is being investigated. Specific properties of models change over time. More comprehensive models may be able to incorporate the variables causing these changes; but generality and comprehensiveness in models is not an unmixed blessing. More on this below. In any event the development of theories and investigation of hypotheses has not proceeded so far that one can think of having anything like complete explanations of economic life. Economists are plagued with a continuing dissatisfaction and restlessness with the existing body of theory and a great desire to replace weak theory with stronger theory and outmoded models with current models.

Misunderstanding of theorizing revolves around the necessity for abstracting from reality and making simplifying assumptions. Ideally theories should have sufficient detail and precision to handle all possible variations and exceptions, make accurate numerical predictions, and have sufficient generality to be applicable in a variety of situations. Yet these properties to a large extent are mutually exclusive. Generality means loss of precision, yet detail means reduction in applicability and an increase in the cumbersomeness of the model. Lack of detail and lack of reality in models go hand in hand. In fact models by definition are unrealistic. A completely realistic model would be an exact reproduction of reality, and by its zealous attention to realism it would forfeit any usefulness as a model. It would be too comprehensive to comprehend. Novices tend to judge models and theories on the basis of their correspondence to reality. Scientists judge theories on the basis of their usefulness, on their ability to provide order out of chaos, and on their power to explain and predict important phenomena.

In subsequent chapters some extremely unrealistic models of international trade will be built, unrealistic both because of what is left out of the model and what is said about what remains in the model. These models represent the main body of conventional international trade theory. But since it has been argued here that theories must be tested, subsequent chapters and sections will be devoted to surveying attempts to test and verify (or refute) this body of theory. The purpose of this is to convey to the reader some of the flavor of scientific research and hopefully an understanding of how one goes about doing research in economics.

It must be acknowledged at this point that there is by no means complete agreement among economists on all theoretical and empirical points. In the first place, it is easier by far to build a model than to test its hypotheses. Models yielding contradictory or at least different explanations of economic phenomena compete for the attention and allegiance of economists. They are different in terms of their definitions, underlying structure, and assumed or postulated functional relationships. The debate on these points goes on; assumptions are questioned; alternatives are proposed. Only the empirical tests of hypotheses can ultimately resolve the debates. Yet the backlog of untested hypotheses is staggering. This is because empirical research is a difficult, time-consuming, and often inconclusive activity. This leads to the second problem, the continuing debate over proper research methods and interpretation of results. As subsequent chapters will show, empirical research and hypothesis testing tend to raise more questions about economic models and theories than they answer.

In short, researchers are continually confronting the magnitude of their ignorance about economic phenomena. On the other hand, teachers and textbook writers are supposed to be transmitting knowledge, not ignorance. Researchers and teachers tend to look at our accumulation of economic knowledge through different ends of the telescope for obvious and necessary reasons. This book tries to present a more balanced view that shows both the extent of and the limits to our understanding. It asks the reader to remember this and understand why it must be so in any frank presentation of the state of knowledge in a scientific field.

A NOTE ON SUPPLEMENTARY MATERIALS

At the end of most of the following chapters there appear lists of additional reading materials. These references are in addition to footnote citations in the bodies of each chapter. The readings are presented in order of increasing sophistication and difficulty. The first are at a level which should be readily accessible to readers of the text. These readings have been chosen to provide alternative points of view, or to demonstrate applications of materials presented in the text, or to provide historical background or discussion of policy issues which have been omitted in the text. Advanced readings go more deeply into some of the theoretical issues raised here. They might provide a start for the student who wished to write a term paper on a theoretical point. They could also provide a useful but incomplete bibliography to students who plan to go further in their study of international economics.

SUPPLEMENTARY READINGS

General Texts and Surveys of the Literature

Kindleberger, Charles, *International Economics,* 4th ed., Homewood, Ill., Irwin, 1968.
Haberler, Gottfried, *A Survey of International Trade Theory,* rev. ed., Princeton, N.J., Princeton University Press, 1961.
Caves, Richard, *Trade and Economic Structure,* Cambridge, Mass., Harvard University Press, 1960.
Meade, J. E., *The Theory of International Economic Policy, Trade and Welfare,* London, Oxford University Press, 1955.

Sources of Data

U.S. Office of Business Economics, *Survey of Current Business* (monthly).
International Monetary Fund, *International Financial Statistics* (monthly).
————, *Directions of Trade* (monthly).
United Nations, *Monthly Bulletin of Statistics* (monthly).
————, *Yearbook of International Trade Statistics* (annual).
Secretariat of the General Agreement on Tariffs and Trade, *International Trade* (annual report).

On Economic Method

Krupp, Sherman R., ed., *The Structure of Economic Science,* Englewood Cliffs, N.J., Prentice-Hall, 1966.
Friedman, Milton, "The Methodology of Positive Economics," in *Essays in Positive Economics,* Chicago, University of Chicago Press, 1953.

Chapter

Comparative Advantage
and Mutually Beneficial Trade

SEEKING A BASIS FOR TRADE

Most of the trade which the theory seeks to explain takes place between private parties, both individuals and firms. International trade is simply voluntary exchange where the two parties happen to reside in different countries. Since it is voluntary, it must take place because of the potential for mutual profit. Buyers buy foreign goods when they are cheaper, or better, or different from goods available from domestic sources. Sellers sell abroad when the foreign price is higher, or at least no lower than the price to be received at home. This simple explanation really does not tell us very much, though, since it does not explain how or why these price differences arise.

Price differences can arise between markets either because of differences in demand conditions, or differences on the supply side of the markets. A simple two-country supply and demand model can be used to illustrate this. Assume a world of only two countries, the United States and the United Kingdom. For simplicity assume that transportation costs between the two countries are zero. The first model, portrayed in Figure 2.1, shows how supply differences can lead to trade in a single commodity. The U.S. supply and demand curves are drawn in the normal fashion in the right-hand part of the figure. All the prices are expressed in dollars. The supply and demand curves for the United Kingdom have been drawn in mirror-image fashion. The demand curves are identical in the two countries; but costs, as represented by S_{UK}, are lower in the United Kingdom.

In the absence of international trade each market would seek its own equilibrium price—P_1 in the United Kingdom and P_2 in the

United States. If the two countries can exchange goods in international trade, U.S. consumers will find that they can purchase their goods more cheaply in the foreign market. Foreign output will rise. Because of the upward sloping supply curve, the increased output in the United Kingdom must be sold at a higher price. At the same time, output and price in the United States will decline because of the reduction in the demand for the more expensive U.S.-produced product. This process continues until the price differential has been eliminated. P_3 is the equilibrium price at which U.K. exports equal U.S. imports.

Price differences can also arise because of differences in demand. In Figure 2.2 the supply curves in the two countries are identical. But there are differences in tastes or incomes which make for greater demand in the United Kingdom at any price. It is this difference in demand conditions which explains the price differential and creates the possibility of trade.

A similar diagram can be used to show that by assuming that transportation costs are zero a great deal is gained in simplification, while very little is lost in terms of fundamental insights. In Figure 2.3 the United States is the low-cost supplier of the good. If trade is permitted, the United Kingdom will increase its imports of the good as long as their price is greater than the price in the United States plus the cost of transportation. Both markets are in equilibrium, with U.S. exports equal to U.K. imports when the U.S. price has risen to P_3 and the U.K. price has fallen to $P_3 + t$, where t is transportation

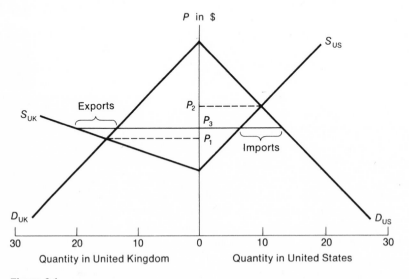

Figure 2.1
Trade in a single commodity based on supply differences

cost per unit. Trade will take place whenever there are domestic price differentials which are greater than the unit cost of transporting goods from one country to the other.

Although the model may be useful as a beginning step, it should be clear that it is an incomplete model. The model leaves unex-

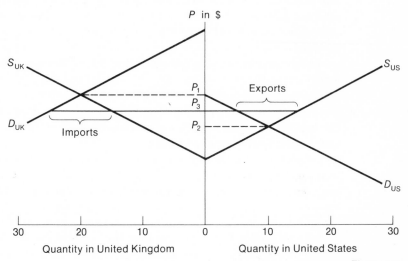

Figure 2.2
Trade in a single commodity based on demand differences

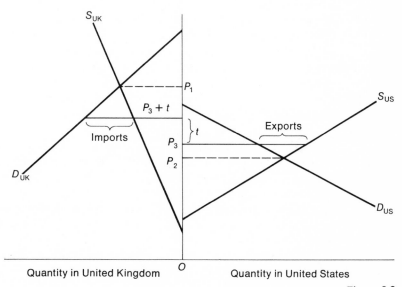

Figure 2.3
Trade in a single commodity with transportation costs

16

plained two things. First, the model says nothing about what causes differences in costs and prices. Alternative explanations of cost differences will be the topic of the next two chapters. A more important omission is that this model explains the trade of only one good in a partial equilibrium setting. There is no way of knowing what the impact of imports or exports of this good will be on the prices and outputs of other commodities or on the prices of factors of production. Also it is not clear from this model that either nation will achieve balance-of-payments equilibrium. Could it happen, for example, that for all goods in the United States the supply curves were all above the supply curves in all other countries? If this were so, the United States would be an importer of all goods and an exporter of none, a clearly untenable position. In the next section it will be shown for a two-country model that when trade between nations exists in more than one commodity, there is some combination of exchange rates for the currencies and domestic price levels at which both countries will export some goods (and import others) and at which both countries will enjoy a balance-of-payments equilibrium.

PRICE ADVANTAGE AND THE FLOW OF GOODS

The next chapter contains an introduction to the oldest and probably the simplest model of international trade, the Ricardian model of comparative cost. The comparative cost model is an explanation of trade which does not explain enough. The model assumes relative differences in the cost of production of the goods being traded but does not explain how these cost differentials arise. The modern theory of international trade which is introduced in Chapter 4 traces these cost differentials to differences in factor endowments among nations. Some nations have *relatively* more capital than labor in comparison with other nations. The modern theory of trade shows how these differences give rise to international trade.

Before turning to these alternative and in a sense competing theories of trade, there is a common core to be introduced. This core does not represent a theory. But without an understanding of this basic principle, the comparative cost and modern theories of trade will be very difficult going. This common principle is known as the principle of *comparative advantage*. Briefly stated it shows that mutually beneficial trade between two nations is possible whenever there are differences in the *relative prices* of goods between the two countries. The remainder of this chapter is devoted to explaining the *comparative advantage* principle and distinguishing it from price advantage. Subsequent chapters outline alternative explanations of *why* situations of comparative advantage exist between countries.

Table 2.1

17

Table 2.1
Price and cost differences—an illustration

Good	U.S. price (cost) ($)	U.K. price (cost) (£)	U.K. price in dollars at exchange rate of $4 = £1	Ratio of U.S. price to U.K. price
Gloves (pairs)	2	1	4	.50
Soybeans (bushels)	2.50	1	4	.625
Rifles	45	15	60	.75
Motor scooters	240	50	200	1.20
Suits	72	12	48	1.50
Stereos	300	45	180	1.67

Table 2.1 shows for six representative commodities the hypothetical cost in dollars of producing them in the United States and the cost in pounds sterling of producing them in the United Kingdom. Under the assumption of competitive markets in the two countries, these costs will also equal the prices at which the goods are sold in their own domestic markets. In order to determine which goods will be exported by each country, prices must be expressed in terms of a common denominator; that is, an exchange rate must be used to convert prices into a common currency.[1] If the exchange rate between the pound and the dollar is $4 per pound, the dollar equivalents of the U.K. prices would be as shown in the third column in Table 2.1.

Comparison of the U.K. and U.S. prices for gloves, for example, shows that U.S. gloves are half the price of U.K. gloves. Similar price differentials in favor of the United States exist for soybeans and rifles. The price differentials in the case of motor scooters, suits, and stereos are in favor of the United Kingdom. One would conclude that the U.S. would export gloves, soybeans, and rifles to the U.K. because it has an advantage in the production of these, and that it would import motor scooters, suits, and stereos from the U.K.

If the exchange rate were $10 per pound, that is, if the pound were very expensive in terms of the dollar, all U.K. goods would become more expensive in dollars. The second column of Table 2.2 shows the ratio of U.S. to U.K. prices at this new exchange rate. Since all U.K. goods are more expensive than their U.S. counterparts, the U.S. would export all six commodities to the U.K. An exchange rate of $.50 per pound would make the pound and con-

[1] A foreign exchange rate is the price one must pay in his currency (e.g., dollars) to obtain one unit of the foreign currency (e.g., pounds). Exchange rates can be expressed in terms of either currency. For example, an exchange rate of pounds of $4/£ is equivalent to one of £.25/$ for dollars.

Table 2.2
Prices and price ratios at alternative exchange rates

Good	U.K. price in dollars at an exchange rate of $10 per £	Ratio of U.S. price to U.K. price	U.K. price in dollars at an exchange rate of $.50 per £	Ratio of U.S. price to U.K. price
Gloves	10	.2	.50	4
Soybeans	10	.25	.50	5
Rifles	150	.3	7.50	6
Motor scooters	500	.48	25	9.6
Suits	120	.6	6	12
Stereos	450	.75	22.50	13.3

sequently all the U.K.-produced goods relatively inexpensive. As the last two columns of Table 2.2 show, at this exchange rate the U.S. would import all six products from the U.K.

Given the underlying cost conditions as expressed by the first two columns of Table 2.1, the pattern of trade is sensitive to the exchange rate. There is an exchange rate which results in no imports from the U.S.; there is an exchange rate which results in no exports from the U.S. But this means that there must be some exchange rate between $10 per pound and $.50 per pound which will result in balanced trade between the two nations. Balanced trade means that the total value of imports is equal to the total value of exports. Also whatever this exchange rate is, it is clear that gloves will be exported and stereos imported by the U.S.

In the example of the two tables *price advantage* has determined whether a good would be exported or imported by a country. Price advantage refers to a simple comparison of prices when both prices are expressed in a common monetary unit. The pattern of price advantage is highly sensitive to the exchange rate, as Table 2.2 shows. Price advantage also depends on monetary factors and price levels in the two countries. Changes in the overall level of prices due to monetary inflation or deflation have the same effect on trade as exchange rate changes. The following example will illustrate this.

Starting with the same price, cost, and exchange rate information as in Table 2.1, assume that there has been a monetary inflation in the United States which has doubled all prices and wage rates. The results of this are shown in the first column of Table 2.3. The exchange rate is still $4 per pound. Now all goods except gloves can be purchased more cheaply in the U.K. than in the U.S. If instead of U.S. inflation the U.K. had experienced price inflation (or the U.S. had experienced price deflation), this could have reversed the flow of goods and made the U.K. import all goods from the U.S.

What would happen if the doubling of money prices in the U.S.

Table 2.3

Table 2.3
Prices and price ratios after inflation

Good	U.S. prices after inflation ($)	U.K. price in dollars at an exchange rate of $4 per £	Ratio of U.S. price to U.K. price
Gloves	4	4	1.0
Soybeans	5	4	1.25
Rifles	90	60	1.50
Motor scooters	480	200	2.40
Suits	144	48	3.0
Stereos	600	180	3.3

had been accompanied by a change in the exchange rate to $8.00/£, raising the price of the pound and U.K. goods? The U.K. price in dollars would have doubled, too, and the ratios in Table 2.3 would have been the same as those in Table 2.1. Exchange rate changes and changes in overall price levels have the same kind of effect on price advantage. If the pattern of price advantage has resulted in one country importing more than it is exporting (running a balance-of-payments deficit), the pattern can be shifted by either a change in the exchange rate or a change in price levels.

The pattern of price advantage is crucial in the determination of the balance of trade; but it is of only superficial importance in determining the structure of trade, that is, which goods will be exported by each country and which will be imported. The structure of trade is determined by the pattern of *comparative advantage.* In other words, at a superficial level all trade flows depend on or can be explained in terms of price advantages. But the resulting flows of trade might be seriously out of balance. To make predictions about (or to explain) the pattern of balanced trade a different kind of information is required, specifically knowledge of patterns of comparative advantage.

COMPARATIVE ADVANTAGE
AND THE REAL MEANING OF "CHEAPER"

Comparative advantage does not depend on money wage rates and prices nor exchange rates in its definition. Comparative advantage is a "real" concept in that it can be defined independently of any monetary variable such as exchange rates. In fact if comparative advantage exists, it is not affected at all by changes in exchange rates or money prices. Consider the two commodities in Table 2.1, gloves and stereos. In the U.S. stereos are 150 times more expensive than gloves; that is, the ratio of the price of stereos to the price of gloves is 150 to 1. In the U.K. this ratio is only 45 to 1. In comparison to gloves, stereos are less expensive in the U.K. than in the U.S. In the U.K. it takes only 45 pairs of gloves to buy one stereo, while in the U.S. it takes 150 pairs of gloves. These ratios are called relative prices. They define the price of stereos relative to or measured in terms of gloves.

None of the relative price ratios for goods in the U.S. changes in Tables 2.1 to 2.3. Relative prices within a country are not affected by changes in exchange rates or absolute price levels. It is this structure of relative prices and costs which actually defines comparative advantage. Whenever the price ratio for a pair of goods in a country is different from the price ratio in a second country, one country has a comparative advantage in the production of one good, and the other country has the comparative advantage in the production of the other good. Which good? Stereos are relatively cheaper in the U.K. than in the U.S. So the U.K.'s comparative advantage lies in stereos. It follows that gloves are relatively more expensive in the U.K.; that is, the U.S. has the comparative advantage in gloves.

Assume for a moment that there is no money and all exchange must be by barter. An individual in the U.S. who wants a stereo must have 150 pairs of gloves to trade for the stereo (or 120 bushels of soybeans). In the U.K. he would only need 45 pairs of gloves (or 45 bushels of soybeans) to trade for a stereo since there the relative price of stereos is lower. If trade between residents of the two nations were possible (with no transportation cost), everyone wanting a stereo would take his business (and his gloves) to the U.K. The U.K. resident wanting gloves could only get 45 pairs of gloves for his stereo in the U.K., but if he traded his stereo for gloves in the U.S. he would be able to get 150 pairs. Stereos are relatively cheaper in the U.K., and the U.S. would tend to import them; while gloves are relatively cheaper in the U.S., and the U.S. would tend to export them.

Where comparative advantage exists, its effect may be obscured by an improper exchange rate, as in the examples of Table 2.2. But this is a problem of balance-of-payments adjustment. In Table 2.2, when the exchange rate was $10/£, the U.S. had a price advantage in the production of all goods. The exchange rate obscured the fact that stereos were still relatively cheaper in the U.K. (in comparison with gloves) than in the U.S. Balance-of-payments adjustment would take the form of lowering the exchange rate or lowering all money prices in the U.K. through monetary deflation. If such adjustments are made, eventually the comparative advantage situation we know to exist because of relative price differences would also be reflected in the money prices (price advantages). Balanced trade would take place.

This demonstrates what might be called a theorem in international trade. If there are differences in the relative prices between countries so that comparative advantage exists, there is an infinite number of combinations of exchange rates and absolute price levels at which balanced trade can take place. Given the relative prices and the price levels of the two countries there is a single exchange rate at which balanced trade will take place. And given relative prices and the exchange rate there is one *ratio* of absolute price levels in the two countries at which balanced trade will take place. To make clear the meaning of this last statement, refer again to Table 2.1. If the exchange rate is $4 per pound and the price levels of columns 1 and 2 produce balanced trade, balanced trade will also occur if *both* price levels in the U.K. and U.S. are doubled (or halved).

The dependence of comparative advantage and trade on relative prices might best be made clear by a negative example. In Table 2.4 domestic prices are given for three goods. At the exchange

Table 2.4
Price differences without comparative advantage

Good	U.S. price (cost) ($)	U.K. price (cost) (£)	U.K. price in dollars at an exchange rate of $4 per £	Ratio of U.S. price to U.K. price
Mead	10	2.50	10	1.0
Malt	20	5.00	20	1.0
Madiera	30	7.50	30	1.0

rate of $4/£, there is no incentive for trade. At any other exchange rate, either the U.S. or the U.K. would have a price advantage in *all* goods. The $4/£ exchange rate is the only rate which does not result in unbalanced trade; but it results in no trade. This is because there is no comparative advantage for either country in any pair of goods. Malt is twice as costly as mead, in both countries. Relative prices are the same in both countries; thus there is no comparative advantage.

To conclude this section, three points should be emphasized. First, comparative advantage results from differences among nations in the relative costs or relative prices of two goods within each country. These differences are invariant to the exchange rate since the exchange rate plays no role in their calculation. Also these relative price or cost ratios are invariant to inflation or deflation in either country, assuming that inflation affects all prices proportionately.

Second, comparative advantage is symmetrical in that if one nation has a comparative advantage in the production of gloves, by definition it has a comparative *dis*advantage in the production of

22   stereos. This must mean that the other country has a comparative advantage in the production of stereos and a comparative disadvantage in the production of gloves. Thus there is a basis for advantageous trade.

Finally, to prevent possible confusion, it would be useful to point out the distinction between two similar terms as they are used here. Some writers treat the terms *comparative advantage* and *comparative cost* as synonyms. Others, this writer included, prefer to reserve the term comparative cost to describe a particular kind of economic model in which comparative advantage is due to *assumed* differences in labor productivities and labor costs. Such a model is developed in the next chapter. Other models, including the one developed in Chapter 4, attribute comparative advantage to differences in factor endowments. Comparative advantage could be due to differences in demand conditions. The existence of comparative advantage provides the basis for mutually beneficial trade; and comparative cost models are one type of explanation for comparative advantage.

Chapter

The Classical Explanation of Comparative Advantage: Comparative Cost

LABOR PRODUCTIVITY, COSTS, AND PRICES

The comparative cost theory of trade can be traced back more than a hundred and fifty years to David Ricardo.[1] This theory begins with the assumption of differences in the costs of production. Given these differences in relative costs, it follows that comparative advantage (a difference in relative prices) exists and will determine the flow of trade. If the comparative cost theory makes a contribution to our understanding of trade flows, it is in its explanation of the differences in costs, that is, in its underlying theory of production and cost.

The original statement of comparative cost was based on an extremely simple cost theory, the labor theory of cost. Simply put, this cost theory hypothesizes that the prices of goods depend upon the cost of labor utilized in their manufacture, and nothing else. If it takes one man working one day to make a bicycle and it takes two men working two days to make a boat, then the price of boats will be four times the price of bicycles. Relative prices are determined by relative labor costs. Knowledge of money wage rates is sufficient to determine money prices. The labor theory of cost does not ignore the fact that tools and materials are also needed to make bicycles and boats. It simply states that the proper measure of the labor used to make these goods includes the labor embodied in the tools and materials, that is, the labor used to produce the means of production.[2]

---

[1] The reference is David Ricardo, *On the Principles of Political Economy and Taxation,* chap. VII. There are many editions of this classic work.

[2] Strictly speaking, all that would be added would be the labor behind that portion of the tool used up or worn out in production, that is, depreciation.

The theory can also be expanded to take into account differences in the quality of the labor services provided by different individuals. Let us call this the pure labor theory of cost.

This pure labor cost theory is unsatisfactory in one fundamental aspect. To say that past labor used to make a tool can simply be added to today's direct labor inputs to obtain total economic cost is to misunderstand the nature of capital. The labor used to make the tool was paid for at the time the tool was made. Yet the returns to having the tool, the greater productivity of the direct labor inputs which can use the tool, are delayed and spread out over time. The owner of this tool must receive payments or returns over and above the labor costs of the tool to compensate him for this waiting.

Another way to look at it is that the past labor used to make the tool had an alternative use, for example producing something for consumption then. The value of the labor embodied in the tool should at least equal this foregone opportunity for consumption. To use a simple example, suppose that labor had an opportunity cost of $10. In other words it could have been used to produce $10 worth of consumption goods at that time. Suppose that instead it was used to make a tool which must "cure" for one year, at which time it is completely used up in growing a crop. Suppose further that the tool improves the farmer's productivity by $10. Is the value (productivity) of the labor in the tool equal to its opportunity cost? If consumption now is generally preferred to consumption later, the answer is no. The tool must make a contribution to productivity of more than $10 to have a value equal to its full opportunity cost because part of the opportunity foregone was consumption then (one year ago). This, in essence, is the return to capital or waiting.[3] Any theory of cost which ignores this, as does the pure labor theory of cost, is seriously incomplete.

However, this simplest form of the labor theory of cost is not necessary for the comparative cost theory. A more general statement of cost conditions for the comparative cost theory requires only these two assumptions: (1) that labor and the other factor inputs, for example capital, are combined in fixed proportions which are the same for all goods; and (2) that production takes place under conditions of constant returns to scale. These two assumptions combine to assure that total costs are always *proportional* to direct labor inputs, and that cost per unit of output is constant.

These assumptions are clearly unrealistic. Factor prices and

[3] A complete treatment of capital and interest theory would place greater emphasis on the productivity of capital. One reason that goods now are preferred to goods later is that they can be invested now, that is, turned into capital or tools which will have returns greater than costs. The opportunity cost of consumption is the foregone alternative of having more later through productive investment.

factor proportions are important variables, not constants, in most theoretical economic structures, including the modern theory of trade to be outlined in the next chapter. However, most economists would agree that the test of a theory is not whether its assumptions pass some rather vague test of realism. All models and theoretical structures involve abstractions from reality and perhaps even distortions of reality. This is how insights are gained. Is this one of those cases where the simplifying assumptions do not distort our vision but actually aid in our understanding? Or is this a case of a misleading oversimplification? This turns out not to be an easy question. And in any event if the test of a theory is the empirical validity of its hypotheses, we should defer a final answer until such tests can be made.

Leaving the question of empirical validity to a later chapter, let us proceed to an explanation of the theory. The following numerical example is based on the pure labor cost theory. Labor is assumed to be the only input; all labor in each country is of identical quality and productivity; and labor productivity is the sole determinant of cost. Labor is freely mobile between industries within a country, but does not move between countries. In addition it is assumed that competition in all markets keeps prices equal to costs. Finally, when trade is introduced, transport costs are assumed to be zero. In the remainder of this section we will examine the relationships among labor productivity, costs, and prices.

Assume that the labor cost and productivity figures for the United States and the United Kingdom are known for the only two goods produced in these two countries. The hypothetical data are presented in Table 3.1. It takes one man-day of labor to manufacture a ton of butter in the United States. It only takes a half a man-day to make the same amount of butter in the United Kingdom. These labor requirements are also reflected in the productivity figures in the lower

Table 3.1
Labor productivity and requirements—U.K. and U.S.

	U.S.	U.K.
Labor required to make 1 ton of butter (in man-days)	1 man-day	.5 man-day
Labor required to make 1 artillery shell (in man-days)	1.5 man-days	1 man-day
Productivity of labor in butter manufacturing	1 ton/man-day	2 tons/man-day
Productivity of labor in shell manufacturing	.67 shell/man-day	1 shell/man-day

half of the table. U.K. labor is twice as productive as U.S. labor in the manufacture of butter. Also in the case of artillery shells it takes 50 percent more man-days of labor to manufacture one artillery shell in the United States than it does in the United Kingdom. Turning it around, U.K. labor is 50 percent more productive than U.S. labor when used to make shells.

The classical theory does not contain an explanation for the differences in labor productivities among either goods or countries. In the pure labor theory of cost they could be attributed to differences in climate or natural resource endowments if these were important to the production of the goods in question. Ricardo's original example was based on cloth and wine in England and Portugal. Productivity and cost differences could also be due to differences in skill levels and education. Under the more general statements of comparative cost, productivity differences could be attributed to differences between nations in the proportions in which labor is used with other inputs, and to differences in the prices of these other factor inputs.

It appears that labor is absolutely more productive in the United Kingdom since in either line of activity the productivity of labor is higher in Britain than it is in the United States. In real terms, the United Kingdom has an *absolute productivity advantage* in the manufacture of both goods. One is tempted to jump to the conclusion that the United Kingdom would produce both goods for the international market, and the United States would import both butter and shells. But this would ignore the points made in the preceding chapter. The U.K. absolute advantage can be offset in international trade by differences in wage rates and prices and by the exchange rate. The U.K. absolute advantage may not result in a price advantage in both goods. Besides, the principle of comparative advantage says that under conditions of balanced trade, trade patterns will be determined by differences in relative prices.

If markets are competitive, prices equal costs; and the productivity data given in Table 3.1 are sufficient to determine the relative prices of butter and shells in each country. As shown in Table 3.2 the relative price of shells is 1.5 in the U.S., indicating that they are 1½ times as expensive to produce as butter. It takes 1½ man-days of labor to make a shell, and this much labor could have produced 1½ tons of butter. The relative price of shells in the U.K. is 2. The relative price of butter is always the reciprocal of the relative price of shells.

If money wages are known, the money prices of both goods can be calculated from the productivity data in Table 3.1. Assume that in the United States the money wage rate is $10 per day. Since it takes one man-day of labor to produce a ton of butter, and labor is the

Table 3.2
Relative prices in both countries before trade

27

	U.S.	U.K.
Relative price of shells in terms of butter (butter required to purchase one artillery shell)	1.5 tons	2 tons
Relative price of butter in terms of shells (artillery shells required to purchase one ton of butter)	⅔ shell	½ shell

only factor input in the production of butter, the price of butter has to be $10 per ton. The price of one artillery shell has to be $15. The money prices of shells and butter have the same relationship to each other as the relative prices shown in Table 3.2. This would be true no matter what wage rate was assumed to hold in the United States.

Tables 3.1 and 3.2 both show that comparative advantage exists as it has been defined in Chapter 2. Relative labor costs and relative prices in the two countries are different because of labor productivity differences. Because there is comparative advantage for both countries, there is some set of money price levels and exchange rates at which each country will have a price advantage in the production of one good and at which mutually beneficial trade will take place. The next two sections will demonstrate that this is so.

LABOR PRODUCTIVITY AND TRADE

The relative price information in Table 3.2 is sufficient to determine the flow of trade in the event that trade is opened up between the United States and the United Kingdom. Which good will the United States export? In the United Kingdom one would have to sell 2 tons of butter to obtain the funds necessary to purchase 1 shell; or one would have to forego the production of 2 tons of butter in order to obtain the labor necessary to produce 1 shell. However, if an individual in the United Kingdom were able to purchase artillery shells at the U.S. set of relative prices, he would be better off, since the cost of one artillery shell in the United States is only 1½ tons of butter. This is sufficient motive for the U.K. to import shells from the U.S., even though its own labor is absolutely more productive in producing shells.

While U.K. labor is absolutely more productive in both goods, the advantage is relatively greater in butter production. In comparison with the U.S., U.K. labor is twice as productive in butter while it is only 1.5 times as productive in shells. Therefore it can make better use of its advantage by producing only butter and trading butter for shells. This is another way of saying that the labor cost of one shell produced in the U.K. is one man-day, but the labor cost of obtaining one shell indirectly by trade is only ¾ of one man-day (since ¾ of one man-day makes 1.5 tons of butter which, if traded at the relative price of the U.S., brings 1 shell in exchange).

In the United States domestic sources of artillery shells are cheaper for U.S. residents than are shells from the United Kingdom. But by the same token, the U.S. citizen finds it cheaper to obtain his butter in the U.K. than to make it himself. A ton of butter costs ⅔ of an artillery shell in the U.S.; it only costs ½ of an artillery shell in the U.K. at the U.K. set of relative prices. It pays U.S. individuals to specialize in the production of shells and obtain the butter that they want by exchange with the U.K. If the U.S. can trade at the U.K. prices, there is a net gain by trade for the U.S. of ⅙ of an artillery shell for each ton of butter imported. This is the difference between the U.S. and the U.K. prices for butter.

This numerical example demonstrates the central proposition of both modern and comparative cost theories of trade. When relative prices in two countries are different in the absence of trade (when comparative advantage exists), trade will be profitable for both countries. Each country will import that which is relatively cheaper in the other country.

Once again it should be emphasized that the comparative advantage which is revealed in this numerical answer is due to *comparative* productivity and cost differences and is independent of the absolute level of productivity in either country. To demonstrate this, suppose that due to some public health measure (e.g., malaria control), labor productivity in both activities in the United States was tripled. The student should be able to construct a new version of Tables 3.1 and 3.2 with this information and predict what would happen to the relative prices in both countries and the direction of trade. The answer is, "Nothing." What about real wages and incomes in the United States? As a more difficult test, what would happen to trade patterns as a result of a change in husbandry techniques which doubled the productivity of labor in butter production in the United States but was not available to the British?

The preceding example can be illustrated with a graphical construct called the production possibilities curve. This curve shows which combinations of outputs are possible for a nation and which are impossible, given its stock or endowment of resources and the state of technology or productivity. Assume that in the United States the total supply of labor which is available per year is 100 man-days. If these 100 man-days were devoted solely to the production of butter, the productivity figures show that the total output of the economy would be 100 tons of butter and no artillery shells. In Figure 3.1 this possible economic situation is represented by point *A* on the butter axis at 100 tons of butter and 0 shells per year. Alternatively, the economy could devote this total supply of labor to the production of artillery shells, in which case the total output of artillery shells would be 67 while the total output of butter would be 0. Of course other combinations are possible. Dividing the labor supply evenly between butter production and shell production would result in 50 tons of butter and 33 shells per year.

The straight line connecting points *A* and *B* in Figure 3.1 is the U.S. production possibilities curve showing all possible alternative combinations of output which could be realized given the stock of labor and the state of technology. Any point above and to the right of the production possibilities curve represents an impossible or un-attainable situation. Any point below and to the left of the curve shows that some resources are unemployed or are being used inefficiently. The efficient use of resources in production is defined as that alloca-tion of resources which leads to a production point on the produc-tion possibilities curve. When resources are being used inefficiently, it is possible by reallocating resources to obtain more of at least one good without reducing the output of the other.

The relative price or cost of shells can be determined from the production possibilities curve. The cost of increasing the output of shells is the reduction in the ouptut of butter which must be made in order to free resources for shell production. The reduction in butter output is an opportunity foregone or the opportunity cost of shells. As the dotted lines forming the triangle show, the opportunity cost for producing ten shells is 15 tons of butter. If markets are competitive, prices equal costs; and the relative price of shells is 1.5.

Figure 3.2 shows the production possibilities curve for the United Kingdom under the assumption that the U.K. labor supply equals

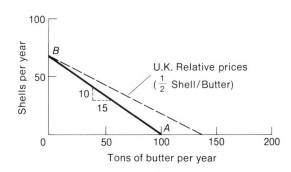

Figure 3.1
Production possibilities curve for the United States

100 man-days per year. In the U.K. the opportunity cost of increasing shell output by 10 is 20 tons of butter.

The production possibilities curve also demonstrates graphically the proposition that whenever relative prices are different trade is profitable. If the United States reduces its domestic output of shells by 10 per year and allocates more resources to the production of butter, it can increase butter production by 15 tons per year. As an alternative, if it were able to sell or trade those 10 shells at the price ratio prevailing in the United Kingdom it would be able to obtain 20 tons of butter for the 10 shells. The dashed line beginning at *B* in Figure 3.1 represents the trading opportunities or the consumption possibilities open to the United States with trade at the U.K. prices. The consumption possibilities curve lies outside the production possibilities curve. If the United States specializes in production by making only shells, and exchanges shells for butter at the U.K. price, it can reach any point on the consumption possibilities curve. Trade with the United Kingdom makes possible higher consumption possibilities than are available by autarkic production and consumption. The United Kingdom can obtain higher consumption possibilities through trading than is possible by autarky by specializing in the production of butter so long as the price ratio at which it can trade is different from its domestic price ratio. If it can trade at the U.S. relative prices, it should produce only butter, that is, at point *A*. It would then be able to obtain consumption combinations above its production possibilities curve and along the dashed line beginning at *A*.

Obviously it can't be both ways: the U.S. engaging in trade at the U.K. relative prices and the U.K. engaging in trade at the U.S. relative prices. All that has been shown is that there is a tendency for trade to take place and that domestic relative prices determine the

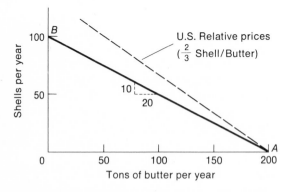

Figure 3.2
Production possibilities curve for the United Kingdom

THE EQUILIBRIUM OF TRADE

An equilibrium in trade is defined as that state in which the quantities traded and their prices are not changing or fluctuating. Trade will be in equilibrium if three conditions are met. These are: that the price ratio be the same in both countries (in the absence of transportation costs); that the quantities offered in trade be equal to the quantities demanded for both goods; and that trade be balanced, that is, that the value of exports equal the value of imports for both countries.

The first step in describing such an equilibrium is to determine the prices at which trade will take place. These prices, like all other prices, will be determined by the interaction of supply and demand. The supply conditions have already been spelled out. They determine the range within which the equilibrium prices must fall. In equilibrium the relative price of any good can be no lower than the relative price of that good in the nation with a comparative advantage in its production, and no higher than its price in the country with a comparative disadvantage. In terms of the example, the price of butter will fall within the interval of ½ to ⅔. The price of a shell will be within the interval 1.5 to 2.0. This is all that supply or cost analysis can tell us. Exactly where in this range the equilibrium price will fall depends on demand conditions in both countries. First a numerical example will be used to illustrate this. Then a more general geometric technique will be employed.

Suppose that with the opening of trade an "auctioneer" is stationed midway between the two countries to cry out different prices until he finds that price which causes the quantities supplied and demanded to be equal. Suppose further that at his first cry the price is experimentally set at $P_B = .6$ shell per ton; and at that price U.S. residents wish to import a total of 50 tons of butter per year. This is equivalent to offering 30 shells (.6 × 50 tons) to the United Kingdom. This relative price is an equilibrium price if, and only if, the U.K. residents wish to import 30 shells per year at that price.

Suppose that they wish to import more at that price. They would also be willing to pay a slightly higher price for shells in order to obtain 30 of them. The butter price of .6 is equivalent to a price for shells of 1.67 tons of butter. Suppose the English were to raise their offer to, say, 1.70 tons of butter. This is equivalent to lowering the price of butter to .588 shell per ton. The effect of lowering the price of butter for U.S. residents would be to encourage them to import more butter, that is, offer more shells for export. This adjustment process would continue until the quantities of shells offered by the

U.S. (a measure of their demand for butter) was exactly equal to the demand for shells on the part of U.K. residents.

The effect of trade on prices can be summarized as follows. For each country the relative price of the product in which it has a comparative advantage will rise with trade. For example, for the U.S. shells rose from 1.5 to 1.7 tons. The relative price of the good in which it has a comparative disadvantage will fall. For the U.S., butter fell from .67 to .588 shell. In other words, each country can obtain its imported good relatively more cheaply with trade than in the absence of trade.

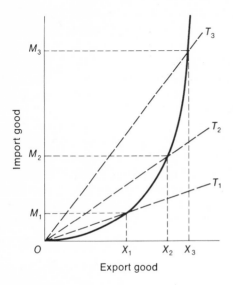

Figure 3.3
The derivation of an offer curve

Demand conditions in international trade can be portrayed with offer curves, or as they are sometimes called, reciprocal demand curves. An offer curve for a country shows the maximum amount of its export good it will offer in exchange for a given amount of the import good, or alternatively the minimum amount of the import good it will accept in return for a given amount of its export good. This derivation is illustrated in Figure 3.3. If $O-M_1$ of the import good is available, the country would offer as much as $O-X_1$ of its export good to obtain it. If the amount available were doubled to $O-M_2$, the offer of the export good would less than double to $O-X_2$. In other words, as more of the import good becomes available, additional amounts of it become relatively less desirable and the offer of the export good will not increase proportionately. The result is that the offer curve will get increasingly steep or be concave upward.[4]

There is another possible interpretation of the offer curve. For various relative prices it shows how much of one good would be exchanged for the other. Any relative price can be represented by a straight line from the origin as in Figure 3.3. The slope of such a line, for example $O–T_1$, is equal to the price of the good measured on the horizontal axis relative to the other good. In Figure 3.3, $O–T_3$ represents a higher price for the export good than $O–T_1$, since, for any quantity of X, the relative price line indicates a larger quantity of M. At the price of $O–T_3$, the offer curve shows that $O–X_3$ would be exported in exchange for $O–M_3$ of the import good. It is also important to note that this trading combination, along with all others which result from an intersection of a price line with the offer curve, represents balanced trade.

Returning to the earlier numerical example, offer curves for the United States and the United Kingdom are presented in Figure 3.4. The U.K.'s import good is on the vertical axis. Each nation's offer curve emerges from the origin with a slope equal to its domestic pretrade relative price. These price ratios are shown by the dashed line extensions, $O–T_{\mathrm{US}}$ and $O–T_{\mathrm{UK}}$. They are the boundaries within which the final trading equilibrium must fall. This equilibrium occurs at the intersection of the two offer curves. At this point the three conditions for an equilibrium are met. There is only one relative price

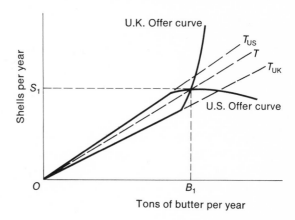

Figure 3.4
Trading equilibrium

[4] A comprehensive derivation of offer curves is presented in the appendix to Chapter 6. The full derivation of the offer curve would show that it extends into the southwest quadrant as well. In this region the so-called export good would be imported because the foreign prices were so favorable.

set, $O–T$. Quantities demanded and supplied (offered) of each good are equal. And because the single price line intersects both offer curves at this point, trade is balanced for both nations. If the price of butter were lower, that is, if the price line were less steep, the United States would demand more butter, while the United Kingdom would offer less. This disparity between quantities demanded and supplied would result in the price of butter being bid up. Similarly, if the price of butter were above $O–T$, the excess supply would push the price down to the equilibrium value.

If the equilibrium price ratio is known, the equilibrium position can also be shown on the production possibilities curves of Figures 3.1 and 3.2. These curves are reproduced as Figure 3.5. Since the new trading equilibrium price is known, the consumption possibilities curves can also be drawn. Each nation is specializing in the production of its comparative advantage good. Production of shells is $O–S_2$ in the United States while butter production is $O–B_2$ in the United Kingdom. The slopes of the dashed consumption possibilities curves are the same (except for sign) as the equilibrium price ratio, $O–T$, in Figure 3.4. Trading and consumption equilibria are shown by C_{US} and C_{UK}. The U.S. is importing and consuming $O–B_1$ of butter. It is consuming $O–S_1$ of shells and exporting the remainder, $S_1–S_2$, to the U.K.

While it is generally expected that both countries would specialize and that the equilibrium price would be different from the price prevailing in either country in the absence of trade, it is not necessary that this be the case. Because of the assumptions underlying the comparative cost model of production, each nation's offer curve emerges from the origin as a straight line. The end of the linear segment marks the beginning of specialization in production. The larger the nation, the longer is this linear segment of the offer curve. If one nation were very large relative to its trading partner, the offer curves

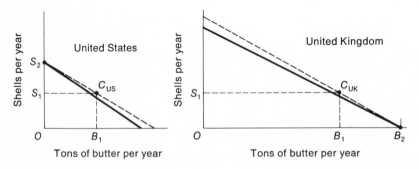

Figure 3.5
The equilibrium of production and consumption

could intersect in this linear portion. Such a case is shown in Figure 3.6. The trading equilibrium price is the same as the pretrade price in the U.S., and the U.S. would continue to produce some of both goods. The smaller nation turns out to be too small to have any effect on the world price. However, smallness has its advantages. As will be shown in the next section, in this case the smaller nation reaps all of the gains from trade.

REAL INCOME AND THE GAINS FROM TRADE

In this section it will be shown that, in general, trade is beneficial to both countries in that labor will have a higher real wage with trade, and that the benefit or the gain from trade will be proportional to the difference between the original pretrade prices and the equilibrium trade prices. Statements about the gains from trade are fairly simple to make in the comparative cost model. Since labor is the only factor of production, all the gains accrue to labor. And since labor is assumed to be homogeneous and a single wage prevails in the nation, the gains are shared more or less equally by all laborers. It will be shown in Chapter 6 that in general it is not this easy to make unqualified statements concerning the gains from trade or whether a nation is better off because of trade.

Consider first the effect of trade on real incomes. Real income is an aggregate measure of the consumption possibilities open to an individual. In an economy with money prices and wages, real income depends on the money wage rate and the hours worked, which determine money income, and upon the prices charged for the goods consumed. An increase in prices, with money wages and hours worked unchanged, will reduce consumption opportunities and real income. A dollar doesn't go as far.

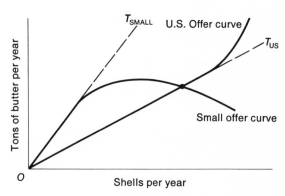

Figure 3.6
Trade equilibrium with only one nation specializing

In an economic model where money prices and wages have not been introduced, real income can be defined in terms of the productivity of labor. Where labor is the only input, it must be paid a wage equal to the value of its output. If the value of output is $10, competition among employers will bid the wage up to $10. If the wage is equal to the value of the output, the laborer can purchase his output with his wage. It is simpler to say that the laborer's wage in real terms is equal to his output or his productivity. This is his real wage. Returning to Table 3.1, the output of a U.S. worker in one day is 1 ton of butter or .67 shell. These are two ways of expressing his real wage rate. Real income is the product of the real wage and the quantity of labor supplied, which is assumed to be fixed. Therefore changes in real wages will be accompanied by proportionate changes in real income.

Since the real income concept actually involves opportunities for consumption of both goods, shells and butter, there is a question of which good should be used to express the real wage rate, shells, butter, or some weighted average of the two? Here comparisons of real wage rates will be expressed alternatively in terms of shells and butter. If the results are the same for both, they will also be the same for any weighted average of the two.

The first results can be quickly seen by examination of Table 3.1. The real wage rate of labor in the United States and United Kingdom in the absence of trade can be expressed alternatively as follows:

Real wage of labor in U.S.	1 ton butter/man-day
	or .67 shell/man-day
Real wage of labor in U.K.	2 tons butter/man-day
	or 1 shell/man-day

By either comparison real wages are higher in the U.K.

If trade is opened and the equilibrium price of butter is, for example, $P_B = .6$ shell per ton, it can be argued that the real wage of labor in the United States has risen. While productivity and real wages as expressed in shells are unchanged, labor is indirectly more productive in terms of butter. One man-day of labor will still produce only .67 shell, but now these shells can be traded for 1.12 tons of butter, a 12 percent increase in the "indirect" productivity of U.S. labor in obtaining butter.[5] The real wage in terms of shells is unchanged, but if it is expressed in terms of butter it is higher. And any weighted average of these two measures of real wage will also be higher. It is not necessarily true that all laborers will benefit equally from the lower price of butter. If all people have identical

[5] If .6 shell can obtain one ton of butter, .67 shell can obtain 1.12 tons.

tastes and preferences, there will be equal gains. But otherwise those who normally purchase more butter benefit.

The real wage in the United Kingdom has also risen. Given the same price for butter as assumed in the preceding paragraph, U.K. labor has a real wage of 2 tons of butter per day or 1.2 shells per day.[6] The real wage as expressed in shells has risen by 20 percent and any weighted average of the two measures has also risen.

In the comparative cost model the gains from trade are in the form of higher real incomes attributable to the opportunity to purchase the imported good at lower prices. This means that, if other things are equal, the greater the change in price the greater the gains from trade. For the large nation which opens trade with a small nation, there may be no gains at all. However, in general, trade raises the real wages and real incomes of workers in both countries, even when one country has an absolute cost advantage in the production of both goods. The absolute cost advantage is reflected in higher real wages; but the introduction of trade when *comparative* advantage exists will raise real wages even higher. The rich country's gain is not the poor country's loss in this case, since real wages and real incomes rise for all workers.

SUPPLEMENTARY READINGS

Kindleberger, Charles, *International Economics,* 4th ed., Homewood, Ill., Irwin, 1968, chaps. 2, 3, appendix C.

Caves, Richard, *Trade and Economic Structure,* Cambridge, Mass., Harvard University Press, 1960, pp. 6–22.

Viner, Jacob, *Studies in the Theory of International Trade,* London, George Allen & Unwin, reprinted in 1955, chap. VIII.

Haberler, Gottfried, *The Theory of International Trade,* London, Macmillan & Co., 1937.

[6] One ton of butter can be sold for .6 shell, and 2 tons will net 1.2 shells.

Chapter

The Modern Theory of Comparative Advantage and Trade

In a fundamental way the comparative cost model of trade is incomplete. In its simplest form it assumes only one factor of production, or at best factors which are combined in fixed, unchangeable proportions. Intercountry productivity differences for the single factor or factor bundle are assumed or postulated at the outset. The direction of trade is determined by these postulates, since the price differences giving rise to comparative advantage follow immediately from the differences in productivity.

A major task of the modern theory of trade is to show how prices are determined and why intercountry price differences might arise. In order to do this we must develop a general model of the domestic economy. The model to be developed in this chapter is complete in that:

1. it permits any number of factor inputs;
2. it deals explicitly with the process of production, including variations in the proportions in which factor inputs are combined; and
3. it is a general equilibrium model which permits the determination of factor prices and quantities of outputs as well as product prices.

Ultimately the nontrade equilibrium of a market economic system depends on only four things: the endowment or available quantities of factor inputs, the available technology, the tastes and preferences of the individuals in the economy, and the pattern of income distribution.[1] The first two are basically supply factors, while the latter two are demand factors. This will be shown below with our general model. In principle differences in relative prices between countries can arise because of intercountry differences in any of these four basic determinants of the equilibrium. However, the most widely accepted version of the modern theory of trade focuses on only one of these, differences in factor endowments. In this chapter we will first develop the general equilibrium model using graphical techniques. We will then show how differences in supply and demand conditions can lead to trade and how they determine the direction of trade. In the next two chapters we will deal with the effects of this trade on product and factor prices and incomes. In Chapter 7 we will examine to what extent these competing hypotheses concerning the causes of trade have found confirmation in empirical testing.

PRODUCTION, COSTS, AND PRICES IN ONE COUNTRY

Isoquants and Production

Since there is a strong consensus among economists that supply elements are more important than demand in explaining the flows of goods in trade, the major part of this section is devoted to developing a model of the production process. First assume that there are two factors of production, labor and perfectly homogeneous capital. All labor is assumed to be identical. Homogeneous capital implies that, at least in the long run, capital can be transferred freely and without cost from one industry or use to another. The model can be generalized mathematically to any number of factor inputs. The assumption of only two factors permits a graphical portrayal of the production process.

Next assume that both capital and labor are required in the production of any good. Take steel for example. The relationship between the inputs of labor and capital and the output of steel can be described by their production function. A production function is a mathematical expression giving the technical or engineering relationship between factor inputs and commodity outputs. It can be expressed as follows: $S = S(K, L)$, where S denotes output of steel per unit of time, and K and L denote the rates of inputs of labor and capital.

This symbolic statement can be translated as follows. The out-

---

[1] In an economy with no government, this in turn depends only on the distribution of ownership of the factor inputs and their market prices.

put of steel per unit of time depends in a particular but unspecified way on the rates at which capital and labor are being used. This production function, as written, assumes a given state of knowledge or level of technology. Any scientific or engineering discoveries or innovations which lead to an improvement in the terms at which inputs can be converted to outputs is a change in technology. Such changes are kept out of the model by assumption until a later chapter, which deals directly with trade, technological change, and growth.

Men are not really being consumed in the production of steel; only the services that men provide. The unit of labor input is the use of one man for one day, that is, one man-day. In the same manner capital is not being directly consumed in the production of steel, only the services that capital provides. Actually, of course, capital machines are gradually worn out or depreciated by their use in production. To simplify the analysis, we can either assume that capital is perfectly durable, or that owners of capital undertake repairs and upkeep sufficient to counter the effects of physical depreciation, so that in either case the stock of capital is not in fact depleted by production.

How is this stock of capital to be measured? Although capital is assumed to be homogeneous, it consists of many kinds of machines, tools, goods in process, inventories, and buildings. Capital can be freely transformed from one form to another over time; but at any point in time the existing stock of capital is in fact heterogeneous. For the purposes of the model there are two possible solutions to this problem. The first is to develop some aggregate measure of the capital stock which adds together its disparate elements. This can only be done through the construction of an index or weighted aggregate. If the capital embodied in a building could be gradually withdrawn and transformed into two turret lathes, buildings must incorporate twice as much capital. Buildings should enter the index number calculation with twice the weight of lathes. The index number which results from these calculations represents a physical stock of capital, not a value. It is in the same dimensional terms as the stock of laborers.[2] The capital input to the production process would then be the services from one unit of this composite capital stock for one day. Call this a "capital day." The other solution is to artificially impose homogeneity by assumption. Suppose that there was a General All Purpose Machine which could be used in the produc-

---

[2] In principle the index number solution to the problem of measuring the capital stock is unsatisfactory. This is because of a fundamental characteristic of all index number calculations. This so-called index number problem is discussed in Chapter 6, pages 84–86. Despite its inherent weaknesses, there is no practical alternative for empirical work.

tion of anything. Then the total capital stock is simply the number of machines, and the unit of capital input is a machine day.

The production function can take many forms. The simplest form is when labor and capital can be combined only in fixed or constant proportions in the output of steel. For example, suppose that the only physically possible way of producing steel is to combine the inputs in the ratio of two man-days to one capital-day. Suppose that two man-days plus one capital-day yield one ton of steel, and the process has constant returns to scale. This production relationship is shown in Figure 4.1.

Point A equals 100 tons and shows the consequences of combining 200 man-days of labor per year with 100 capital-days of capital per year. The long dashed lines forming a corner at point A represent an isoquant. An isoquant shows all possible combinations of inputs of labor and capital which will produce 100 tons of steel. If 300 man-days of labor are combined with 100 capital-days, 100 tons of steel will be produced and 100 man-days of labor will be superfluous. There is a family of isoquants of similar shape, each one showing the quantities of inputs required to produce a different quantity of steel. Their "corners" all lie on the line emerging from the origin which signifies a capital/labor ratio of ½. This family of isoquants is a graphical mapping or presentation of the production function described above.

Now assume that steel can be produced by two quite different processes. The first is as described above; in the second process a ton of steel can be produced by combining 1½ man-days of labor

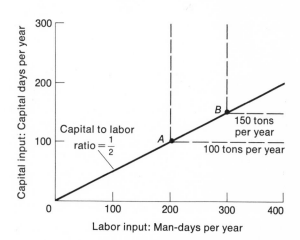

Figure 4.1
Production function for steel—fixed proportions and constant returns to scale

and 1½ capital-days of capital. This second production process is described by the point A′ at the corner of the dashed line isoquant in Figure 4.2. At point A′ 150 man-days plus 150 capital-days can be combined to produce 100 tons of steel. As before, there is a whole family of such isoquants whose corners lie on the one-to-one capital/labor ratio line. In considering production theories, there is no valid reason for assuming only one or only two or only any small number of production functions or production combinations. It is a techno-logical fact of life there are many ways to "skin a cat," and there are many ways to produce a ton of steel. A third way of combining labor and capital to produce 100 tons of steel is represented by A″. Now if we consider that these three processes can be used simul-taneously or in some combination, the isoquant for 100 tons of steel becomes the connection of the points A, A′, and A″ in Figure 4.2. In fact, if there is an infinite number of ways to skin a cat, that is, if continuous variation of the input proportions is possible, the iso-quants for any given level of output will be smooth, continuously curved, and convex to the origin. Figure 4.3 shows a family of con-tinuous isoquants representing such a production function for steel.

With the aid of Figure 4.3 we are ready to answer the question, What combination of inputs of labor and capital will be used to pro-duce steel? We must assume that producers have some incentive, such as profit, to choose the most economical combination of inputs. The production process chosen will depend upon the relative prices of the factor inputs. Assume at first that the price of one capital-day

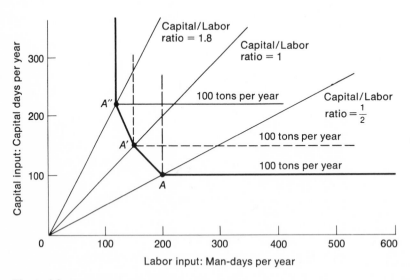

Figure 4.2
A two-process production function for steel

of capital services is $1.00, and the price of one man-day of labor services is $1.00.[3] The relative price of capital to labor is one to one. With this information a family of isocost lines can be drawn in Figure 4.3. Two of these are shown. Each of these shows the various combinations of capital and labor services that could be purchased with a given sum of money. if the total budget or total cost is $300, and the prices are as shown, a firm could purchase 300 capital-days of capital services and no labor, or could purchase 300 man-days of labor and no capital, or 150 days of each, or any other combination which amounted to a total expenditure of $300.

There are two ways to approach the question of the efficient use of factor inputs in production. The first is to ask how to allocate factor inputs so as to minimize the cost of producing some given or target output. This is equivalent to finding the lowest isocost line which touches the given isoquant or target output curve. Alternatively, we should ask how to maximize the output of steel for a given total cost or total expenditure. This is equivalent to finding the highest possible isoquant which touches a given isocost line. Either way the question is approached the answer is the same. Production is efficient in the sense that it is not possible to get a higher output

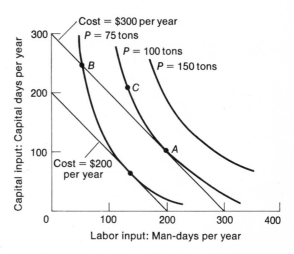

Figure 4.3
The production function for steel with continuous input substitution

[3] The price of labor is the wage rate, or the price of renting a man and his services for one day. Similarly, for capital imagine a gigantic *United Rent-All Agency* owning the whole capital stock and leasing machines to producers as needed. The rent charged is the price of capital services. If markets are competitive it does not matter whether the producer owns his own machine and charges himself an implicit rent, or rents it from someone else. In either case the rental over the life of the machine will sum to the cost of the machine plus the interest on the investment.

without increasing total cost whenever an isoquant is tangent to an isocost line. Point *A* is such a tangency.

With this analysis the effects of changes in relative factor prices can be shown. If capital were to become more expensive relative to labor, the isocost lines would be rotated or twisted counterclockwise. See Figure 4.4. To say that capital has become relatively more expensive is identical to saying that labor has become relatively less expensive. What matters is the ratio of the price of labor to the price of capital, which is shown graphically by the slope of the isocost line.[4] In the example in Figure 4.4, the price of capital has risen from $1 per capital-day to $2 per capital-day. It has also induced a substitution effect in that the new efficient production point for an output of 100 tons of steel is now at point *B*. At this point more labor is being used and less capital than at the old relative prices. In conclusion, changes in the relative prices of factors of production induce changes in the proportions in which they are combined in the productive process, as producers economize on the factor with the increased price.

The factor intensity of a production function is one characteristic which plays an important role in explaining flows of goods in international trade. Factor intensity refers to the *ratio* of capital to labor in a production process at a *given set* of relative factor prices. More specifically, it refers to comparisons of these capital/labor ratios among production processes for different goods using the same factors at a given set of factor prices. Figure 4.5 shows one isoquant

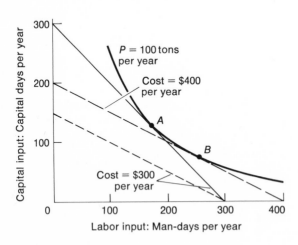

Figure 4.4
The effect of changes in relative factor prices

[4] Ignoring the minus sign.

each for the steel and cloth industries. The factor price ratio, shown by the isocost line *X–Y*, is the same for both industries since both industries purchase their capital and labor in the same market. Steel has a higher capital/labor ratio (shown by the angle θ_S) *at that set of factor prices* than does cloth. The *comparison* of capital/labor ratios in steel and cloth reveals steel to be capital intensive relative to cloth at that set of factor prices.

In Figure 4.6 the relative prices of labor and capital have been changed to make labor relatively less expensive. At the new set of relative factor prices steel is still capital intensive *relative* to cloth since θ'_S is still greater than θ'_C.

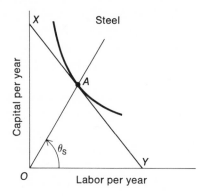
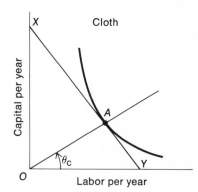

Figure 4.5
Relative factor intensities

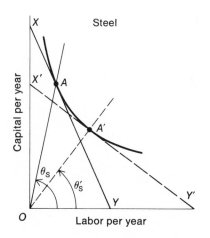
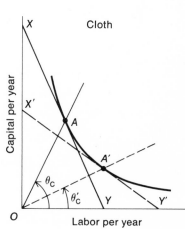

Figure 4.6
Unchanged relative factor intensities with different relative prices

There is no reason why relative factor intensities must remain unchanged as factor prices change. In Figure 4.7 the cloth and steel isoquants are placed in the same diagram to compare their shapes. In this example when capital is cheap relative to labor (see the isocost lines in the upper left portion), cloth is capital intensive relative to steel, as shown by θ_C being greater than θ_S. However when labor becomes cheap relative to capital, cloth becomes relatively labor intensive in comparison with steel. At any point to the right of the ray O–T, cloth is the labor intensive good; but to the left of O–T, steel is labor intensive. This phenomenon is known as *factor intensity reversal;* and it arises because labor and capital are relatively good substitutes in production of cloth while they are not relatively good substitutes in the production of steel. Hence, a change in relative factor prices brings about a greater substitution effect in cloth than in steel and this is sometimes sufficient to reverse factor intensities.

One other concept regarding production theory should be mentioned now, lest it lead to confusion later. This is the concept of returns to *scale* in production. Returns to *scale* refers to what happens to output if *all* inputs are changed proportionately. If when all inputs are changed proportionately, output changes by the *same* proportion, this is constant returns to scale. Increasing returns to scale refers to that case where a proportionate increase (decrease) in all factor inputs leads to a more than proportionate increase (decrease) in output. Constant returns to scale are assumed throughout.

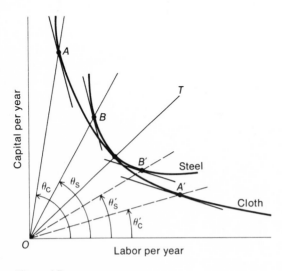

Figure 4.7
Factor intensity reversal

We are now ready to examine the interrelationships between two industries in production, under the assumption that there are only two goods produced and that there are only two factors of production, capital and labor. To portray the production relations we utilize a graphic device sometimes known as an Edgeworth-Bowley box. As shown in Figure 4.8, the box itself can only be drawn if the quantities of both inputs in the economy are known and fixed. The endowments of the two factors determine the size and shape of the box. The axes or dimensions of the box show the total quantities of labor and capital available to the economy. They are assumed to be 500 man-days and 300 capital-days per year.

The box is drawn to show how labor and capital are divided or allocated between the production of steel on the one hand and cloth on the other. The sides of the box are drawn to be just like the axes of an isoquant diagram such as were shown earlier in this chapter. The left-hand and lower edges represent the vertical and horizontal axes for the isoquant diagram for steel. Point A, when referred to these two axes, shows that 300 man-days of labor and 100 capital-days of capital are being utilized in the production of steel. When the page is turned upside down, it can be seen that the other two axes represent the isoquant diagram for cloth production. When point A is referred to the upper right-hand corner or the origin with respect to cloth, it represents an allocation of 200 man-days of labor and 200

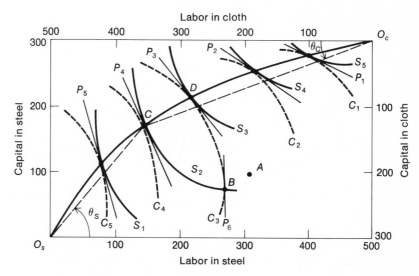

Figure 4.8
Production in a two-factor/two-good world—the Edgeworth-Bowley box

48 capital-days of capital to cloth production. Point A shows that 300 man-days of labor are allocated to steel and 200 man-days of labor are allocated to cloth; and this exhausts the total supply of 500 man-days of labor. Similarly, point A represents a full employment allocation of capital between steel and cloth. Any point within the box represents an allocation of resources which uses up the total quantities available.

In the box the solid line isoquants are for steel, while the dotted line isoquants represent alternative outputs of cloth where the total output of cloth increases, moving from upper right to lower left. The isoquants or production functions in cloth and steel are different in that at any factor price ratio such as P_4 in Figure 4.8, the capital/labor ratio is higher in steel. In other words steel is relatively more capital intensive. At point C this is shown by the angle θ_S being greater than θ_C. The significance of the assumption that factor intensities are different will be shown below.

The box can be used to distinguish between those allocations of resources and outputs which are efficient and those which are not. Inefficient outputs are those where it is possible to increase the output of one good costlessly, that is, without any offsetting decrease in the output of the other good. Point B in the diagram represents an inefficient allocation of resources between steel and cloth production. It would be possible, in fact desirable, to withdraw about 60 man-days of labor from steel production and use them in the production of cloth. At the same time, by withdrawing capital from the production of cloth and utilizing it in the production of steel, the economy could be moved along the cloth isoquant to point D. Here the output of steel would be higher while the output of cloth would *not* have been diminished. Alternatively, the economy could have moved from point B to point C increasing the output of cloth while holding the output of steel constant. Points C and D both are efficient production points. There is a whole family of these efficient production points located along the curved line from O_s to O_c. This line is called the *efficiency locus.* Each of these efficient points can be found by locating a tangency point between a cloth isoquant and a steel isoquant. At such a tangency point, it is impossible to increase the output of one good, that is, move to a higher isoquant for that good, without simultaneously moving to a lower isoquant for the other good.

A market economy will naturally tend to move to a point somewhere on the efficiency locus, O_s–O_c. Which point along the locus is actually chosen will depend upon the demand conditions in the economy. To see why an economy will tend to move toward the efficiency locus we must recall the point made earlier about tangencies between isoquants and isocost lines. We must also impose the condition that labor and capital markets function smoothly so that both industries can buy a factor at the same price. An isocost line has been drawn through each of those tangency points actually drawn in Figure 4.8 representing the relative factor prices that will prevail at that point. Each isocost line, labeled P_1, P_2, etc., is simultaneously tangent to both isoquants at their point of tangency. Therefore, at the efficient points both industries have reached their optima for the given set of factor prices.

At point B, where the relative factor prices are given by the line P_6, the steel industry is not in equilibrium. At this set of factor prices, with capital being relatively cheap compared to labor, steel producers would like to use more capital relative to labor and would be willing to pay more than the going price for capital. The steel industry's attempts to obtain more capital will bid up the price of capital services. But this process will continue as long as the isocost line cuts the steel isoquant, S_2, rather than being tangent to it. At the same time in the steel industry labor is relatively expensive. The steel industry will wish to use relatively less labor at the going wage rate and will be discharging labor. The net effect will be that the steel industry will be moving to a point somewhere upward and to the left of point B. As the price of capital rises the cloth industry will find that capital is relatively expensive to it, and labor is relatively inexpensive. The cloth industry will be buying less capital services and buying more labor services moving up and to the left of point B. This process will continue until both industries have reached a point which is on the efficiency locus. There will be no incentive for either industry to change the quantities of capital and labor taken by it when the isocost line is tangent to both isoquants at their point of tangency to each other.

The Production Possibilities Curve

The Edgeworth-Bowley box in Figure 4.8 shows the production possibilities open to an economy given technology and factor supplies. This information can be used to draw a production possibilities curve such as the one shown in Figure 4.9. At each point on the efficiency locus of Figure 4.8, there is one steel and one cloth isoquant. The pairs of values from these isoquants, outputs of steel and cloth, can be used to locate points in Figure 4.9. Each such point represents an efficient output combination; and all such points make up the production possibilities curve. All the labeled points in Figure 4.9 have their counterparts in Figure 4.8. Point B in Figure 4.9 is inefficient because, given the factor endowment, it would be possible to move up to the right producing either more steel or more cloth or more of both.

Figure 4.8 does not give a clear picture of the concept of costs of production. However, Figure 4.9 does. The cost of increasing the output of steel is the reduction in the output of cloth which must take place in order to free the resources for increased steel production. In moving from point D to point E in Figure 4.9, steel production is increased by ΔS. The cost of ΔS is the reduction in cloth production ΔC. The marginal cost of steel production is $\Delta C/\Delta S$, or the negative of the slope of the production possibilities curve at that point. Similarly, the marginal cost of cloth production at any point is the negative reciprocal of the slope of the production possibilities curve. In this example the marginal cost of steel ($\Delta C/\Delta S$) increases with increasing steel output. Also the marginal cost of cloth ($\Delta S/\Delta C$) is an increasing function of cloth output.

Let us consider further some of the things which influence the shape and the position of the production possibilities curve. One is obviously the total factor endowment of the economy. An increase in the quantity of labor available to the economy would shift out the production possibilities curve at all points. If both factors of production were to increase in quantity over time as the consequence of economic growth, the box would get larger and larger and the production possibilities curve would shift continuously farther up and to the right. The exact effect of this depends upon the relative growth rates of capital and labor. In the example used above, if the growth rate of capital is higher than the growth rate of labor, the Edgeworth-Bowley box in Figure 4.8 will gradually become more square. Also the outward movement of the production possibilities curve will be biased in favor of the capital intensive good, steel.

The state of technology is the other major determinant of the supply conditions portrayed by the production possibilities curve.

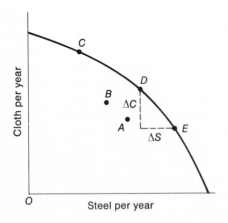

Figure 4.9
Production possibilities and opportunity costs

Technological change will shift all of the isoquants within the Edge-worth-Bowley box so as to make possible greater outputs with an unchanged total factor supply. This will also result in an outward movement of the production possibilities curve. These matters will be given greater attention in Chapter 12.

Finally we must consider why the production possibilities curve is concave to the origin, that is, why there are increasing marginal costs. The condition of increasing costs is the consequence of two things, both of which are necessary conditions for a concave produc-tion possibilities curve. These are first the presence of two factors of production which can be combined in variable proportions, and second the fact that at any factor price ratio the two goods have dif-ferent factor intensities or capital/labor ratios. When steel output is increased, cloth output must be reduced simultaneously. This reduction frees both capital and labor from cloth production but relatively more labor, since cloth is labor intensive. Steel would try to absorb relatively more capital, but it cannot. This "conflict" would be resolved by an increase in the relative price of capital and a de-crease in the capital/labor ratio in steel; that is, steel would become more labor intensive relative to its own earlier position. Both of these changes are adverse to steel production, putting it on increasingly disadvantageous terms relative to cloth production, hence increasing the opportunity cost of steel production.

If there is only one factor of production, as in the simple com-parative cost model, this phenomenon cannot arise, provided pro-duction takes place under constant returns to scale. In this case opportunity costs are constant and the production possibilities curve is a straight line (see Chapter 3). The same conclusion holds for the case of two factors combined in fixed proportions, since they can be treated as one composite factor bundle. If there are decreasing returns to scale, with a single factor, the production possibilities curve will be concave to the origin. And if there are increasing re-turns to scale throughout, the curve will be convex to the origin.

If there are two factor inputs, but the factor intensities are the same for both goods, then as the output of one is increased it ab-sorbs factors in the same proportions that they are being released by the other good. There are no changes in factor prices or capital/labor ratios, and opportunity costs are constant, again provided that there are constant returns to scale.

In the two-factor case where there are increasing returns to scale, it is possible that the general expectation of concavity to the origin can be upset. The effect of increasing returns is to make the production possibilities curve concave upward while the presence of two factors and different factor intensities has the opposite effect. Whether the production possibilities curve turns out to be concave or convex depends upon the relative strengths of these two tendencies.

To summarize the influences on the conditions of cost:

—increasing returns to scale tends to lead to decreasing opportunity costs, and vice versa;

—different factor intensities among goods tends to lead to increasing opportunity costs and concavity, even with constant returns to scale;

—identical factor intensities or a single factor tend to lead to constant cost.

Equilibrium in a Closed Economy

Up to this point the discussion has been relevant to any economic system, from a strictly private enterprise capitalistic system to a planned economy where outputs are determined by fiat from the central authority. We did describe how market forces would tend to move a market economy toward the efficiency locus and production possibilities curve. In a command economy authorities have to figure out how to get there by using techniques like linear programming. In this section and in the remainder of the book we deal only with market economies. We assume that there is no government to interfere with resource allocation (except for tariffs, later), that all markets are competitive, and that factors can move freely and costlessly from one industry to another. In this respect the analysis is long run in nature.

In a market economy the money price of any good is determined by the intersection of a supply curve and demand curve. This market demand curve is the summation or horizontal addition of all individuals' demand curves. Each of these depends in part on the level of income for that individual. Therefore the market demand curve for each good must depend on both the tastes and preferences of all individuals, and the distribution of income among them.

While the analysis of the market for a single good assumes that all other prices are taken as given, in general equilibrium analysis of an economic system this assumption is not valid. All prices are variables to be determined simultaneously. In effect the general equilibrium of an economy can be represented by a large system of equations where there are separate demand and supply equations for each good and for each factor input. This system must be solved simultaneously for the unknowns, the prices and quantities. One of the most important characteristics of market economies is that they contain equilibrating mechanisms which automatically seek out the solution values for the economy.

In this set of equations the demand equations reflect the distribution of income and the tastes and preferences which shape what people do with their incomes. The supply equations reflect factor endowments and the state of technology which determines what can be done with the available resources.[5] In a two-good model of the economy these supply conditions are portrayed by the production possibilities curve. Unfortunately it is quite difficult to obtain a comparable graphical portrayal of the general equilibrium conditions of demand.[6] Here we will outline the conditions which define an equilibrium and describe the mechanisms which will guide a market economy toward that position. The graphical tools we will use do not permit us to determine where that equilibrium will be in advance.

In the full equilibrium of our two-good world the prices of goods in both markets are such that the quantities supplied equal the quantities demanded, and there is no tendency for any of the variables to change. It can be shown that this economy will be in equilibrium whenever the ratio of the prices is equal to the ratio of the marginal costs. Graphically the price ratios or relative prices can be represented by price lines such as P_1-P_3 in Figure 4.10. These lines are similar to the isocost lines of Figures 4.3 to 4.8. The steep line, P_1, shows a high price of steel relative to cloth.

To see how the adjustment process works, suppose that producers of steel and cloth initially decide to produce a combination of outputs shown by point A. When this output is placed on the market there will be some set of prices of steel and cloth which will just clear the market. Suppose that the market can be cleared only at a low price of cloth relative to the price of steel, as shown by the price line P_1. At point A the terms at which consumers are willing to give up cloth for steel are higher than the opportunity cost of steel. Hence producers will see an opportunity for profit in producing larger quantities of steel. Similarly, the opportunity cost of cloth exceeds the willingness of consumers to exchange steel for cloth, so cloth production will decline.[7] The combined actions of steel and cloth producers will move the economy from point A toward point B.

[5] In fact supply and demand are interrelated through the effect of factor prices on incomes and demand. A given set of product prices determines a set of factor prices. Factor prices are incomes to the recipients and changes in these affect income, demand, and product prices. In sum the system is completely interdependent.

[6] Community indifference curves are often used as a pedagogical device to represent demand. However, community indifference curves can only be drawn under very limiting assumptions about the distribution of income. These assumptions seriously impair their usefulness. Unless these limitations are kept clearly in mind by the student, he is likely to reach invalid conclusions about the effects of trade. It is my view that the extra trouble required to discuss demand in the absence of community indifference curves is worth it. However, for those who wish to see these curves in action, they are derived and used to portray the equilibrium of trade and the gains from trade in the appendix to Chapter 6.

[7] In terms of money prices the price of steel exceeds its marginal cost, which is a signal for steel producers to expand output, assuming competition. In cloth, price is below marginal cost.

54 At the same time, the increased output of steel will tend to depress the price of steel, and the reduced output of cloth will tend to increase the price of cloth, so that the price line will be rotating counterclockwise. Eventually there will be some point where the price line will be tangent to the production possibilities curve rather than cutting it. Such a tangency point is shown at point B with price line P_2. In comparison with P_1, P_2 shows a lower price of steel and a higher price of cloth. Since the price line and the production possibilities curve are tangent at this point, the ratio of prices is equal to the ratio of marginal costs, or, in money terms, price equals marginal cost in both industries. Therefore both industries are at equilibrium. Point B represents an equilibrium position for the economy determined by the interaction of supply and demand.

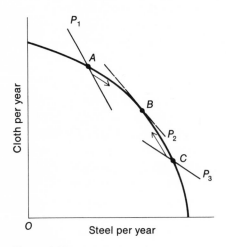

Figure 4.10
The equilibrium of a closed economy

At point C steel is relatively abundant and the price of steel is relatively low, but at the same time because of increasing costs the marginal cost of steel is quite high relative to the marginal cost of cloth. Steel producers are not in equilibrium since marginal cost exceeds price. The adjustment process works just as before. Steel producers reduce output and the price of steel rises. Cloth producers increase output and the price of cloth falls; eventually an equilibrium will be reached at point B where price ratios equal cost ratios.

A TWO-COUNTRY MODEL OF TRADE

It was shown in Chapter 2 that differences in the relative prices and costs of producing a commodity in two countries are sufficient to induce the flow of trade. Now that we have outlined the elements of a theory of production and a model of general equilibrium within one country, we can see how price and cost differences might arise. Given the production conditions and the production possibilities curve in one country, the prices in that country will vary as the tastes of consumers vary and as the distribution of income varies. Differences in demand conditions are sufficient to explain differences in prices and cost, unless of course the production possibilities curve is linear. In that case, demand determines only quantities and supply determines prices as in Chapter 3.

With identical patterns of demand, price differences and cost differences can arise if supply conditions are different. Supply differences could arise if in two countries the production functions were different, or if there were differences in factor endowments. The remainder of this chapter will be devoted to examining in more detail the two cases of trade between two nations with different factor endowments and production possibilities curves and with identical production possibilities curves but different demands.

In both models the following set of assumptions will be made: there are two countries, two goods, and two homogeneous factors in fixed supply; both countries have the same production function (that is, the isoquants are the same shape and pattern); transportation costs between countries are zero; in both countries product and factor markets are perfectly competitive; factor intensity reversals do not occur; factors are mobile within countries but immobile between countries; and finally, in both countries production goes on with constant returns to scale but increasing costs.

Trade with Different Factor Endowments

In addition to the general assumptions made above, it is assumed in this subsection that the two countries have different relative factor endowments; that is, the ratio of the total capital supply to the total labor supply is different between the two countries. Assume that the two countries are the United States and the United Kingdom. Further assume that the ratio of capital to labor in the United States is higher than the capital/labor ratio in the United Kingdom. In other words, the United States is relatively capital rich *in comparison with* the United Kingdom. Finally, assume that the demand conditions are the same in both countries.

The first step is to show the effect of factor endowments on the production possibilities curves. In brief, each country will have relatively lower marginal opportunity costs in that good using its relatively abundant factor more intensively. See Figure 4.11. The capital abundant United States will have lower costs in steel production, which is capital intensive relative to cloth. This is because capital abundance yields a relatively lower price for capital. While this lower price affects costs in both goods, it has a greater effect on the cost of the good using more capital. At any ratio of cloth production to steel production the marginal cost of cloth in the United Kingdom is lower than in the United States. Conversely, at any ratio of cloth to steel output the United States has a lower marginal cost of production of steel. This can be seen by drawing a line from the origin to the production possibilities curve at that point (see Figure 4.11). For any line so drawn, that is, for any ratio of cloth and steel outputs, the slope of the U.K. production possibilities curve will be steeper; it will show greater marginal cost for steel or lower marginal cost for cloth production. In simpler but less precise terms each production possibilities curve tends to be bowed out or extended relatively farther in the direction of the good using its abundant factor more intensively.

In the absence of trade the equilibrium position in each country will be determined by the interaction of domestic demand and supply conditions. The domestic or pretrade equilibrium positions are denoted by the two points A in Figure 4.11. A dashed line representing the price ratios in the opposite country has been drawn through each country's equilibrium position. This allows easy visual comparison of price ratios between the two nations. In the United States the domestic price of cloth relative to steel is quite high in comparison with the United Kingdom.

These price differences which exist in the absence of trade are sufficient to generate trade if the situation permits. Let us assume that some diplomatic maneuver or revolution in transportation technology has occurred and that now trade can take place between the

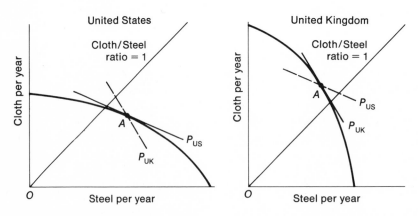

Figure 4.11
Pretrade equilibria with different factor endowments

two countries. U.S. producers will see that they can sell steel at a higher price (measured in cloth) in the United Kingdom than they can obtain at home. This also means that cloth is cheaper in the United Kingdom. At the same time the British will see that they can buy steel more cheaply in the United States than they can at home. Both forces will encourage an increase in the U.S. production of steel and a contraction in the production of steel in the United Kingdom. It is the contraction in steel production which is necessary and provides the resources for the expansion in cloth production in the United Kingdom. Correspondingly in the United States, cloth contraction is necessary before resources can be freed for expansion in steel.

The law of a single price tells us that the price of steel relative to the price of cloth must be the same in the United States and the United Kingdom after trade. Both countries will adjust their consumption and production of steel and cloth until the new equilibrium is reached where quantities demanded and supplied are equal, the relative prices in the U.S. and the U.K. are equal, and trade is balanced in value terms. As in Chapter 3, offer curves can be derived. Their intersection will determine the equilibrium price ratio and quantities traded.[8]

The new world price ratio is shown by the solid line labeled P_W for both countries in Figure 4.12. P_W is tangent to the production possibilities curve of both countries at point B_P. The subscript means production point. We have yet to determine the consumption positions in both countries. If trade is taking place in steel, the United States must be consuming a different amount of steel than it is producing. The points B_C on the new price lines show the consumption position of the United States and United Kingdom. The exact location of point B_C depends on demand conditions—tastes and incomes. The United States is consuming O–S_3 of steel and O–C_3 of cloth. The difference between domestic production and domestic consumption is being exported to the United Kingdom. Similarly the difference between cloth consumption, which is larger than cloth production, is made up by imports from the United Kingdom. Another way of looking at it is that at the price ratio which emerges in trade and the resulting output of producers in the United States, U.S consumers are not in equilibrium. At the relatively high price of steel that results, they would wish to consume less steel than is being produced and more cloth than is being produced. They can make this adjustment by trading the excess production of steel with the United Kingdom and obtaining cloth in return. Steel can be exchanged for cloth through trade with the latter on more favorable

[8] See pp. 32–35.

THE MODERN THEORY OF COMPARATIVE ADVANTAGE AND TRADE

terms than it could be transformed into cloth by resource reallocation in the United States. This is because steel could be exchanged
for cloth in the United States in the absence of trade only by moving
along the production possibilities curve.

In the United Kingdom, British consumers are not satisfied with
the output B_P but are able to trade cloth for steel at the world price
ratio, P_W. This is more favorable to them than their domestic trans-
formation possibilities. They export the excess of cloth production
over consumption.

Can we say anything more precise about the location of the
consumption point B_C? While Figure 4.12 shows the consumption

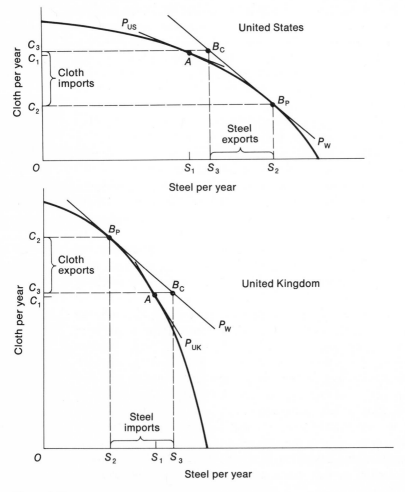

Figure 4.12
Trade with different factor endowments

points for both countries to be above and to the right of the pretrade equilibria, it does not always have to turn out this way. Take the case of the United States. Trade lowers the price of cloth, so we would expect the consumption of cloth to increase with trade.[9] Steel consumption might either increase or decrease. The higher average real income resulting from trade would tend to increase steel consumption; but its higher relative price works in the opposite direction. To summarize the U.S. case, with the exception of the possibility mentioned in the footnote, the consumption point will be above the old equilibrium point and either to the right or left of it depending on the strength of the income and price effects on steel consumption.

Notice that in this example trade does not lead to complete specialization in either country. Both countries are still producing both commodities after trade. This would be considered a likely outcome but not a necessary one. It is a consequence of increasing costs in both countries. As a country tends to specialize relatively in the production of its export goods, because of increasing costs and changing factor prices the good becomes relatively more expensive. This gradually eliminates the cost advantage. Unless the country is very small relative to its trading partner, or the production possibilities curve has a low degree of curvature (costs increase slowly), this process will halt the move toward specialization before the point of complete specialization is reached.

Trade might be said to have benefited both countries because it has enabled them to arrive at consumption positions which are unattainable in the absence of trade. Trade has enabled both countries to move outside their production possibilities curve by relatively specializing in the production of a good in which they have a comparative advantage. However, one should be cautioned against making too much of statements such as this. Nothing has been said as yet about how the increments to cloth and steel consumption have been distributed among individuals. At this point we cannot rule out the possibility that some individuals might be worse off with trade in the sense that they have *less* of both steel and cloth to consume. This question of the gains from trade and their distribution will be taken up in the next two chapters.

In this section our attention has been directed toward supply conditions as an explanation for trade between nations. We have assumed throughout that technical knowledge was freely available

[9] There is an exception. It will be shown in the next chapter that some individuals may experience a reduction in income with the opening of trade. If the individuals in this group all had very high income elasticities of demand for cloth, and were major consumers of cloth, their adverse income effect may more than offset the effect of the lower price of cloth. In this case the new consumption equilibrium would be below and to the right of point A.

60 and therefore that production functions were identical. In other words, differences in available technology were ruled out. We also have assumed that factor inputs were homogeneous, or of similar quality in both nations. Therefore differences in relative factor endowments turned out to be the only remaining supply condition which could account for relative cost differences and trade.

In summary the model of trade developed here states that trade flows can be explained by differences in the relative abundance of factor inputs—measured in physical, not value terms. Differences in factor endowments yield differences in factor prices and costs which give rise to comparative advantage. A nation will have a comparative advantage and will tend to export that good using its abundant factor more intensively.

The modern theory of trade as presented here has been attributed to two Swedish economists, Heckscher and Ohlin, and is widely known as the Heckscher-Ohlin theory of trade.[10] The Heckscher-Ohlin model has become the most widely used and highly developed theory of trade in the economist's kit of analytical tools. Whether this has been warranted by the model's success in empirical tests of its hypotheses is a question left for a subsequent chapter. Here we will only note that much of the theoretical framework developed in this chapter could also be used to build models based on differences in factor quality or technology on the supply side or on differences in demand. This last possibility will now be demonstrated.

Demand Differences and Trade

Assume two countries with similar relative endowments of factor inputs. In other words the total capital/labor ratios of the two countries are the same. This would give rise to similar or proportional production possibilities curves. For convenience assume that the factor endowments are identical in magnitude. Then given identical production functions and technology, the two nations would have the same production possibilities curve. This is shown in Figure 4.13. If demand conditions were the same, prices would be the same in both countries and there would be no basis for trade. If there are demand differences, they could arise either because of differences in the underlying patterns of tastes and preferences or because of differences in the level and/or distribution of income.

Assume that U.S. consumers tend to prefer cloth over steel at

[10] See Eli F. Heckscher, "The Effect of Foreign Trade on the Distribution of Income," first published in Swedish in 1919 and reprinted in translation in *Readings in the Theory of International Trade,* eds. H. S. Ellis and L. A. Metzler, Philadelphia, Blakiston, 1949; and Bertil Ohlin, *Interregional and International Trade,* Cambridge, Mass., Harvard University Press, 1933.

any relative price of cloth in comparison with U.K. consumers. The latter have a relative preference for steel over cloth at any relative price of steel. This would lead to different equilibrium outputs and price ratios in each country in the absence of trade. The United States might be at point *A* with a price line represented by P_{US1}. The output and consumption of steel would be $O-S_{US1}$ and the output of cloth would be $O-C_{US1}$. Similarly, the equilibrium position in the absence of trade for the United Kingdom is assumed to be at point *B*.

Opportunities for trade are present because of the differences in the relative prices and costs in the two countries. Trade results in a single price ratio in both countries which we will assume to be represented by P_W. At this price ratio the production in both countries will be the same at point *C*, with cloth production at $O-C_{P2}$ and steel production at $O-S_{P2}$. At P_W the price of cloth is cheaper in the United States than before, and cloth consumption will increase even though cloth production has decreased. This is permitted because the U.S. consumers substitute the cheaper British cloth for more expensive domestically produced cloth. In fact, the U.S. consumption point will be at a point like *D* on the line P_W. At the same time the British consumption point will move outward to a point such as *E*. $O-S_{UK2}$ shows the consumption of steel in the United Kingdom after trade,

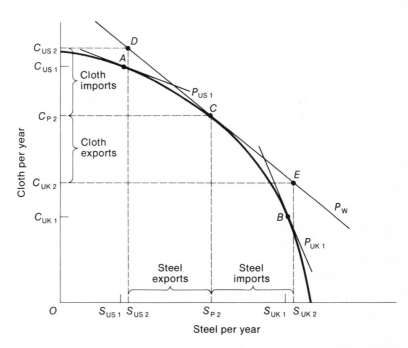

Figure 4.13
Trade with different demands but identical factor endowments

and $O\text{--}S_{US2}$ shows the consumption of steel within the United States after trade. Also indicated along the horizontal axis are the imports and exports of steel. Similarly, on the vertical axis we can find the amount of cloth being exported from the United Kingdom and imported by the United States.

Trade arises because of differences in patterns of taste, and each country tends to import that good which it has a comparative preference for in consumption; and each country exports the other good.

Differences in demand can also play a role in the Heckscher-Ohlin model of trade. Assume that there is a relatively capital rich nation with a production possibilities curve such as shown in Figure 4.14. Assume, however, that patterns of demand in the country are such that the domestic equilibrium in the absence of trade is at point A with very high production and consumption of steel. At the domestic equilibrium the price of steel is quite high relative to the price of cloth. If this country's potential trading partner has a lower relative price of steel, the United States would import steel and export cloth, even though steel were produced with its relatively abundant factor of production. In other words, the Heckscher-Ohlin hypothesis that countries tend to export the good which uses its most abundant factor of production intensively can be upset if patterns of demand are sufficiently biased toward the same good. For a capital rich country a strong bias in demand toward the capital intensive good can reverse the Heckscher-Ohlin finding, and this can lead to that nation importing rather than exporting it.

Although some economists have argued that patterns of taste should be roughly similar among nations, a situation such as that

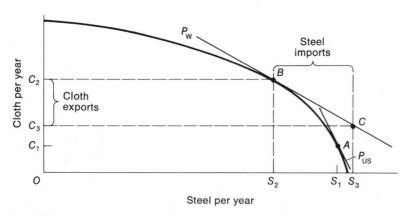

Figure 4.14
Reversal of the Heckscher-Ohlin prediction because of biased demand

shown above could arise, for example, because of differences in real income levels and in the income elasticity of demand for goods. If the income elasticity of demand for goods made of steel is quite high, the bias in demand shown in Figure 4.12 could be explained if real incomes were high in the country in question compared to other countries. Differences in patterns of demand can also be explained by differences in the distribution of real income.

CONCLUSIONS

In this chapter we have developed a general equilibrium model of a domestic economy in graphic form. The model reveals that there are four fundamental determinants of the market equilibrium costs, prices, and outputs. They are factor endowments, technology, tastes and preferences, and incomes. When two economies are juxtaposed in the model and there are price differences, trade will take place according to comparative advantage. In principle the price differences and the trade could be due to intercountry differences in any of the four fundamental determinants of equilibrium.

Most of our attention has been devoted to the Heckscher-Ohlin version of the model which rules out all possible explanations of trade except differences in factor endowments. This model leads to the hypothesis that each nation will export that good which utilizes its abundant factor more intensively. We have also shown how demand can influence trade in the context of the model.

For supplementary readings, see the end of Chapter 5.

Chapter

The Modern Theory: Factor Prices and Factor Incomes

The main purpose of the theory of international trade is to discover the effects of trade on prices and incomes in both countries. It is only through an understanding of the changes in real incomes and prices which result from trade that we can say anything meaningful about the gains from trade. The important effects of trade which are predicted by the modern Heckscher-Ohlin model can be summarized in three statements about product prices, factor prices, and the gains from trade. The first statement is the almost trivial one that trade will make product price ratios equal between countries. As we saw in the last chapter, differences in product price ratios provide the incentives for altering the flows of trade, and these incentives continue until product price ratios are equalized. The second statement is a theorem concerning factor prices. The theorem states that under a certain set of assumptions free international trade will equalize factor prices among countries. The third statement might be termed the fundamental theorem of international trade. It states that free trade is better for a country than no trade, that is, that under free trade real incomes will be higher than in the absence of trade. In the next chapter we will attempt to show not only what this theorem says but what it does not say about the welfare of individuals in a country.

CHANGES IN FACTOR PRICES

In the first part of Chapter 4 the foundation was laid for predicting the impact of trade on factor prices. Factor prices and product prices are directly related. In one country, trade causes the price of the export good to rise and that of the import good to fall, unless the special case of constant cost prevails.[1] In response, the output of the export good rises and that of the import good falls. The factor price changes depend on the relative quantities of the factors of production being released (laid off) in one industry and absorbed in the other.

If this nation is relatively capital abundant, it will tend to export the capital intensive good and import the labor intensive good. From all this it follows that the export industry which already is using relatively more capital will be trying to absorb the abundant factor in relatively greater amounts than it is being released by the contracting import industry. The scarce factor, labor, is used intensively in the import industry and will be released in relatively higher proportion than it can be absorbed elsewhere. The price of the abundant factor must rise in these circumstances; and the price of the scarce factor must fall. The prices of the export good and the factor used more intensively in its production will both rise as a consequence of trade. The price of the scarce factor will fall as the import good falls in price.

From this general discussion of the direction of movement of factor prices, two interesting questions emerge. First, since one country's abundant factor is the other's scarce factor, the price of any one factor is rising in one country and falling in the other. Are they diverging or moving toward equality? Can any more be said about the international tendencies of factor prices? The answer to these questions can be stated as the factor price equalization theorem. This will be taken up in the next section. The other question concerns factor prices and the gains from trade. Since any factor price is somebody's wage rate, or land rent, or return on capital, is it possible that falling prices for scarce factors mean some people are made worse off by trade? This possibility is examined in the third section of this chapter.

The reader may be able to grasp intuitively the relationships among product prices, outputs, and factor prices which are described above. The next several pages represent a digression to make more explicit the forces at work as output changes and resources are shifted from one industry to another. Assume a country is in domestic equilibrium in the absence of trade, as shown in Figure 5.1. If changes in consumer preferences or perhaps international trade raise the price of steel relative to the price of cloth, more steel will be produced. Starting at point A this means that the economy is moving toward point B. What will be the effects on factor prices of this change in output? As the price of cloth falls the clothing industry will be reducing output and releasing both capital and labor from production. At the same time the increased price of steel will

---

[1] This exception will be dealt with below.

cause the steel industry to expand production and increase its demand for both factors of production. However, as can be seen from the diagram, at all factor price ratios steel production is relatively capital intensive in comparison with cloth production. This means that as cloth production is reduced the clothing industry is releasing relatively more labor than the steel industry is absorbing at given factor prices.

Figure 5.2 is an expansion or enlargement of the region around point *A* in Figure 5.1. It shows the pressures on wage rates and the price for capital as the output of steel expands and the output of cloth contracts. As long as relative factor prices do not change, the clothing industry will contract along the dashed line from point *A* toward O_c, e.g., from point *A* to point *C*. This means that the clothing industry is releasing labor and capital in a ratio equal to the tangent of the angle θ_C in Figure 5.1. At the same time the steel industry is expanding and attempting to absorb resources at a different capital/labor ratio given by the tangent of the angle θ_S in Figure 5.1. As long as factor prices do not change, the steel industry will attempt to expand along the line from O_s through point *A* toward point *D*. But as the steel industry does this it is demanding or requiring more capital relative to labor than is being made available by the clothing industry. If factor prices do not change, the steel industry will try to reach point *D* while the clothing industry will try to reach point *C*. At these positions, the clothing industry has released more labor than the steel industry wants to absorb; but it has released less capital than the steel industry wants to absorb. There is an excess

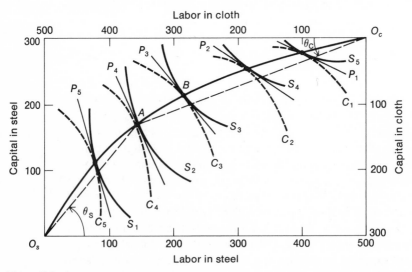

Figure 5.1
The effect of changing output on factor prices

supply of labor and an excess demand for capital. The excess demand for capital will tend to force up the price of capital relative to labor; and this effect is reinforced by the downward pressure on wage rates because of unemployment. The expansion of the capital intensive industry, steel, will result in an increase in the price of capital *relative to* labor.

This is an important theorem which will be used later to discuss the effects of free trade and tariffs. The student would be well advised to be sure that he understands it at this point. To summarize, the expansion of output in an industry can only take place with a corresponding contraction of output in the other industry. The expansion of output will tend to increase the price of that factor which is used most intensively in the expanding industry. The contracting of output will tend to reduce the price of that factor which is used most intensively in the contracting industry. This is true whenever relative factor intensities are different. The fact of different capital/labor ratios in two industries means that factors are not being released for one industry in the same proportions in which they are being absorbed in the other industry. Thus there will be some excess

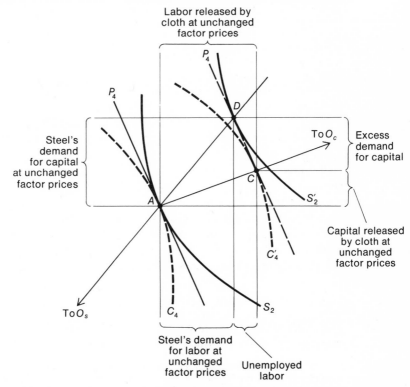

Figure 5.2
The effects of changes in output on factor prices—enlarged

THE MODERN THEORY: FACTOR PRICES AND FACTOR INCOMES

supply of one and excess demand for the other. It is these excess supplies and demands which work through market forces to alter the factor price ratio.

Figure 5.1 clearly shows the systematic variation in factor price ratios as output levels change. Starting near the lower left-hand corner, with a relatively high output of cloth and low output of steel, capital is relatively cheap compared to labor. Moving upward to the right, increasing the output of capital intensive steel, the price lines become less and less steeply sloped, showing a rising price of capital and a falling price of labor. Larger and larger outputs of steel tend to bid up the price of capital and force down the price of labor. Each point on the efficiency locus implies a different factor price ratio and corresponds to a point on the production possibilities curve. And each point on this curve corresponds to a single set of opportunity costs and product prices. In other words there is a unique relationship between product prices and factor prices. The proof of the factor price equilization theorem offered in the next section will rest in part on this important point.

The one exception to these conclusions occurs where the economy has constant costs and the production possibilities curve is a straight line. Of course in this case changes in output due to demand changes or international trade have no effect on relative product prices until and unless the economy completely specializes in producing one good. More importantly for our present purpose, such changes do not affect relative factor prices. This is because with constant costs the efficiency locus in the Edgeworth-Bowley box is a straight line connecting the corners. In Chapter 4 it was explained that constant costs would occur only if the production functions for the two goods were identical in the sense that at any set of relative factor prices the capital/labor ratios in the two goods would be identical. This is equivalent to saying that the isoquants must be so shaped that the efficiency locus is a straight line. In this case contraction of the output of one good releases capital and labor in the same proportions as they are being absorbed in production of the other good. There is no excess demand or supply of either factor, and relative factor prices do not change.[2]

THE FACTOR PRICE EQUALIZATION THEOREM

The proof of the factor price equalization theorem rests on a set of assumptions, some of which turn out to be quite restrictive in prac-

[2] With complete specialization the link between product and factor prices is broken. When the corner of the Edgeworth-Bowley box is reached, relative factor prices remain constant no matter what further changes in product prices occur. Relative factor prices will still be equal to the slope of the isoquant through the corner point. If one factor were to temporarily become more expensive, producers would attempt to substitute the new,

this set of assumptions is the same as the full set of assumptions underlying the Heckscher-Ohlin model of trade. The list of assumptions follows:

1. As in Chapter 4 we assume a two-factor, two-commodity, two-country model;[3]
2. The production functions for each good are the same in both countries and exhibit constant returns to scale;
3. The factor inputs are of identical quality in both countries;
4. The factor inputs are in fixed supply;[4]
5. The production functions for the two goods are different, that is, have different capital/labor ratios, so that the production possibilities curve is concave;
6. Factor intensity reversal as described in Chapter 4 does not occur;
7. Product and factor markets are perfectly competitive;
8. The free flow of goods in trade with no transportation costs is assumed; but factors of production are not mobile between countries;
9. It is assumed that with trade no country specializes in the production of one good, or to put it in another way, with trade both goods must still be produced in both countries.

The first step in the proof is to show that, given the production functions for the two goods, there is a unique relationship between relative product prices and relative factor prices. The general nature of this relationship has been outlined above. An increase in the price of one product relative to the price of the other will cause a reallocation of resources and an increase in the price of that factor of production used intensively in the good with rising price.

In each country for every possible product price ratio, given the production functions, there is a uniquely determined factor price ratio. If the production functions are the same in both countries, and this is one of the assumptions made above, the factor price ratios will be the same whenever the product price ratios are the same. Since trade equalizes product price ratios between two countries, trade must also equalize factor price ratios.

---

relatively cheaper one for it. But the only effect of this increased demand for the other factor would be to raise its price until their relative price was once again at its equilibrium value.

[3] There is a mathematical statement of the proof which is valid for any number of factors as long as the number of products traded equals or exceeds the number of factors of production.

[4] This assumption is only necessary for the graphical version of the model. In a general mathematical version, if factor supplies depend in part on factor prices, equalization of these prices will still occur.

While equalizing factor price *ratios* is not the same thing as equalizing absolute factor prices, the latter follows from the assumption of identical production functions. With competitive factor and product markets a factor is paid its value of marginal product. In other words the factor's price equals its marginal physical product multiplied by product price. With the kind of production functions assumed for the proof, marginal products depend only on the proportions in which factors are combined. With factor price *ratios* the same in both countries, factor proportions, and therefore marginal products, will be the same in both countries, and this means absolute factor prices are equalized. Hence the theorem is proven.[5]

An interesting close relative to the factor price equalization theorem is the product price equalization theorem. With appropriate assumptions drawn from the list above the product price equalization theorem states that in the absence of trade in products, the free flow of factors of production among countries would equalize not only factor prices but product prices. The student should see that the proof of this theorem is symmetrical with the proof of the factor price equalization theorem.

The factor price equalization theorem is interesting as an exercise in abstract economic reasoning. No one claims that factor prices are in fact equalized by trade. The list of assumptions necessary for deriving the proof is quite restrictive. The ensuing discussion will not only raise some issues which will help to keep the factor price equalization theorem in proper perspective; it will also point out some problems in applying the Heckscher-Ohlin model of trade to observed phenomena.

The main problems stem from our inability to define and to distinguish conceptually the two most important elements of the modern model, factor inputs and production functions. The model from which the theorem is deduced assumes that production functions are identical in all countries and that factors of production are identical or homogeneous among countries. But this leads us into an intellectual cul-de-sac. If production functions are to be identical among different countries, it must be because a production function is defined as representing the existing state of technological and scientific knowledge. This knowledge is freely available to all, and

---

[5] This verbal argument does not constitute a rigorous proof in the mathematical sense. Because of the relatively limited role this theorem plays in understanding observed patterns of trade flows and factor price differences among nations, a more rigorous proof has been omitted. Interested students are referred to the original statements of the proof by Paul Samuelson, "International Trade and the Equalization of Factor Prices," *Economic Journal*, 58 (June, 1948), 163–184; and "International Factor-Price Equalization Once Again," *Economic Journal*, 59 (June, 1949), 181–197. Also M. O. Clement, R. L. Pfister, and K. J. Rothwell provide a comprehensive presentation and discussion of the theorem in *Theoretical Issues in International Economics*, Boston, Houghton Mifflin, 1967, chap. 1.

all countries have the same opportunities for utilizing the given state of the art. But then how are differences between countries in climate and other aspects of the environment to be reflected in production theory? Is climate a factor of production? If so, then not all factors of production are homogeneous among countries.

Furthermore, what about differences in the quality of labor, or in the quality of existing capital equipment? As an empirical matter labor is not homogeneous within countries, let alone among countries. Can we get around this by defining different classes of labor as being different productive factors? How about skilled labor, semi-skilled labor, and unskilled labor? In order to do this successfully we have to show that differences in labor quality within a class are insignificant. In addition we have to show for each class of labor that we have defined as a separate factor that some quantity of the factor is available in both countries.

Some of these questions are more important for the fate of the factor price equalization theorem and the Heckscher-Ohlin hypothesis than they are for the modern theory of trade as a whole. For example, since trade flows depend upon relative price differences, production functions can be defined so as to be different among countries with different climatic conditions. Then we can say that trade arises because of differences in relative factor endowments, or differences in demand, or differences in the underlying production functions, or some combination of all three. But the factor price equalization theorem rests squarely on the assumption of identical production functions among countries. For it is here that the unique relationship between relative product prices and factor prices is found. If production functions are defined so that they are different, factor price equalization will not occur except by chance.

There are other conditions under which factor price equalization will not occur. These all involve violations of the original set of assumptions. Going down the list assumptions 1 and 4 are not required in a general mathematical statement of the theorem. The main problems with assumptions 2 and 3 have already been discussed. As for assumption 5, constant costs would result in at least one country completely specializing in one good. When specialization occurs, the link between product and factor prices is broken. Geometrically, specialization in production is a corner solution where the production point with trade lies on one axis of the production possibilities curve. The process of adjustment toward factor price equalization is halted as the system bumps into the corner.

Assumption 6 rules out factor intensity reversals. In other words, if an industry is the capital intensive industry in one country, it must also be relatively capital intensive in the other country. If the capital intensive industry in one country is the labor intensive industry in the other, factor price ratios in both countries may move in the same direction with trade and may or may not get closer to each other. In any event equalization of factor prices will not occur. It continues to be true that for any given factor price ratio, there is only one possible product price ratio. However, where factor intensity reversals occur the converse is not true. A given product price ratio is consistent with two different factor price ratios, one on each side of the reversal. In the country where the industry is capital intensive, the relative price of capital for any given product price ratio will be higher than in the country where the industry is labor intensive.

Monopoly power can cause a divergence between prices and costs which will also break the link between product prices and factor prices. If there are transportation costs, product prices will not be made exactly equal nor will factor prices. All we can say in the face of transportation costs is that there is a tendency toward factor price equalization. The proof also requires that every country have at least some of every factor of production included in its factor endowment. Almost by definition without this assumption factor prices cannot be equalized among countries.

What is left of the theorem? As a theorem, it follows logically from its assumptions and postulates. As a piece of logic and deduction, it is above reproach and not without some intellectual beauty. As a theory supposedly descriptive of real world economic processes, it is something else again. We can see that international trade makes economies and markets interdependent. There normally is some tendency for factor prices to be drawn closer together although in practice certainly not to equality.[6] Low factor prices in countries are raised with trade; correspondingly, in other countries high factor prices tend to be lowered when trade occurs. And this is obvious enough. If the price of the factor in a country is high, it is because of relative scarcity in that country. Trade which presents the opportunity to purchase the good using the scarce factor intensively at a price below the domestic price has the effect of reducing this scarcity. Consequently the price of the factor will tend to fall.

The significance of the factor price equalization theorem lies not in the realism of its assumptions or the likelihood that empirical testing might lead to its verification, but in its role as a price of abstract economic reasoning in aiding our understanding of the mechanisms and adjustment processes of the modern theory of trade. By proving the theorem, and by finding out what restrictive assumptions are necessary to this proof, hopefully we will have sharpened our analytical tools and strengthened our powers of economic reasoning.

[6] Even this tendency toward equalization could be thwarted if factor intensity reversals occurred.

TRADE AND THE REAL INCOME OF INDIVIDUALS

We have seen that the introduction of trade will raise the price of that factor of production which is used intensively in the export good and lower the price of the other factor. But since the prices of goods are also changing, this information is not sufficient to tell us in which direction the real incomes of factor owners are changing. Rather than work with relative factor prices or factor prices expressed in monetary terms, we must introduce the concept of real factor returns. Real factor returns are what matter to consumers because they are the purchasing power or the command over goods conferred by receipt of the monetary factor reward. We must find out what happens to the absolute factor prices and real factor returns before we can arrive at any more conclusions about the gains from trade.

Take labor for an example. The real value of the money wage payment to the recipient is what it will buy. Real wage rates then are money wage rates adjusted for the price level:

$$\text{Real wage rate} = w = \frac{W}{\overline{P}} \tag{5.1}$$

W is the money wage rate; $\overline{P}$ is an index of consumer prices. Real income is:

$$\text{Real income} = wH = \frac{W}{\overline{P}}H \tag{5.2}$$

where H is the number of hours worked per period and has been assumed to be constant. The money wage rate in any industry is related to the productivity of labor in the following way:

$$W_c = (MPP_{lc})\,P_c \tag{5.3}$$

where MPP_{lc} is the marginal productivity of labor in cloth. The right-hand term gives the value to the firm of hiring one more unit of labor. If this were greater than the wage, firms would want to hire more labor. And the wage rate would be bid up until (5.3) was satisfied. Now we are ready to move to a demonstration of a theorem concerning the effects of trade on the real incomes of factors of production in trade.

This theorem, which is based on the work of Samuelson and Stolper,[7] states that the opening of trade will not only increase the relative return to the factor used intensively in the export good, but

---

[7] Wolfgang Stolper and Paul A. Samuelson, "Protection and Real Wages," *Review of Economic Studies*, 9, No. 1 (November, 1941); reprinted in American Economic Association, *Readings in the Theory of International Trade*, Philadelphia, Blakiston, 1949, pp. 333–357.

will also absolutely increase the rate of return and therefore the real income of this factor. The assumptions underlying the theorem are: two goods and two factors, no factor intensity reversals, increasing costs, and no specialization with trade. The example developed in Chapter 4 will be used; in it the United States is relatively capital rich and exports steel—the capital intensive good. The question is: What happens to the real wage rate of labor after trade is opened? The opening of trade will bring about an increase in the price of steel relative to the price of cloth at the same time that wages are falling relative to the price of capital. One is tempted to say that the effect of these changes on the real wage rate can be found by calculating a price index incorporating the prices of steel and cloth and using equation (5.1) above. Might it be that the falling price of cloth will more than offset the falling wage rate and thus produce an increase in the real wage rate? An index number calculation seemingly would be able to provide the answer to this question. However, because of the inherent problems in index numbers,[8] more confidence in the results could be held if the use of indexes could be avoided altogether. The contribution of Samuelson and Stolper is to show how this can be done.

Assume temporarily that workers consume only cloth so that the price index relevant to calculating the real wage rate is identical to the price of cloth. If this is so then the real wage rate of laborers in cloth can be found by combining equations (5.1) and (5.3):

$$w_c = \frac{MPP_{lc} \cdot P_c}{P_c} = MPP_{lc} \tag{5.4}$$

This states that when cloth is the only good consumed by wage earners, the real wage rate of cloth laborers is equal to the marginal physical product of labor in cloth. The introduction of trade causes a reduction in the output of cloth and a change in the capital/labor ratio in the production of cloth in favor of labor; that is, the cloth industry uses labor more intensively.[9] Because of the law of diminishing returns, this increase in the amount of labor per capital unit results in a decrease in the marginal product of labor, and according to equation (5.4) a decrease in the real wage and real income of labor. An extension of the law of single price shows that if the real wage rate of clothing workers is falling, so is the real wage rate and real income of steel workers. The introduction of trade reduces the real income of the scarce factor.

The student might be tempted to ask what happens if we make steel the wage good instead. If it is assumed that workers consume

[8] See Chapter 6, pp. 84–86.
[9] If this is not clear, review Figures 5.1 and 5.2.

only steel, then a combination of equations (5.1) and (5.3) will give the real wage rate of laborers in steel in terms of their marginal physical product, as follows:

$$w_s = \frac{MPP_{ls} \cdot P_s}{P_s} = MPP_{lc} \qquad (5.5)$$

The introduction of trade results in an expansion in the output of steel, and an increase in the ratio of labor to capital in that industry. In other words, labor is being used relatively more intensively in both steel and cloth production with trade in comparison with the before trade position. In both industries this change in the capital/labor ratio results in a fall in the marginal physical product of labor. If labor consumes only steel, the decline in the *MPP* of labor in steel means that labor's real wage has fallen. Also if labor consumes only cloth, the decline in the *MPP* of labor in cloth means that labor's real wage has fallen. Since real wage rates fall for all laborers no matter whether they are assumed to consume only cloth or only steel, they must fall for any combination of cloth and steel in consumption.

The theorem can be restated in general terms now. The introduction of trade will decrease the real price and the real income of that factor which is used intensively in the import good. The real income of the scarce factor will fall with trade. Also the real factor return and real income of the factor used intensively in the export good will rise as a consequence of trade.[10] Finally if factor prices are equalized, real factor returns will be equalized among countries as well.

To summarize, trade raises factor prices and incomes for the abundant factors and lowers them for the relatively scarce factors. In Chapter 4 we showed that trade expanded the consumption possibilities for the nation as a whole. But it is now clear that not all factors share in these "gains" from trade. In the next chapter we turn to an evaluation of these gains from trade and how they are distributed.

Trade with Changing Quantities of the Factor Inputs

In the Heckscher-Ohlin model we assumed that the quantity supplied of a factor was given and did not change when factor prices changed. In other words we assumed that the supply curve for the factor was vertical, or had an elasticity of zero. This was necessary to define

[10] The converse is not always the case. The reduction of trade by a tariff on imports usually but not always will increase the real income of the scarce factor. The exception is pointed out in Lloyd A. Metzler, "Tariffs, the Terms of Trade, and the Distribution of Income," *Journal of Political Economy*, 57, No. 1 (February, 1949), 1–29. See also Chapter 9, pp. 142–143.

76 uniquely the Edgeworth-Bowley box of Chapter 4. Suppose, however, that starting from an equilibrium without trade the opening of trade caused an increase in the available quantity of the abundant factor in response to the predicted increase in its price. In other words, suppose the supply curve sloped upwards to the right. It turns out that while this complication is fatal to an easy geometric presentation of the Heckscher-Ohlin model and to its principal hypothesis, it does not destroy the model itself. The model can still be expressed mathematically. If the quantity supplied of each factor depends on its own price and nothing else, an equilibrium exists. If the other assumptions are still valid, the factor price equalization and Samuelson-Stolper theorems will still be true. The hypothesis that countries export the good using their abundant factor intensively is valid only if factor supply curves slope up to the right. Then trade raises the price of the abundant factor and increases its supply and degree of relative abundance. However, if the relationship between factor price and quantity supplied is inverse, for example, the backward bending supply curve of labor, relative factor intensity cannot be defined uniquely for a country.

FACTOR MOBILITY AND FACTOR PRICES

Let us leave the universe of abstract economic worlds and examine some practical consequences of opening trade. In the abstract models it was assumed that labor and capital were perfectly mobile among alternative uses. There was no cost of transferring capital from one line of production to another; labor and capital moved instantaneously from one occupation to another in response to marginal changes in demand. This is obviously a heroic assumption to make if the analysis is to have any relevance to the real world.

At the opposite extreme it could be assumed that each product is produced by combining a particular kind of capital and a particular kind of labor. It could be assumed that these kinds of labor and capital are specific to the production of one good; that is, they cannot be used in the production of any other good. In this situation a reduction in the demand for cloth, for example, would not reduce the output of cloth, since the supply curve of cloth would be completely inelastic. The price of cloth would fall and the returns to the capital, labor, and other factors specific to cloth production would also fall. As long as the price of cloth remained above zero these factors of production would earn some income but perhaps not very much. But by assumption they would continue to work for any real return above zero because they had no alternative.

The assumption of completely immobile factors probably more closely approximates the real world in the short run than the alternative assumption of perfect mobility. Capital can only be transferred from one industry to another slowly and normally not without cost. Labor is also less than perfectly mobile among occupations, industries, and regions. This is particularly true of older workers, less educated workers, and workers in those relatively isolated areas dependent on one industry. Another point to consider is that wages tend to be inflexible downward, so the short-run effect of a decrease in the demand for labor could be unemployment rather than a fall in wages which would tend to maintain full employment. Average incomes would fall, but the impact would be unevenly distributed between those who maintained their jobs at the old wage rates and the newly unemployed.

The effect of opening trade where factors are relatively immobile in the short run could be to lower the incomes of owners of both capital and labor employed in the production of the import type good, and to raise the incomes of both factors in the export industry. In the long run both capital and labor would flow out of the import industry. The longer the period allowed for adjustment the more closely the observed results would approximate those predicted by the model. But the adjustment would be slow and painful. In the short run at least, one can see why both capital and labor in an industry would oppose any policy change which would increase the imports of that type of good.

SUPPLEMENTARY READINGS

Kindleberger, Charles, *International Economics,* 4th ed., Homewood, Ill., Irwin, 1968, chap. 2, appendixes A and B.

Clement, M. O., Pfister, Richard L., and Rothwell, Kenneth J., *Theoretical Issues in International Economics,* Boston, Houghton Mifflin, 1967, chap. 1.

Caves, Richard, *Trade and Economic Structure,* Cambridge, Mass., Harvard University Press, 1960, chaps. 2–3.

The following are all reprinted in American Economic Association, *Readings in International Economics,* Homewood, Ill., Irwin, 1968:

Robinson, Romney, "Factor Proportions and Comparative Advantage," *Quarterly Journal of Economics,* 70, No. 2 (May, 1956), 169–192.

Johnson, Harry G., "Factor Endowments, International Trade, and Factor Prices," *The Manchester School of Economic and Social Studies,* 25, No. 3 (September, 1957), 270–283.

Haberler, Gottfried, "Some Problems in the Pure Theory of International Trade," *Economic Journal,* 60, No. 238 (June, 1950), 223–240.

Chapter

The Evaluation of the Gains from Trade

THE GAINS

The Size of the Pie

To speak of the gains from trade implies that trade is good. This in turn implies that there is agreement on a criterion which defines good and bad. It is time now to consider this problem of the choice of a criterion explicitly. At the beginning of Chapter 5 we said that the third major conclusion of the modern theory of trade was that free trade was better than no trade at all. What definition of good is required to justify such a statement? The criterion is the size of the nation's economic pie, or the efficiency criterion as it was described in Chapter 1.[1] By the size of the pie we mean the national income or the aggregate value of the total of goods available for consumption.

In Chapter 4 it was pointed out that through trade both countries achieved consumption positions that were outside their production possibilities curves and that in some sense this was an improvement for both countries.[2]

Figure 6.1 reproduces the trading equilibrium of the United Kingdom from Figure 4.12. Before trade, domestic production and

---

[1] See p. 7.

[2] As usual there is an exception to this generalization. If one country has constant costs, there is no change in product prices in that country. The production point is moved; but the consumption possibilities line through that point lies along rather than outside the production possibilities curve. In this case the other country reaps all of the gains from trade. Similarly, if one country is very large relative to its trading partner, the quantities traded may be too small to influence product prices in the large country. Here the small nation reaps all the gains.

consumption were represented by point A. After trade the consumption possibilities line is P_W. Without knowing the new equilibrium consumption point, the gains from trade can still be measured in terms of the imported good, steel. Before trade the nation consumed $O–C$ of cloth and $O–S_1$ of steel. Postulating a constant consumption of cloth at $O–C$, trade permits an increase in the consumption of steel of $S_1–S_2$. This potential increase in aggregate steel consumption is a measure of the physical gains from trade. But the true measure of the gains must be in terms of individuals' welfare or utilities. And the size of the pie measure of the gains sheds no light on this.

Assume that after trade, domestic consumption is given by point C_1, which is upward and to the right of point A. This means that with trade U.K. producers and consumers have reallocated their resources and carried out trade in such a way as to have more *collectively* of both goods than they could obtain in the absence of trade. By the criterion of efficiency or the size of the pie, point C_1 or any other point above and to the right of A is an unambiguous improvement.

If instead the equilibrium is C_2, the situation is less clear. U.K. consumers have more steel to consume after trade than they did before; but the domestic consumption of cloth has fallen. Under the efficiency criterion it can still be argued that the United Kingdom is in a better position than previously on the following grounds. The

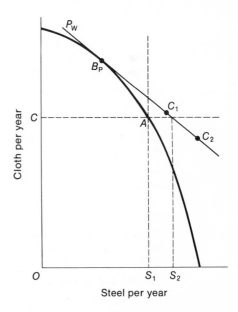

Figure 6.1
The gains from trade—an aggregate approach

price line P_W which represents the consumption alternative of the United Kingdom extends upward and to the right of point A. This shows that U.K. consumers had the opportunity to reach a clearly preferred position such as C_1. The fact that they could have chosen position C_1 but chose C_2 instead must mean that C_2 is preferred to C_1 and therefore also to A.

But what does it mean to say that a "nation" is better off? What does it mean to say that a nation prefers C_2 to C_1? Does this mean everybody? or a majority of the people? or the political leadership? The notion of a national or community preference is a tricky one. Chapter 5 taught us that some factors of production will experience a decline in real incomes in moving from A to C_1 or C_2. How are the preferences of these individuals weighted in determining the national preferences?

Under certain artificial restrictions and assumptions it is possible to speak of the set of national preferences as if the nation acted as a single individual. If these conditions are met, it is valid to speak of a community choosing C_1 or C_2 over A without worrying about adverse effects on some members of the community. These assumptions permit the construction of what are called community indifference curves which have most of the same properties of the indifference curves of individuals. Community indifference curves are useful in that they permit one to draw conclusions about such questions as the gains from trade, or the effects of tariffs or economic integration on community welfare. However, this usefulness is gained at the expense of sweeping under the rug or assuming away the troublesome questions about income distribution which have already been alluded to and are discussed in the next section. A derivation of community indifference curves, including a discussion of the required assumptions, is included in an appendix to this chapter. The appendix also shows how offer curves can be derived when the community indifference curves are known, and how these can be used to find the equilibrium of trade, the gains from trade, and their distribution between the trading countries.

In summary, the gains from trade are in the form of a larger aggregate consumption. For any one country, the gains are positive where free trade is compared with no trade (see Figure 6.1). However it is possible that one country can increase its gains from trade by moving from free trade to a position of restricted trade through the use of an optimal set of tariffs. This possibility is shown in Chapter 9. In addition we can make a statement about the gains from trade from a global point of view. The size of the world pie is maximized by the free trade; that is, free trade maximizes the global gains from trade. This statement is a simple extension of the conclusion that perfect competition leads to the most efficient allocation of resources in the domestic economy.[3] Any restrictions on trade have the same effect on global efficiency as monopolizing practices would have on the efficiency of the domestic economy. Just as the monopolist's gains come at the expense of the efficiency of the national economy, the increased gains that would accrue to a nation from restricting its trade come at the expense of its trading partners. And the decrease in the size of the global pie is greater than the increase in the size of the slice going to the restricting nation.

The Distribution Question

Now we come to the crux of the matter. We have said that there are gains from trade; and we have also said that the owners of the scarce factor of production experience a reduction in the factor return and their real income as a result of trade. Can it be said that they gain? Obviously not. The trade that brings a larger pie also reslices it so that some individuals may get shorter rations. The so-called gains from trade are distributed in a very unequal way. The statement that a nation gains by trade involves some kind of implicit or explicit value judgment which in some way compares the gains of one group and the losses of another. This can be a tricky business.

This is another way of saying that the efficiency criterion with its exclusive attention to the size of the pie irrespective of how it gets sliced is at best incomplete. Actually, unqualified acceptance of the efficiency criterion in the case of the gains from trade implies the value judgment that losses to some individuals, no matter how large, are all right so long as the aggregate of individual gains is greater than the losses. But one could as legitimately feel that any economic change which brought losses to any individual was undesirable no matter how large the potential gains for others.

The problem of income distribution value judgments has been the major concern of a branch of economics called welfare economics. Welfare economics has attempted to establish the conditions under which it can be said that an economic change has resulted in an unambiguous improvement for the members of the society or economic system. The unsolved problem here is how to define and measure the welfare of the society as a whole in such a way that the effect on welfare of a variety of economic changes such as trade can be predicted.

We will not attempt a thorough discussion of welfare economics at this point. We will attempt to outline briefly three possible

---

[3] Two good elementary proofs of this can be found in Lloyd Reynolds, *Economics,* 3rd ed., Homewood, Ill., Irwin, 1969, chap. 24; and Heinz Köhler, *Welfare and Planning,* New York, Wiley, 1966, chaps. 1, 2, and 4.

approaches to the selection of a welfare criterion. One of these is absolute. The criterion says that welfare is improved if and only if no individual in the economy finds himself worse off after the change, and at least one individual finds himself better off than before. This criterion is the economic analogue of a unanimous consent political system. Very few potential economic policy changes in the real world would be able to pass this criterion. Almost any change that we might contemplate, even though we feel certain that it is a good change in some sense, is likely to have adverse economic effects on some individuals. Some examples are: the enforced dissolution or regulation of a monopoly, the regulation of pollution discharges into the water and air, the building of roads, and taxes.

The second approach to welfare criteria involves the *potential* for compensation. It can be stated in several ways. For one, a policy change is deemed good if those who would gain by it are willing and able to pay a bribe or compensation to those who would lose by it. In other words, if the potential gainers can afford to bribe the potential losers for their unanimous consent and still have something left over for themselves, the change is deemed good. This is the rationale for acceptance of the efficiency criterion. Another way to put it is that any change which increases national income, given the available supply of factor inputs, is deemed good or an improvement. This is because this increment to national income in principle provides a pool out of which the losers could be compensated and still have a residual to be distributed to the gainers. These are two ways of stating the same criterion.[4] Note that neither way of expressing the criterion says that these bribes or compensating payments have to be made. In this way the gut issue of what is a just or equitable income distribution is avoided. Whether you think that in any particular case the compensating payments should be made or not depends upon your personal evaluation of the alternative income distributions, the one that results from nonpayment and the one that results from payment.

The third approach to the problem of evaluating income distribution is to place different weights or values on changes in the incomes of different individuals where the weights depend on their original income levels or some other relevant characteristic of the individuals. For example, one might feel that a $1 change in the income of a $1,000 per year man should have ten times the weight of

---

[4] However, there is one problem with the criterion stated in GNP terms. The policy change may result in a change in income distribution, product prices, and the composition of output, in which case the change in GNP cannot be measured without some ambiguity. In addition the compensation test has been found to give ambiguous answers in some situations. It is possible that given the initial set of prices and incomes the gainers could bribe the losers to move from state A to B, while at the new prices, etc., prevailing at B the losers could bribe everyone to go back to A.

a $1 change affecting a $10,000 per year man. In other words if the poor man lost $1, the economic change that caused this loss would be deemed bad unless at least ten people in the $10,000 per year class gained $1. Conversely if the poor man gained, the change would be good so long as no more than ten $10,000 per year men lost (or one $10,000 man lost no more than $10). It can be seen that the use of a set of weights is a middle ground between the extremes of the "unanimous consent" rule with its infinite weights on all losses and the compensation/efficiency criterion which weights all gains and losses equally.

A set of weights, or a social welfare function, could be drawn up to reflect any conceivable ethical viewpoint on income distribution. The problem is whose set of weights should be used to make public policy decisions where some gain and others lose. To discuss this question would carry us too far afield. But it should be pointed out that the question itself has both normative (how should we be making these decisions) and positive elements (how are we actually making these decisions).

In order to evaluate the income distribution consequences of trade we must know what they are. The distribution of the gains and losses accompanying trade cannot be predicted directly from the model because the distribution of income depends upon the distribution of factor ownership. No assumptions about factor ownership distribution have been made. It could be assumed that there are two groups of individuals in the economy: laborers, that is, owners of the factor service labor, and capitalists, the owners of the factor service capital. If it is assumed that the ownership of capital is evenly distributed among capitalists and the ownership of labor services is evenly distributed among laborers, then the distribution of income among individuals is determined by factor prices. If labor is used intensively in the import good, trade will redistribute income away from laborers and toward capitalists. One might reasonably expect that laborers would oppose the opening of trade. When it is said that there are gains from trade, what is meant in this instance is that the capitalists as a group could afford to transfer income to laborers as a group in a sufficient amount to restore laborers at least to their pretrade level of income. Capitalists would still have some additional income left over after making this transfer payment. It is this increment which represents the real value of the gains from trade. Once again it must be emphasized that whether the transfer payment should actually be made or not is a value judgment which cannot be decided on economic grounds alone.

While we are playing around with abstract economic models, we could make a different set of assumptions about the distribution of factor ownership. Suppose that capital were evenly distributed among

84 all individuals, and that labor were evenly distributed among all individuals. Then the opening of trade would cause equal reductions in the labor income for all individuals and equal increases in the income from capital for all individuals. Since the gains from trade are positive, each individual would find that his gains exceeded his losses; that is, he would be better off with the opening of trade. This example passes the strong welfare criterion mentioned first, since no one is made worse off and someone, and in this case everyone, is better off by the change. But this happy result was obtained by making an extreme assumption about the distribution of factor ownership, which had the effect of eliminating any real distribution problem.

What is left of the notion of the "gains" from trade after we have opened the box on the income distribution question? We can say that trade makes the available pie bigger for a nation, and free trade maximizes the size of the total world pie. This constitutes the core of the economists' logical case for free trade. But until we have found a universally accepted measure of welfare which is capable of judging alternative income distributions where some people lose, we have no logical or objective basis for concluding that the larger pie is really better.

THE TERMS OF TRADE
AS A MEASURE OF THE GAINS

The Terms of Trade

In the preceding section the concern has been with the comparison of two alternatives: autarky or no trade on the one hand, and free trade on the other. Those whose task it is to measure the effects of trade are seldom concerned with such stark comparisons. Rather, they are interested in the accumulation of many changes in economic variables and their effects over time on the existing flows of trade. Several analytical tools have been developed to aid the investigator in describing these changes in some quantifiable form. One of these is a measure called the *terms of trade.* In this section several concepts of the terms of trade are presented; the impact of several kinds of economic change on these measures is shown; and the extent to which changes in the terms of trade signal corresponding changes in economic welfare is discussed.

The terms of trade is an index number *comparison* showing changes *over time* in the conditions under which trade takes place. There are several formulations of the terms of trade, each measuring a different facet of trading conditions. Three such indexes will be considered here. But first let us review the concept of an index number.

An index number is a way of adding up dissimilar things to obtain a single valued measure for the aggregation. An index number is a weighted average. GNP is an index of the total output of many kinds of commodities and services in an economy where the weights are the prices used in valuation. A price index is an average of all those prices selected for inclusion where the weights are the quantities of the commodities that are sold in a particular period of time. Changes in an index number from one period to another tell us something, but not everything, about changes in the components making up the aggregate or index figure. Index numbers of prices, for example, are distorted or have a bias because when prices change demand theory tells us that quantities purchased change in an opposite direction, other things being equal. Yet the quantity weights used in constructing the index do not change from period to period.

To trace the trend of the volume of imports over time, for example, an import quantity index could be developed. Since imports consist of many physically noncomparable items, physical quantities would have to be converted to comparable dollar quantities by using the prices of the goods. The total value of imports in year 0 is:

$$\text{Value in year } 0 = \Sigma P_m^0 Q_m^0 \tag{6.1}$$

where the Σ is an operator meaning a summation of all of the following terms, P_m^0 is the price of each of the import goods in the year 0, and Q_m^0 represents each of the physical quantities in year 0. An index number is a comparison of terms similar to equation (6.1) for pairs of years. To compare the quantity of imports in year 1 with those in year 0 equation (6.2) would be used:

$$\text{Import quantity index} = Q_m^{01} = \frac{\Sigma P_m^0 Q_m^1}{\Sigma P_m^0 Q_m^0} \tag{6.2}$$

The ratio would be expressed as a single number. If the number were greater than 1 this would indicate that the aggregate physical volume of the imports was higher in year 1 than year 0. If the number were less than 1 this would indicate a fall in the physical quantity of imports.

Several inherent problems in index number calculations must be considered before turning to the use of index numbers in defining terms of trade. The first concerns the choice of weights. In the above index the base year prices were used as weights. Prices from other years could have been chosen and the results of the index number calculation might have been somewhat different. Also this index would be distorted if prices changed over time, because the weights used in the index would not reflect the changing importance of various goods. Further consideration of this point gets us into some rather fine questions in index number theory which we should not go into here.[5]

More importantly, an index number has no inherent way of recognizing changes in the quality of the goods entering into the index number calculation. It is possible by continually revising the method of calculation of the index to make some rough approximation to an adjustment for quality. But unless this is done, any index number can become seriously biased over time when the qualities of the goods entering into the index are changing. Another problem is that in a growing and changing world the composition of the class of goods in the index calculation may be changing. In the above example new goods may be added to the list of imports, and old goods may become obsolete and be dropped from the list of imports. Index number calculations must be revised continually to reflect this changing composition of imports.

These three problems, weights, quality, and composition, combine to make comparisons of index numbers over a fairly long period of time almost meaningless. Quality and composition changes might safely be ignored in making a year-to-year comparison, but very rarely could they be safely ignored in making comparisons from decade to decade, for example. Long-term trends in index numbers must be interpreted with considerable care and skepticism.

What kind of index numbers might be used to measure changes in the gains from trade over time? Quantity indexes for imports and exports do not provide enough information to answer questions about gains from trade, or improving or deteriorating conditions of trade. Quantity indexes do not provide information on changes in the values of exports and imports, or foreign exchange earnings, or the real resource costs of traded goods.

The most common index number used in terms of trade comparisons is a simple import and export price index. It is known as the *net barter terms of trade* or, sometimes, the *commodity terms of trade*.

$$\text{Net barter terms of trade} = B^{01} = \frac{P_x^{01}}{P_m^{01}} \tag{6.3}$$

where

$$P_x^{01} = \frac{\Sigma P_x^1 Q_x^0}{\Sigma P_x^0 Q_x^0}$$

and P_m^{01} is defined similarly for imports.

<hr>

[5] For a theoretical discussion at the intermediate level see C. E. Ferguson, *Microeconomic Theory*, rev. ed., Homewood, Ill., Irwin, 1969, pp. 67–72.

The net barter terms of trade is a ratio of an export price index and an import price index, each calculated in the manner shown above, where quantities are used to weight the changing prices. Since index numbers are always comparisons between two years, equation (6.3) should be interpreted as showing the net barter terms of trade for year 1 relative to the base year, year 0.[6] If on average the prices received by a country for its export goods rise further over a given period of time than the prices of that country's imported goods, then the net barter terms of trade will be greater than 1. Rising export prices give rise to higher net barter terms of trade and improving terms of trade for a nation. Rising import prices contribute to deteriorating terms of trade for a nation.

Although net barter terms of trade data may be interesting, one cannot safely use them to come to conclusions about the welfare of a country over time. In addition to the problems confronting all index number comparisons mentioned above, the net barter terms of trade are made less useful because of two important omissions. The net barter terms of trade do not say anything about the capacity to import, that is, the total foreign exchange earnings from exports; nor do they give any indication of the opportunity cost of a given bundle of imports. These problems can be illustrated with an example drawn from a domestic situation, the farm problem.

The net barter terms of trade for farmers as a sector in the economy have been calculated by the Department of Agriculture since 1910. Farmers' terms of trade is a ratio of an index of prices received for farm products to an index of prices paid for materials and consumer goods. It is called the parity ratio. The terms of trade have shown a marked but erratic deterioration over the sixty years since their first publication. The price index for exports is comparable to the index of prices received for agricultural commodities by farmers; our import price index is analogous to the index of prices paid for all goods by farmers. Nobody would argue that farmers economically are worse off today than they were fifty-five years ago simply because their terms of trade have deteriorated. For one thing, although the prices of their "imports" have been rising, so have their incomes. Their capacity to buy or import is higher now by far than before. Another concept of the terms of trade has been developed to reflect just this fact. It is called the *income terms of trade.*

$$\text{Income terms of trade} = I^{01} = B^{01} \cdot Q_x^{01} = \frac{P_x^{01} \cdot Q_x^{01}}{P_m^{01}} \tag{6.4}$$

[6] Saying simply that the terms of trade for a country are 132 (or any other number) in 1966 has no meaning since the base year is not specified. That would be just like saying that consumer prices were 114.8 in February, 1967, without comparing this with the average of 100 for 1957–1959 (the base years) or 111.6 for February, 1966.

where
$$Q_x^{01} = \frac{\Sigma P_x^0 Q_x^1}{\Sigma P_x^0 Q_x^0}$$

The income terms of trade differ from the net barter terms of trade by the addition of an export quantity index in the numerator. The income terms of trade are really a ratio of the value of exports or the income from exports to the price of imports. They show the purchasing power of a nation's exports. In other words, if the prices of exports decline, the ability of a country to import can be maintained if the quantity of exports rises by an offsetting amount maintaining the income terms of trade at a constant value.

The true cost of imports is not their price but the opportunities for domestic consumption foregone by producing exports for trade. Another concept of terms of trade reflects these opportunity costs. It reflects, for example, the impact of technological change in an export industry which might lower the price of exports but also lower the resource cost of exports. This concept is known as the *single factoral terms of trade.*

Single factoral terms of trade $= F^{01} = B^{01} \cdot T_x^{01}$

where T_x^{01} is an index of productivity in the export goods industries. If prices of export goods fall by a given percentage amount but the average productivity of the factors of production in the export industry rises by an equal percentage, the single factoral terms of trade will be unchanged. Although exports are earning less in unit terms, they are costing less in terms of factor inputs and opportunities foregone as well. If productivity rises faster than export prices fall, other things being equal, the single factoral terms of trade will improve for a nation. Of course productivity improvements have been a major factor in mitigating the effects of the deterioration of agriculture's net barter terms of trade. The major barrier to greater use of the single factoral terms of trade is the difficulty of measuring productivity change by industry.

The principal reason for the continuing theoretical interest in the various measures of terms of trade is their possible use in evaluating the gains from trade or the welfare effects of changes in trade. Two important reservations about using the terms of trade as a measure of welfare change must be kept in mind throughout the subsequent discussion. The first is that empirically the terms of trade are imperfect because of the index number problems discussed above. The second, perhaps more fundamental, reservation is that the terms of trade can only be related to an efficiency measure of welfare, that is, one which ignores the distribution of gains and costs among individuals within the nation. When we say that a certain terms of trade measure has given a "correct" indication of the welfare change, we mean only that it has correctly signalled the change in national income or the size of the pie. Terms of trade measures can shed no light on the welfare implications of the way in which that change was distributed among individuals.

The theoretical exploration of the terms of trade has been concerned with two things: predicting the effect of various economic changes on the several terms of trade measures; and interpreting the movements of the terms of trade as welfare indicators. In this section we will not deal with the first kind of question; it will be treated where appropriate in the last five chapters on tariffs, integration, and growth. Here we will consider the welfare implications of several kinds of movements of the terms of trade and use them as examples to illustrate the problems involved.

For our first example suppose that the foreign demand for a nation's exports increases. Unless the supply of exports is completely elastic the immediate effect is an increase in the price of exports. The quantity of exports must increase. But the effect on the net barter terms of trade is not clear. The change in demand conditions must be analyzed in the context of the general equilibrium of the economy. The increase in exports will increase domestic prices, incomes, or both. This in turn will lead to an increase in the demand for imports. Import prices are likely to rise, depending on the foreign supply elasticity for imports and the domestic price and income elasticities of demand for imports. Depending on how much import prices rise, the net barter terms of trade could either increase or decrease. If the net barter terms of trade increase, welfare is improved. A bundle of resources devoted to export production will now be able to purchase a larger quantity of imports. Also, the income terms of trade must have increased. In this case the measures move in the same direction and give the same, "correct," answer to the welfare question.

But suppose in the above case that the prices of imports rise sufficiently to cause a decline in the net barter terms of trade. It is possible for the income terms of trade to have either risen or fallen so that these two measures give conflicting signals.[7] The welfare impact is still correctly signalled by the net barter terms of trade.

---

[7] For an example, suppose that export prices rise 10 percent, export quantities rise 5 percent, and import prices rise 12 percent. The net barter terms of trade are:

$$\frac{(1.10)}{(1.12)} = .98$$

The income terms of trade are:

$$\frac{(1.10)\,(1.05)}{(1.12)} = 1.03$$

While the revenue generating capacity of exports has risen faster than import prices, the nation must now devote more of its scarce resources to export production to maintain the same level of imports.

As a rule, when a change in the net barter terms of trade is due to an autonomous change in foreign demand or supply conditions, the direction of their change correctly indicates the welfare effect. However, when the net barter terms of trade change because of an autonomous change within the country, such as improving technology, they are an unreliable indicator of welfare changes. If export prices are falling no faster than productivity is rising, the foreign purchasing power of a bundle of resources is better measured by the single factoral terms of trade.

The effects of a tariff on the terms of trade provide another example. If the foreign supply of imports is less than perfectly elastic, a tariff can improve the net barter terms of trade. The larger the tariff, the greater the improvement, until the tariff becomes prohibitive, that is, until there are no imports. Up to a point, the rising tariff improves the welfare of the tariff-imposing nation.[8] The net barter terms of trade give a correct signal. But beyond the point of the "optimum" tariff, improving terms of trade are associated with a deteriorating welfare position.

With all of the index number problems, qualifications, and chances for misinterpretation, it is a wonder that economists pay any attention at all to these data. The fact is that imperfect as these measures may be, they are all that are available to the practicing economist who has something important he wants to measure. Before one arrives at any conclusions based on terms of trade data, he must familiarize himself with the procedures used in constructing the indexes and with the sources of data. And he must try to determine the causes of the observed movements in terms of trade, for it is only when these are understood that he can offer judgments about the welfare significance of these movements. It was pointed out above that the net barter terms of trade are better for evaluating external changes, while the single factoral terms of trade are appropriate where technology is affecting the domestic export industry. Unfortunately for the economist doing empirical work, both kinds of changes are likely to be occurring simultaneously.

SUPPLEMENTARY READINGS

Kindleberger, Charles, *International Economics,* 4th ed., Homewood, Ill., Irwin, 1968, chap. 3, appendix C.

[8] This argument and the necessary qualifying assumptions are found in Chapter 9, pp. 143–146.

Clement, M. O., Pfister, Richard L., and Rothwell, Kenneth J., *Theoretical Issues in International Economics,* Boston, Houghton Mifflin, 1967, chap. 3, pp. 126–150.

Samuelson, Paul A., "The Gains from International Trade," *Canadian Journal of Economics and Political Science,* 5 (May, 1939), 195–205; reprinted in American Economic Association, *Readings in the Theory of International Trade,* Philadelphia, Blakiston, 1950, pp. 239–252.

Kenen, Peter B., "Distribution, Demand, and Equilibrium in International Trade: A Diagramatic Analysis," *Kyklos,* 12 (1959), 629–638; reprinted in American Economic Association, *Readings in International Economics,* Homewood, Ill., Irwin, 1968.

Viner, Jacob, *Studies in the Theory of International Trade,* London, George Allen & Unwin, 1955, chap. 9.

APPENDIX
TO CHAPTER 6

COMMUNITY INDIFFERENCE CURVES, OFFER CURVES, AND THE EQUILIBRIUM OF TRADE

Because community indifference curves are derived from and have properties similar to individuals' indifference curves, we shall begin with a brief review of the latter. Assume for our two-dimensional diagram that there are two goods, cloth and steel, and that there is an individual who is consuming cloth and steel in the combination shown by point A in Figure 6.2. A rational individual would prefer any combination above and to the right of A, such as D, if he were given a choice. There is some point above and to the left of A, say point B, involving less cloth but more steel, which the individual would neither

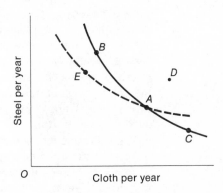

Figure 6.2
An individual's indifference curve

prefer nor reject in comparision with *A*. He would be indifferent between them. An indifference curve through points *A* and *B* connects all points having this indifference property. The individual would experience the same level of satisfaction or utility with any combination of cloth and steel located on that curve. Individuals' indifference curves have four important properties.

1. They slope downward to the right showing that a reduction in the amount of steel consumed by an individual must be compensated for by an increase in the amount of cloth if he is to experience the same level of satisfaction.
2. They are convex to the origin indicating a diminishing willingness to substitute additional cloth for steel as the quantity of cloth rises relative to steel.
3. The area is dense with indifference curves, each one representing a set of cloth-steel combinations which are preferred to any combination on a lower indifference curve. If a change places a person on a higher indifference curve, he is said to be better off, and it is assumed that persons will allocate their expenditures so as to place themselves on their highest attainable indifference curve.
4. No two indifference curves intersect. Intersecting indifference curves contradict the underlying premises of indifference curve analysis. In Figure 6.2 the dashed line indifference curve implies that the individual is indifferent between combinations *E* and *A*, while the solid indifference curve implies indifference between *A* and *B*. But the individual cannot be indifferent among *A*, *B*, and *E*, because combination *B* is clearly superior to *E*. Thus the indifference curve with *E* cannot pass through point *A*.

Knowledge of the shape of an individual's indifference map enables us to predict how he will divide his expenditure between the two goods for any given level of money income and prices. The situation of an individual with a given income and confronted by a given set of prices can be portrayed by a budget line similar to the isocost lines of Figure 4.3 (see pp. 42–44). The individual's utility is maximized, given his limited income and positive prices, when he chooses the combination of goods where an indifference curve is just tangent to his budget line. In a similar manner, community welfare will be maximized when the community reaches a tangency point between its price line and a community indifference curve.

A community indifference curve represents a locus of all points of total or aggregate consumption among which we can somehow say the society is indifferent. We must be able to envision a social system where dictatorially, collectively, or through the combined effect of individual actions the attainable consumption positions are examined at least hypothetically, and the "most preferred" one is somehow selected. In addition, these community indifference curves which govern or are at least consistent with these choices must have the same four properties that individual indifference curves have. Four possible situations meet this test.

The first is where there is only one individual in the society. His tastes and individual indifference curves coincide with society's. The problem of income distribution is finessed because there is only one possible recipient of the economy's output. The second situation is where the society is ruled by one individual, a czar, commissar, or a colonel. He may impose his views of what the society should consume on the other members. In this paternalistic or dictatorial world the chief can decide how much of each good each individual will receive. The aggregation of these decisions may result in a set of convex, nonintersecting community indifference curves, but it is not necessary that they do so.

Both of the above cases define the community's indifference curves as the indifference curves of a single person. We are interested in systems where there are many people, and they are free to make their own choices. For simplicity assume that there are two people, A and B, and that they have attained consumption points that yield them utilities of U_a and U_b, respectively. Under these assumptions define a community indifference curve as the locus of points of total or aggregate consumption where both individuals continue at U_a and U_b.

To make this clear refer to Figure 6.3. Mr. A's indifference map is shown in the normal fashion, while Mr. B's is inverted, with the origin, O_b, in the upper right. Point O_b is located so that the indifference curves corresponding to U_a and U_b are just tangent at point X. Point O_b, when referred to the normal axes, indicates the total consumption of cloth and steel, in this case O_a–C of cloth and O_a–S of steel. Point X shows how it is distributed among A and B to yield the postulated levels of utility, U_a and U_b. Now imagine sliding O_b and U_b from northwest to southeast so as to keep the two indifference curves always in contact. Point O_b will trace out the set of total consumptions of steel and cloth which will just be sufficient to maintain both A and B at their original utility levels. As O_b moves down to the right, both individuals would receive more cloth and less steel but be indifferent between these new combinations and the original ones at Point X. Thus the path traced by O_b constitutes a community indifference curve as defined in the last paragraph.

Unless further restrictions are placed on the system, it is possible to derive in this way community indifference curves which intersect, and it is instructive to see why this is so. Assume a total consumption of O_a–C of cloth and O_a–S of steel distributed between A and B so as to give U_a and U_b (see Figure 6.4). Through this total consumption point there lies a community indifference curve, CIC, which can be derived in the way described above. Now assume a different distribution of the original endowment such as to raise A to indifference curve U'_a and to lower B to U'_b. Again a community indifference curve can be derived, such as CIC' which has a different slope and intersects CIC, thus violating one of the required properties of community

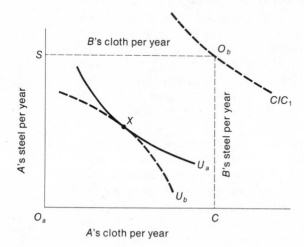

Figure 6.3
Deriving a community indifference curve for a
two-person world

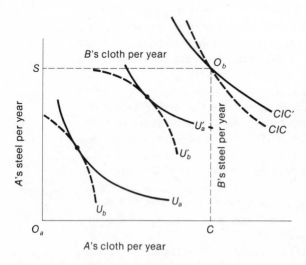

Figure 6.4
Intersecting community indifference curves

indifference curves. In general any redistribution of the original endowment will result in a new community indifference map which intersects the old one. There is no unique community indifference curve through point O_b. The total consumption represented by O_b does not correspond to a unique level of community welfare. The only way to avoid this is to place further restrictions on the system.

One such set of restrictions is to assume that all individuals have the same tastes and preferences (same shapes to their indifference maps), and that all individuals have the same income level. This means that all goods are distributed equally to all individuals, and all individuals choose to consume goods in exactly the same combination. If there are n people in the economy, the community indifference map is simply an n-fold expansion of any one individual's indifference map. The community indifference map is unique and nonintersecting. But this is gained at some cost, since once again the income distribution question has been finessed. Equal incomes could occur if all individuals owned equal amounts of all factors of production. Then they would share equally in the gains and losses associated with factor price changes. Also having identical tastes, they are equally affected by changes in the prices of any goods. On the other hand, if it is assumed that the equal income distribution results from a policy decision, the income distribution question has already been answered, the optimal distribution decided upon, and policy carried out. In this version this system becomes a special case of the fourth possible system for constructing community indifference curves.[9]

The fourth possible way to construct a valid set of community indifference curves is to confront the redistribution question head on, and to assume that society through some political process has agreed upon what constitutes an optimal income distribution (or has agreed upon the set of weights to be used in public policy desisions). In addition it is necessary to assume that society has actually made the necessary redistributions and will continue to make them as necessary in response to economic changes. Then a unique, nonintersecting, convex set of community indifference curves can be derived which will reflect the society's value judgments.

To recapitulate, the central issue in constructing community in-

---

[9] It can also be shown that if individuals have the same tastes and their indifference maps have the property of homogeneity (which means all income and price elasticities of demand are unitary among other things), a nonintersecting set of community indifferences can be constructed. The proof of this can be found in H. Robert Heller, *International Trade: Theory and Empirical Relevance,* Englewood Cliffs, N.J., Prentice-Hall, 1968, pp. 48–51, 178–179. Unfortunately community indifference curves derived in this manner lack one of the properties of individual indifference maps. Specifically, a move from a lower to a higher community indifference curve cannot be interpreted as an improvement in the community's welfare unless a value judgment about income distributions is also invoked. This seems to be where we came in.

difference curves is the articulation of a set of community-wide value judgments about income distribution. There are four kinds of assumptions upon which one could base the construction of community indifference curves. They are:

1. There is only one individual in the society;
2. A dictator decides for everybody;
3. All persons have the same incomes and identical preferences;
4. Society has adopted a social welfare function governing income distribution and acts upon it to assure the optimal distribution of income at all times.

The first three assumptions evade or finesse the distribution question, while the fourth assumes that it has been answered in advance.

Whatever the justification, we assume from here on that a unique set of nonintersecting community indifference curves exists. With them it is a simple matter to show the equilibrium of a closed economy, trading equilibrium, and the gains from trade. In Figure 6.5 we continue the example developed in Chapter 4, where the United States and the United Kingdom exchange cloth and steel. The U.S. production possibilities curve and community indifference map are shown. In the absence of trading opportunities, the United States reaches the highest possible community welfare position when it produces and consumes at the point of tangency between a community indifference curve and the production possibilities curve. This is shown as point A where consumption and production are $O–S_1$ of steel and $O–C_1$ of cloth. This point of tangency also determines the relative prices of cloth and steel, since for this to be an equilibrium position the slope of the price line P_{US} must equal the slopes of the production possibilities curve and community indifference curve at their tangency.

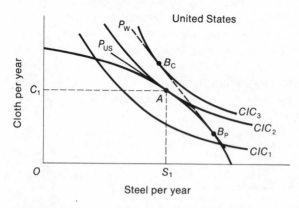

Figure 6.5
The equilibrium of trade

INTERNATIONAL TRADE: Appendix to Chapter Six

The difference between this depiction of the equilibrium and the one used in Chapter 4 can now be pointed out. There we said at any point on the production possibilities curve relative prices would be such that the markets for both steel and cloth would be cleared, given the supplies of each. If the resulting price line was not tangent to the production possibilities curve at that point, producers would have an incentive to alter the quantities supplied by moving to a new production point and causing changes in the market clearing relative prices. This would go on until the price line was tangent to the production possibilities curve. This description of the adjustment process can be applied to Figure 6.5 as well. In Chapter 4 we did not claim that this equilibrium was in any sense an optimum, because we had no means of judging the underlying distribution of the output. Here we do. Here we know, by assumption, that the distribution of income which affects the markets for cloth and steel and helps to determine the relative prices has society's sanction.

Similarly, when trade is opened and the new world equilibrium price ratio is reached, producers have responded by moving to point B_P on the production possibilities curve. Again the highest level of community welfare is attained at a tangency between a community indifference curve, CIC_3, and the consumption possibilities line at world prices, P_W. Whether or not the consumption point, B_C, is to the right or left of point A, the nation has gained by attaining the higher community indifference curve.

This account of the trade equilibrium does not touch upon the determination of the world price ratio. This omission can be corrected by utilizing the community indifference map to derive the offer curves of the United States and United Kingdom. Their intersection determines both the price ratio, or net barter terms of trade, and the quantities exchanged.

Given the community indifference map and the production possibilities curve we can derive a set of trade indifference curves. Each trade indifference curve is the locus of combinations of exports and imports which will leave the country on the same community indifference curve. A unique and simple relationship exists between each community indifference curve and its associated trade indifference curve. This is shown in Figure 6.6. The vertical and left-hand horizontal axis show the U.S.'s consumption of cloth and steel and its community indifference map. Point A shows the social optimum on CIC_1 given the production possibilities curve and no trade. The horizontal axis to the right and the vertical axis represent quantities of exports of steel and imports of cloth, respectively.

Imagine sliding the production possibilities curve up to the right along CIC_1 so that they touch at A'. In order to achieve this level of cloth consumption, $O-C$, the United States would have to produce $B-C$ ($= O'-D$) itself and import $O-B$. With its remaining resources the production possibilities curve shows that it could produce $O'-E$ of steel, consuming $B-E$ ($= O-F$) itself and exporting the remainder, $O'-B$ ($= O-G$). The combination of exports, $O-G$, and imports, $O-B$, provides a second point on the trade indifference curve, TIC_1. The first point is the origin. Any export-import combination on TIC_1 will enable the country to reach CIC_1 when combined with production for domestic consumption. The process can be repeated with higher level community indifference curves to generate a whole map of trade indifference curves. Each trade indifference curve will slope up to the right and be concave upward, and the set will be nonintersecting and represent higher levels of welfare moving upward to the left—provided that the set of community indifference curves have the required properties.

In Figure 6.7 the trade indifference map is used to derive the offer curve of the United States. Price lines represent opportunities to trade at given prices. For any given price line such as $O-T_3$ the United States maximizes social welfare by choosing the export-import bundle where the price line is tangent to a trade indifference curve, in this case TIC_3. The offer curve is the locus of all possible tangency points.

If the United Kingdom exports cloth, its trade indifference map and offer curve will be concave downward. Figure 6.8 shows both countries' offer curves and trade indifference maps. The equilibrium prices and quantities in trade are shown by the intersection of the

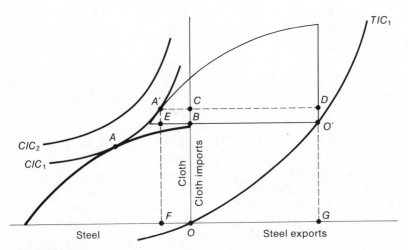

Figure 6.6
Deriving trade indifference curves

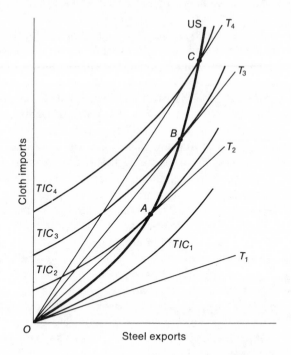

Figure 6.7
Deriving an offer curve from the trade indifference map

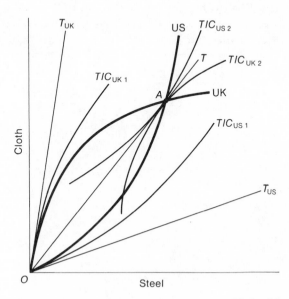

Figure 6.8
The equilibrium of trade and the terms of trade

THE EVALUATION OF THE GAINS FROM TRADE

offer curves at *A*. The net barter terms of trade are given by the price line *O–T*.

It is also possible to discuss the net barter terms of trade as a measure of the gains from trade in terms of this diagram. For instance, the relationship between the terms of trade and the pre-trade prices, $O–T_{UK}$ and $O–T_{US}$, correctly signal the division of the gains between the two countries. For example, if the U.S. offer curve were straight or nearly so, the terms of trade would favor the United Kingdom, and the latter would reap the larger share of the gains from trade. If the U.K. offer curve were to shift because of a change in demand or productivity there, the change in the slope of *O–T* would correctly signal the welfare effect on the United States. Rising terms of trade mean moving to a higher trade indifference curve. However if the U.S. offer curve shifts, it is because of a shift in the U.S. trade indifference map. A rise in the terms of trade may or may not coincide with an improvement in welfare. We cannot tell without consulting the new trade indifference map itself.

This appendix has shown that community indifference curves are quite useful in that they make the full determination of the equilibrium trade position possible in our geometric model, and they make it possible to make fairly strong statements about the gains from trade, the optimality of free trade, etc. They greatly increase the analytical power of our models both in making predictions and in normative evaluations. But this power is more apparent than real because of the nature of the assumptions necessary to justify their use. The assumptions assert, in effect, that the questions that we are trying to answer about welfare effects have already been answered. They convert the search for answers into a kind of mechanical exercise where the answers are already provided by assumption.

Chapter

The Empirical Relevance
of Trade Models

MAKING EMPIRICAL TESTS

In the opening chapter we asserted that theories were made to be
tested, and that empirical testing was essential to determine the
validity and usefulness of economic models. So far in this text we
have not met our obligation to confront the theories that have been
developed with evidence gathered from observation of real world
phenomena. We have two models or alternative descriptions of economic systems. The formal properties of these models have been
analyzed, and theorems and proofs have been developed. The development of the formal models has been both interesting and useful
in its own right. However, if the study of international economics is
to have any more policy relevance than, for example, non-Euclidean
geometry, it must go beyond the analysis of formal properties of
models. It must confront these models with tests of their empirical
content. It must find out, if it can, which of these two models is more
consistent with observed phenomena and better explains the observed flows of goods and services in international trade.

Before proceeding further the difference between a theorem and
a hypothesis should be made clear. A theorem is a logical extension
of the basic properties of a model. It follows necessarily from the
initial assumptions and definitions. It exists and is proven independently of any empirical relevance it might have. In contrast, an
hypothesis is a tentative statement about the way things really are.
Hypotheses are also derived from models and must follow logically
from the initial statement of assumptions, definitions, and relationships. The difference between a theorem and an hypothesis is that

the latter makes the tentative assertion that the model describes or explains the real world. The test of an hypothesis is whether or not the facts are consistent with it.

Theorems and hypotheses can be derived in the same way and stated in similar terms; the difference is in the uses to which they are put. For example, we showed that in an economic system described by the set of assumptions and relationships listed in Chapter 5, factor prices will be equalized by trade among nations. In this form the statement is a theorem. Alternatively, one might make the tentative statement that the world can, for certain purposes, be described by that same list of assumptions and relationships. Then the hypothesis that factor prices would be equalized could be deduced as a consequence of these assertions about the real world. Such a statement demands testing. In the case of the "factor price equalization hypothesis" the test is apparently failed. We observe that factor prices are not equalized; and the model from which the hypothesis was derived must not be a useful description of the real world.[1]

While this is not intended to be a text in statistical methods or econometrics, there are some useful points to be made concerning how economists go about testing hypotheses. These points can be illustrated by comparing the approaches used and the problems faced by an economist with the approaches available to a laboratory scientist.

If the laboratory scientist has a hypothesized relationship between two variables which he would like to test, through controlled experiment he can systematically change one variable, holding all other things constant, and observe and record the results. The economist is faced with a world which for the most part he can neither recreate in a laboratory nor control for experimental purposes. Further, most economic variables are influenced by not one but many forces, all of which can in principle be changing simultaneously. Systematic variation between two variables, say A and B, may not be apparent to the observer if a third variable C also influences B and has also been changing. This makes testing of hypotheses in economics rather difficult and sometimes frustrating. If it is A that is thought to cause changes in B, the economist must find a period in the past when A changed. Further, either C must not have changed during this period, or he must be able to use statistical techniques such as multiple regression which will enable him to isolate the

---

[1] Actually the rejection of the factor price equalization hypothesis might be traced to its being overambitious. A weaker statement based on the same line of reasoning perhaps could be supported by the data. For example, we could hypothesize that although many things actually affect factor prices (all but one of which are ruled out by assumption in the theorem), the economic mechanisms associated with trade, which are described in the model, will tend to reduce the divergence between factor prices, other things held constant. While this form of the hypothesis has not been directly tested, at last it is not obviously false.

separate effects of C and A on B. Finally, he must find enough instances of changes in A being accompanied by changes in B to satisfy himself and other economists that what he observed was not simply due to chance or coincidence.

Another set of problems arises because of the economist's reliance on data supplied by others. Economic data collection is a recent development. The statistical estimation of Gross National Product is less than forty years old in the United States. More esoteric but nevertheless useful economic data are recorded infrequently, such as during decennial censuses. Some data are not collected at all because of difficulty, expense, or perhaps oversight. Too often the things actually measured do not correspond to the economist's theoretical concepts. Finally, necessary aggregation in data collection may hide economically relevant detail or distort conclusions based on the data.

Aggregation problems are particularly relevant in the field of international trade. Consider data on exports and imports broken down by product. A product is defined as that class of goods for which the cross elasticity of demand is infinite, that is, all those items which are perfect substitutes for one another. The definition is unambiguous. The definition also requires us to say that Number 2 ordinary hard Kansas City wheat is a different product from Number 1 ordinary hard Kansas City wheat. If this rule for defining products is strictly followed, the total number of products in an economic system is astronomical. Economically unimportant distinctions among products which are very close substitutes are recognized by this definition. Analysis becomes extremely cumbersome. How much more simple to carry out an analysis in terms of, for example, wheat or grains.

The degree to which the investigator lumps together closely similar products into an aggregate product class such as wheat depends upon the purposes and aims of the investigation. One must remember, though, when an aggregation like this is carried out a certain amount of precision is lost. The loss of precision is more severe the greater the degree of aggregation and the greater the dissimilarity among components in the aggregates. For some kinds of questions these hidden differences may be crucial; for other kinds they surely can be ignored. These aggregation problems are equally applicable to the measurement of factor inputs of various descriptions and qualities. The problem facing the empirical investigator when he sets out to define a product or input class is to evaluate the distortions inherent in his particular definition and decide whether or not these are crucial to his purpose.

To summarize, there are four kinds of problems or difficulties which together make hypothesis testing in economics a demanding art. These are: the reliance for data on historical events which may

104   not exactly correspond to the hypothesized situation; the interrelationships among and multiple determination of economic variables; the possibility that observations were the result of coincidence; and the problems of data and measurement. While this is an imposing list of difficulties, the situation is not as bad as some make it out to be. Some people assert that while the laboratory sciences deal with subjects which act in a predictable way, the social sciences, economics in particular, deal with humans who are unpredictable because they are too complex, or may act irrationally, or have free will, or something. While this may be true of all humans as individuals, it does not necessarily mean that the aggregate behavior of individuals is unpredictable. Our hypotheses in economics refer not to the acts of specific individuals but to the general tendencies of large groups. For example, if the price of a good rises, we cannot point to any one man and say how much his consumption will decrease, or even if it will decrease at all. But we can predict that the total quantity purchased by all individuals will be smaller, provided, of course, that no other variables change simultaneously.

TESTING THE COMPARATIVE COST MODEL

It might be instructive for the student to stop at this point and ask himself how he would handle the assignment of testing the comparative cost model. What kind of data would he seek? What comparisons would he make? It is not sufficient to seek out one or two examples of pairs of nations where trade seems to follow the pattern of comparative cost. The method of scientific inquiry requires that we find a larger number of cases so that we might observe a consistent pattern of trade flows which we can attribute to the workings of the model rather than to chance. We will also be confronted with the problem that the data that are available frequently do not conform to the theoretical definitions employed in the model. As an extreme example, in one of the studies cited below horsepower per worker was used as a measure of the capital/labor ratio in a test of the Heckscher-Ohlin model.

The model of Chapter 3 yielded the hypothesis that for two countries trading with each other, each country would export that commodity for which its labor was relatively more productive. This hypothesis can be expressed in symbolic form.

Let M_a = man-days of labor required per unit of output of commodity A

M_b = man-days/unit of B

and let P_a = output per man-day in A or productivity

$$= \frac{1}{M_a}$$

Capital letters refer to country I; small letters (m) refer to country II. M is the labor cost of output or the inverse (reciprocal) of labor productivity. High values for M mean low productivity.

In Chapter 3 we assumed that labor was homogeneous within one country, and therefore the wage rate was the same in both industries in that country. Comparative advantage was expressed in terms of the ratios of labor cost. Country I has a comparative advantage in the production of A if the ratio of labor cost of A to B is lower in country I than in country II. This can be expressed symbolically in the following form:

$$\text{If } \frac{M_a}{M_b} < \frac{m_a}{m_b} \qquad \text{country I exports A} \tag{7.1}$$

This can be rearranged to give:

$$\text{If } \frac{M_a}{m_a} < \frac{M_b}{m_b} \qquad \text{country I exports A} \tag{7.2}$$

or by substituting:

$$\text{If } \frac{P_a}{p_a} > \frac{P_b}{p_b} \qquad \text{country I exports A} \tag{7.3}$$

Equations (7.1)–(7.3) represent three equivalent ways of stating the comparative cost hypothesis. The choice of which is used depends on convenience and the form in which the data to be used have been compiled. Since labor productivity data are more readily available than data expressed in terms of labor costs, most empirical tests of the comparative cost hypothesis have used equation (7.3). This equation says that if we compare the productivity of labor in the production of each good, for all goods produced in both countries, country I will export that good where its productivity relative to the other country is the highest, and it will import that good where its relative productivity is the lowest.

Three tests of the comparative cost hypothesis have been carried out in this form. The first was carried out by MacDougall.[2] He utilized data on the productivity of labor in twenty-five industries in both the United States and the United Kingdom in 1937. These data were compiled by other researchers. Obviously the test can be no better than the productivity data on which it is based. Measuring the productivity of factor inputs raises statistical and methodological problems which are beyond the scope of this text. Another problem that MacDougall and other investigators have had to face is that both of these countries have tariffs on imports of manufactured goods. As one would

---

[2] G. D. A. MacDougall, "British and American Exports: A Study Suggested by the Theory of Comparative Costs," *Economic Journal*, 61, No. 244 (December, 1951), 697–724.

106   expect, the tariff structures of each nation tend to offset the true comparative advantages of the other nation—as measured by labor productivity. The result is that neither country sends a large percentage of its exports of any good to the other country. It is unlikely then that a test of equation (7.3) based on trade between the United States and the United Kingdom would lead to any conclusive results. However, both these countries export manufactured goods to third countries. If the United States had a comparative advantage vis-à-vis the United Kingdom in the production of a good, one would predict that U.S. exports of this good to third countries would be larger than U.K. exports of this good to third countries. The converse would hold for those goods in which the United Kingdom had a comparative advantage vis-à-vis the United States. It is this third-country hypothesis concerning shares of the world market that MacDougall and other investigators have tested. Table 7.1 is based on MacDougall's data. The twenty-five industries are ranked by the ratio of output per worker in the U.S. to output per worker in the U.K., that is, by the ratio P_a to p_a. For each industry the second column shows the ratio of exports from the U.S. to exports from the U.K. by physical quantity. For example, for electric lamps, U.S. exports were equal to 94 percent of U.K. exports. The comparative cost hypothesis states that high values in column 1 should be associated with high values in column 2. Inspection of the table tends to support the hypothesis, although such an informal test does not rule out the possibility that the observed correlation actually happened by chance. A statistical test based on the Kendall rank correlation coefficient confirms that the relationship between the productivity ratios and the export ratios is more than coincidental.

There is one major divergence between the data and the theory which must be explained. In 1937, the year on which the study is based, the average level of wages in manufacturing in the United States was approximately twice that of the average in Britain. This suggests that where the relative productivity is greater than two, the U.S. comparative advantage would enable it to dominate the world markets in those commodities, and where the relative productivity is less than two the advantage given to Britain by its lower wage rates would allow it to dominate world markets. In other words, we would expect the relative exports of the United States for electric lamps through paper to approach infinity, and for linoleum through cement to approach zero. However, rather than the discontinuous relationship, the data suggest a rather smooth and perhaps linear relationship between relative productivity and relative export shares. To explain this feature of the data we must recognize that the kind of world in which trade takes place is not the perfectly competitive frictionless world of our models. Similar products produced by the United States

Table 7.1

Relative labor productivities and export ratios for the United States and
the United Kingdom

Industry	Output per worker in U.S./Output per worker in U.K.	Exports of U.S. ÷ Exports of U.K.
Electric lamps	5.4	.94
Tin cans	5.25	3.0
Pig iron	3.6	5.1
Wireless receiving sets	3.5	7.6
Motor cars	3.1	4.3
Biscuits	3.1	.23
Matches	3.1	.09
Machinery	2.7	1.5
Rubber tires	2.7	.74
Soap	2.7	.35
Glass containers	2.4	3.5
Paper	2.2	1.0
Beer	2.0	.06
Linoleum	1.9	.34
Coke	1.9	.19
Hosiery	1.8	.30
Cigarettes	1.7	.47
Rayon weaving	1.5	.20
Cotton spinning-weaving	1.5	.11
Leather footwear	1.4	.32
Rayon making	1.4	.09
Woollen and worsted	1.35	.004
Men's and boys' outer clothing of wool	1.25	.04
Margarine	1.2	.03
Cement	1.1	.09

Source: Adapted with permission from G. D. A. MacDougall, "British and American Exports. A Study Suggested by the Theory of Comparative Costs," Economic Journal, 61 (December, 1951), 697–724, Table II.

and the United Kingdom are differentiated to varying degrees. Also
there are transport costs; and these can be expected to shift comparative price advantages in particular cases. These factors help to
explain why we do not observe the complete specialization in particular export markets that the naive comparative cost model might
suggest.[3]

[3] There is an as yet unexplained puzzle concerning MacDougall's results (as well as those cited in footnote 4). While he found that labor productivity ratios were correlated with export shares, another investigator has found that these same productivity ratios are not correlated with export price ratios. See Jagdish Bhagwati, "The Pure Theory of International Trade: A Survey." Economic Journal, 74, No. 1 (March, 1969), 10–17. The question is, if labor productivity does not affect price, how does it affect exports? Bhagwati argues that MacDougall's indirect test is inappropriate.

108   After testing the simple comparative cost model, MacDougall recognized that one of the basic assumptions of the simple model, namely that wages are constant across all industries in a particular country, is not met in reality. Subsequent studies have also gone further by recognizing that in reality labor is not the only factor input. The questions raised by these investigators are: (1) Can some part of the trade of nations be explained by differences in wage rates among industries within a country? (2) Can some part of the trade of a nation be explained by relative differences in capital costs among products? Before we can attempt to answer these questions, we must introduce some new concepts and some new notation.

The letters M and P have the same meaning as above. Also let:

W_a = money wages in industry A

$W_a M_a$ = labor cost per unit of A expressed in money terms

T_a = total cost per unit of A in money terms

R_a = ratio of total cost to labor cost per unit of A

$$R_a = \frac{T_a}{W_a M_a}$$

$$T_a = W_a M_a R_a$$

In making comparisons between countries of the above values, money values are converted to a common denominator through the use of exchange rates. This in itself is a possible source of error in the measurements, because in a system of fixed exchange rates the observed exchange rates may not be equilibrium rates.

We can restate the comparative advantage conditions for two products between two countries in terms of total costs, T, rather than in labor productivities as before.

$$\text{If } \frac{T_a}{T_b} < \frac{t_a}{t_b} \qquad \text{country I will export A} \tag{7.4}$$

Rearranging gives:

$$\text{If } \frac{T_a}{t_a} < \frac{T_b}{t_b} \qquad \text{country I will export A} \tag{7.5}$$

and recalling the definition of T gives:

$$\text{If } \frac{W_a M_a R_a}{w_a m_a r_a} < \frac{W_b M_b R_b}{w_b m_b r_b} \qquad \text{country I will export A} \tag{7.6}$$

Any one of the following inequalities is sufficient to cause country I to export A and import B, provided neither of the other pairs of ratios offsets it.

If $\dfrac{W_a}{w_a} < \dfrac{W_b}{w_b}$ $\qquad\qquad\qquad\qquad$ (7.7)

or if $\dfrac{M_a}{m_a} < \dfrac{M_b}{m_b}$ $\qquad\qquad\qquad\qquad$ (7.8)

or if $\dfrac{R_a}{r_a} < \dfrac{R_b}{r_b}$ $\qquad\qquad\qquad\qquad$ (7.9)

country I will export A. You will recall that our original statement of the comparative cost model assumed that:

$$\frac{W_a}{W_b} = 1 = \frac{w_a}{w_b}$$

therefore,

$$\frac{W_a}{w_a} = \frac{W_b}{w_b} \qquad\qquad\qquad\qquad (7.10)$$

Also if labor is the only input, all the R terms would be equal to one. In the classical statement, only inequality (7.8) can hold. However, we know that in reality we have no grounds for assuming that the inequalities (7.7) and (7.9) will not hold. In fact we know that the R terms will be greater than one; that is, there are other costs besides labor costs. We do know that wage rates are different in different industries in any one country. It is an empirical question whether or not these other factors are sufficiently different among countries that they add to our understanding of the flows of trade.

MacDougall also investigated the combined explanatory power of relative wage rates and relative labor productivities. He calculated relative labor costs, equal to *WM,* for each product, and compared these with relative export shares of the United States and the United Kingdom. He found what he thought to be a better correspondence between relative labor costs and export shares than he had between relative labor productivity and export shares. However, he did not conduct a statistical analysis of the rank correlation. Robert Stern repeated the MacDougall tests using labor productivity data for the United States and the United Kingdom for the year 1950.[4] His results were substantially the same as MacDougall's. Simultaneously Balassa was conducting a similar test using the same data.[5] Balassa's approach was more systematic, and it enabled him to say something concrete about the ability of relative wage differences and relative

[4] Robert Stern, "British and American Productivity and Comparative Costs in International Trade," *Oxford Economic Papers,* 14 (October, 1962), 275–296.
[5] Bela Balassa, "An Empirical Demonstration of Classical Comparative Cost Theory," *Review of Economics and Statistics,* 45, No. 4 (August, 1965), 231–238.

110   capital costs (as measured by the R terms) to explain flows of trade. He found that neither relative wage differences nor differences in the R terms could add significantly to the explanatory power of the comparative cost model.

These results deserve some further comment. As Balassa concedes, his measure of capital cost does not correspond to the theoretical definition. Therefore his results regarding the impact of the R terms cannot be considered as conclusive. As for the effect of relative wages, it is one thing to recognize that wage rates within one country are different among industries. But this cannot be sufficient to explain trade unless we can also show that the structures of relative wages are different between nations. In fact, what evidence we have suggests that relative wage structures are quite similar in comparisons among nations. In terms of our notation,

$$\frac{W_a}{W_b} \neq 1 \quad \text{but} \quad \frac{W_a}{W_b} \simeq \frac{w_a}{w_b} \quad \text{and} \quad \frac{W_a}{w_a} \simeq \frac{W_b}{w_b}$$

In summarizing this survey of tests of the comparative cost model, we have learned something both about the model itself and about some of the general problems of testing models. Concerning the problems of testing, sometimes the data on hand measure something other than the theoretical concept; and this lack of correspondence between the reality that is measured and the demands of the theory weakens the power of any empirical tests.

Imperfections in the real world such as tariffs and transportation costs may require us to ask indirect questions to test the model rather than direct questions. In MacDougall's study it was inappropriate to compare flows of trade between the United States and the United Kingdom; therefore he had to compare export shares of these two countries in third markets. When indirect questions are used in a test there is always the danger that the answers may not also be applicable to the direct questions which were initially of concern. It becomes a matter of logical analysis to determine whether or not the indirect answers are applicable to the direct questions as well. This logical analysis usually involves some formal manipulation of the original model in such a way as to produce indirect questions which are answerable.

As for the model itself, we found a way of expanding the model to incorporate relative wage differences and nonlabor costs. This confrontation of model and reality which results in changes in the model is one of the most important processes in economic research. This importance cannot be discounted in the case of the comparative cost model tested here. Although we found that generalizing the model did not add significantly to its explanatory power, two things must be remembered. Future tests based on better definitions of capital and better measurement may well yield significantly different results. And in any event we learned something in the attempt, and that is what it is all about.

THE HECKSCHER-OHLIN MODEL

In the Heckscher-Ohlin model of trade we assumed certain conditions: constant returns to scale, competition, homogeneity and mobility of factors within countries, homogeneity but no mobility of factors between countries, homogeneity of products between countries, identical production functions, and no factor intensity reversals. Out of this model we derived the hypothesis that a nation would tend to export that good which used the nation's abundant factor intensively. We must either find a way of directly testing that hypothesis or, if it proves impossible to get a meaningful answer to the direct question, we must devise some kind of indirect question to test.

Factor Intensity Reversals

The assumption that no factor intensity reversals occur is important to the Heckscher-Ohlin model. If factor intensity reversal is a common occurrence, the predictions concerning the direction of trade do not follow. Several researchers have attempted to discover whether factor intensity reversals do occur. In principle this should not be too difficult a question to answer. At any given set of factor prices all industries in a country can be ranked by their realized capital/labor ratios. If this ranking is unchanged for all possible factor price ratios, we say that factor intensity reversal does not occur. In other words if factor intensity reversals do not occur, the ranking of industries by capital/labor ratios is unique.

Another assumption of the Heckscher-Ohlin model is that production functions are identical among all countries. It follows that for any two countries with the same production functions the ranking of industries by capital/labor ratios will be identical, if there is no factor intensity reversal. If we can find two nations with sufficiently different relative factor prices and compare their industry rankings, we can test the hypothesis that no factor intensity reversals occur. If rankings are essentially the same, allowing for measurement errors, we can conclude that factor intensity reversals do not occur.[6]

[6] This conclusion, of course, rests on the assumption that the production functions are identical in both countries. Variations in the industry rankings could also be interpreted to mean that the production functions are different among countries. That this alternative interpretation was ruled out by assumption should be borne in mind throughout the rest of the analysis.

Minhas has published the results of such a comparison.[7] He compared the rankings of twenty industries by capital intensity in the United States and Japan. Although the hypothesis of no factor intensity reversals predicts a perfect correspondence in the rankings, Minhas found that the rankings had virtually no correspondence. If these results can be accepted, then the Heckscher-Ohlin version of the model has no value. For if the relative factor intensity of a good depends on factor price ratios, we cannot pin the "capital intensive" and "labor intensive" tags on any goods. And without these tags there is no content to the Heckscher-Ohlin hypothesis. However, Minhas' results have not gone unchallenged. At one level his work has been criticized on technical mathematical and statistical grounds.[8] At another level Minhas' choice of industries to be included in the ranking has been questioned by David Ball.[9] Ball argues that Minhas' negative results arise primarily because three industries were included in the twenty-industry ranking which theory suggests should not have been included. The three are agriculture, and two agricultural-processing industries, grain mill products and processed foods. Ball finds that if these three industries are removed from the ranking, the correlation between the remaining seventeen in Japan and the United States is significant. The grounds for deleting these three industries are as follows. First, the classification agriculture is too broad. It consists of many nonhomogeneous products in both countries. Also natural resource conditions are quite different in Japan in comparison with the United States. Thus the assumption that production functions as normally defined are identical is least plausible in the case of agriculture and agriculture-based industries. Ball also argues that while the assumption that available technical knowledge is approximately the same everywhere probably holds for manufacturing industries, it is much less likely to be true in agriculture. Finally he raises the measurement problem; measures of factor inputs are likely to be less accurate, that is, less reliable, in the case of agriculture. Since agricultural products are a main input in the agricultural-processing industries, Ball also argues that these too should be excluded from the list.

Can we come to any conclusions regarding the factor intensity reversal problem? At this point it seems prudent to say we do not

[7] B. S. Minhas, "The Homohypallagic Production Function, Factor-Intensity Reversals, and the Heckscher-Ohlin Theorem," *Journal of Political Economy*, 70, No. 2 (April, 1962), 138–156; and *An International Comparison of Factor Costs and Factor Use*, Amsterdam, North-Holland, 1963.

[8] See Wassily Leontief, "An International Comparison of Factor Costs and Factor Use: A Review Article," *American Economic Review*, 54, No. 4 (June, 1964), 335–345; and Perry Shapiro, "International Factor Costs and Factor Use: A Comment," *American Economic Review*, 56, No. 3 (June, 1966), 546–549.

[9] David S. Ball, "Factor-Intensity Reversals in International Comparison of Factor Costs and Factor Use," *Journal of Political Economy*, 76, No. 1 (February, 1966), 77–80.

really know. The art of measuring production functions and determining capital/labor ratios industry by industry is not so far advanced that we can have perfect confidence in the numbers being used. One reason is the aggregation of data into industry groups which may not have the same composition in the two countries. Also differences in the quality of products and, more importantly, factor inputs pose serious problems in measurement and in interpretation of the results. The points raised by Ball do have considerable merit. Where natural resources are important factor inputs in the production of particular kinds of goods, the Heckscher-Ohlin model stands on very shaky legs with its assumption of identical factor qualities. The question of how to include differences in natural resource endowments in empirically relevant versions of the Heckscher-Ohlin model is one of the most important questions in applied international economic theory.

Direct tests of the validity of the assumption that factor intensity rankings are unique (no reversals) have not been conclusive. Pending better results on this we must turn to indirect evidence produced by tests of other aspects of the Heckscher-Ohlin model. If other tests are successful, this would imply that factor intensity reversals were not significant. But if the tests do not support the Heckscher-Ohlin hypothesis, then reversals offer one of several possible explanations for the failure.

The Leontief Paradox

Perhaps the most spectacular controversy concerning an empirical test of the Heckscher-Ohlin model has revolved around the results of Wassily Leontief.[10] His studies of the structure of American industry and the pattern of interindustry relationships led him to conclude that the United States tended to export relatively labor intensive goods and to import capital intensive goods.

Leontief's results were based on an analytical technique known as input-output analysis. This is a powerful mathematical technique for tracing the effects of an increase in the demand for one product on the outputs of other industries which supply intermediate inputs. For example, an increase in the output of steel will require not only increases in the direct capital and labor inputs to that industry but also increases in the production of coal and rail transportation. These

---

[10] His results were first published in Wassily Leontief, "Domestic Production and Foreign Trade: The American Capital Position Reexamined," *Economia Internazionale*, 7, No. 1 (February, 1954), 3–32; reprinted in American Economic Association, *Readings in International Economics*, Homewood, Ill., Irwin, 1968, pp. 503–527. A subsequent article based on more detailed analysis confirmed the earlier results. See his "Factor Proportions and the Structure of American Trade: Further Theoretical and Empirical Analysis," *Review of Economics and Statistics*, 38, No. 4 (November, 1956), 386–407.

in turn may require additional inputs of steel in mining and transportation. These secondary effects in related industries give rise to a set of indirect requirements for labor and capital inputs. These indirect requirements may be far larger than the direct requirements. For example Leontief estimated that the direct capital requirements in automoblie production were only about one-fourth of the total capital inputs.[11] Total resouce requirements are the sums of the direct and indirect inputs. Given sufficient information on the pattern and structure of production, input-output analysis can determine direct and indirect factor requirements for any postulated change in the level and/or composition of output.[12]

Leontief constructed an input-output table for the United States based on 1947 data. He then posed the following two questions: If exports of the United States are reduced across the board by one million dollars, that is, a proportionate reduction in the value of all exports, how much capital and how much labor will be released by the export industries and by those related to them through the input-output table? At the same time, if there is a one million dollar proportionate increase in the domestic production of goods being imported, what will be the total capital and labor inputs needed to support this increase in output?[13] If, as is commonly assumed, the United States is a capital abundant nation, the Heckscher-Ohlin model yields the hypothesis that the reduction in export production will release more capital and less labor than will be absorbed by the increase in import competing goods production.

Leontief surprised himself and the rest of the economics profession by finding that the postulated shift from export production to import competing production released more labor than was being absorbed and relatively less capital than could be absorbed. In other words, the United States tends to export its labor intensive goods and import capital intensive goods. These results quickly earned the title "Leontief's Paradox."

Before turning to an analysis and proposed explanations of Leontief's paradox, we might briefly cite the results of studies of other national economies. A similar test based on an input-output model for Japan revealed that Japanese exports were capital intensive and her imports were relatively labor intensive.[14] Japan was commonly

---

[11] Leontief, "Domestic Production," pp. 8–10.

[12] Good introductions to input-output analysis are: William H. Miernyk, *The Elements of Input-Output Analysis,* New York, Random House, 1965; and more succinctly, Heinz Köhler, *Welfare and Planning,* New York, Wiley, 1966, chap. 7.

[13] The questions posed by Leontief can be analyzed graphically in terms of Figures 5.1 and 5.2. See pages 67–68.

[14] Masahiro Tatemoto and Shinichi Ichimura, "Factor Proportions and Foreign Trade; The Case of Japan," *Review of Economics and Statistics,* 41, No. 4 (November, 1959), 442–446.

supposed at the time of the study to be a labor abundant nation, hence the paradox was repeated. However, closer analysis of the composition of exports showed that Japanese exports to relatively undeveloped nations tended to be capital intensive, while her exports to the United States and other Western countries tended to be labor intensive. This situation is consistent with the Heckscher-Ohlin hypothesis if, as is commonly supposed, Japan is labor abundant relative to the United States but capital abundant relative to her less developed trading partners. In other words, a more careful analysis of Japan's trade causes the paradox to disappear.

This particular instance points up another peril in empirical research. The initial statement of the Heckscher-Ohlin model in its simple form assumes two nations, so that one comparison of factor abundance is all that is required to determine the direction of trade. In a multination setting with multilateral trade, a set of comparisons must be made for each country between itself and each other country before the patterns of trade can be predicted. This, of course, also complicates the matter of empirical testing. This explanation does not appear to be useful in explaining the U.S. paradox. While Japan is midway between underdeveloped and industrialized nations in the hierarchy of capital abundance, the United States by all accounts is at the top of the heap.

Three other tests of the Heckscher-Ohlin hypothesis based on input-output studies give conflicting results. One by Stolper and Roskamp of East German trade supports the Heckscher-Ohlin hypothesis.[15] Two others, one of Canadian–United States trade[16] and one of Indian–United States trade,[17] also reveal a Leontief type paradox. In both instances the imports of the other countries from the United States tend to be labor intensive and the exports of the other countries to the United States tend to be capital intensive.

An extensive and sometimes confused literature has grown up around the Leontief paradox. Much effort has been devoted to attempting to interpret the Leontief paradox within the context of the Heckscher-Ohlin model. A major purpose has been to try to show that the paradox does not really refute the basic Heckscher-Ohlin hypothesis. The following paragraphs review some of the most important points in this literature.

1. If factor intensity reversals are a common phenomenon, the

[15] Wolfgang Stolper and K. Roskamp, "An Input-Output Table for East Germany with Applications to Foreign Trade," *Bulletin of the Oxford University Institute of Statistics,* 23 (November, 1961), 379–392.

[16] D. F. Wahl, "Capital and Labor Requirements for Canada's Foreign Trade," *Canadian Journal of Economics and Political Science,* 27 (August, 1961), 349–358.

[17] R. Bharadwaj, "Factor Proportions and the Structure of Indo-U.S. Trade," *Indian Economic Journal,* 10 (October, 1962), 105–116.

116   hypothesis that a nation will export that good using its abundant factor intensively cannot simultaneously hold for both countries. Suppose steel were capital intensive in the capital rich U.S. and labor intensive in the labor rich U.K. In a two-country model, both countries cannot simultaneously export steel as the Heckscher-Ohlin model would predict. The direction of trade in steel could not be predicted without more knowledge of prices or opportunity costs. But it would be quite possible in that case for the United States to import steel, thus establishing a "paradox." We saw earlier that the evidence on the factor intensity reversal question is far from conclusive. It would seem that the burden of proof must still lie with those who would show reversals to be common.

2. At the end of Chapter 4 we showed that if demand conditions were biased in one country toward the good using the abundant factor intensively, that nation might actually import that good. In other words, unusual demand conditions can convert physical abundance into economic scarcity. If the United States had a very high domestic demand for capital intensive goods relative to labor intensive goods, it might import capital intensive goods even though it were a capital abundant nation. However, a corollary of that hypothesis is that the price of capital will be high relative to the price of labor. This seems not to be the case in the United States. Therefore although biased demand conditions offer an explanation of the paradox in principle, there is no evidence to support the contention that this is the best explanation of the paradox in the United States case.

3. A substantial portion of U.S. trade is a consequence of past direct investment of U.S. companies in the economies of other nations. It has been argued that a substantial portion of U.S. imports actually comes from extensions of the U.S. economy abroad rather than from other economies in the sense implied by the Heckscher-Ohlin model. The best example is probably the petroleum industry. It is argued that these imports reflect U.S. technology and U.S. factor abundance rather than the technologies and factor endowments of the source countries. The industries are located abroad because of the location of natural resources required in the industry. The problem of natural resources will crop up again below when we consider another interpretation of the paradox. It has been argued, but never proven, that if imports of this type were eliminated from the Leontief calculations the paradox would disappear.

4. Leontief's own explanation of the paradox is that labor in the United States is more efficient than in other countries perhaps by a factor of two or three. If the U.S. labor supply were adjusted for this presumed greater efficiency, the United States would actually turn out to be labor abundant. Why is labor more efficient? Perhaps be-

cause of superior skills due to greater investment in education and training.[18]

5. One of the most crucial assumptions of the Heckscher-Ohlin model is that production functions are the same in all countries. If production functions are different, the assumptions of the Heckscher-Ohlin model are not met, and the Leontief results cannot be said to pose a paradox. Actually, production functions have to be different in a particular way in order to "explain" the paradox. If the isoquants in two countries are alike in shape and differ only in scale, that is, total outputs for given inputs are different, then the only part of the Heckscher-Ohlin model that fails is factor price equalization. If the isoquants are different in shape, the situation could be like that described above under factor intensity reversal, and no predictions can be made on the basis of factor endowments. But if what we call a production function does exhibit that kind of international difference, it is because of how we have chosen to define it.

This and the previous point taken together have returned us to the intellectual cul-de-sac which we identified in Chapter 5. Either we choose to say that production functions are the same in all countries, in which case we have to admit of differences in factor quality; or we can say that what we call factors of production are essentially the same in all countries, in which case production functions have to be different to incorporate, for example, differences in climate or abundance of natural resources. My preference is to define the production function as the embodiment of the current state of knowledge about how inputs can be combined to make outputs. In the absence of restriction on the international flow of information, production functions are the same everywhere. This sets the stage for the last and perhaps most convincing explanation of the paradox.

6. To put it briefly the production theory underlying the Heckscher-Ohlin model is incompletely specified. At least two things are left out. The first is environment, where this is construed to include the endowment of natural resources as well as climate, location, fertility, and etc. As a practical matter there can be no doubt that a significant portion of international trade arises because of differences in natural resource endowments. Samuelson once said that tropical countries export tropical commodities because they have a relative abundance of the factor of production called tropical conditions. Leontief says, ". . . invisible in all these tables but ever present as a third factor . . . determining this country's productive capacity and . . . its comparative advantage vis-à-vis the rest of the world, are the natural resources: agricultural land, forests, rivers, and our

[18] Leontief, "Domestic Production," pp. 25–28.

rich mineral deposits."[19] Leontief himself found that adjusting his calculations to remove the impact of natural resource oriented trade also removed the paradox.[20]

A second thing left out of the production theory employed here is the level of investment in humans to enhance their skills, knowledge, and productivity. The productivity of labor can be increased by utilizing more physical capital per unit of labor or by combining more human capital, that is, investment in education and training, public health, and so forth, with each unit of basic labor. The higher productivity of labor that Leontief alluded to could be the result of a high rate of investment in human capital. In other words if the human capital inputs to U.S. production could be identified in Leontief's input-output table, the United States might still be found to be exporting capital intensive goods.

The discussion of the Leontief paradox suggests that a substantial part of international trade takes place because of intercountry differences which do not fit easily into the simple production theory of the modern model. If these differences are permitted to show in the admission of differences in production functions or factor qualities, the model loses its elegant simplicity; and generally applicable hypotheses such as the Heckscher-Ohlin hypothesis cannot be deduced. These observations may point the way toward a reformulation of the theory of production which retains a place for differences in resource endowments and resource bases, and which recognizes the many different forms which capital can take. One effort in this direction by Peter Kenen will be discussed in the next chapter.

A Regional Test of the Hypothesis

It has often been said that theories of international trade can be applied with appropriate modification to trade between regions within a national unit. The less regional mobility of factors there is, particularly for labor, the more appropriate international economic theory appears to be in analyzing regional flows of trade. Moroney and Walker have used regional data from the United States to conduct an interesting test of the Heckscher-Ohlin hypothesis.[21] They point out that by using an interregional test rather than an international test they avoid several of the problems which have arisen in attempting to explain or interpret the Leontief paradox. Particularly there is much less reason to suspect that production functions or efficiencies of factors of production should be markedly different between re-

[19] *Ibid.,* p. 35.
[20] Leontief, "Factor Proportions," p. 398.
[21] John R. Moroney and James M. Walker, "A Regional Test of the Heckscher-Ohlin Hypothesis," *Journal of Political Economy,* 74, No. 6 (December, 1966), 573–586.

gions within one country. Also demand conditions among regions are likely to be similar so that the problems of biased demand are not likely to arise. They also present evidence that factor intensity reversals do not occur within the range of factor price ratios found in the United States.

Their test is carried out in two successive steps. The focus of attention is on the South and the non-South as two distinct economic regions. They cite data on lower wages in the South to support their assumption that the South is relatively labor abundant in comparison with the rest of the nation.[22] This assumption in combination with the Heckscher-Ohlin model yields the hypothesis that industries with low capital/labor ratios will tend to have higher location coefficients than industries with high capital/labor ratios. The location coefficient is the percentage of total U.S. output of that industry which was produced in the South.

It is disappointing to find that the data are not consistent with this first hypothesis. In fact, in the twenty industries used in the study, there is some support for the hypothesis that capital intensive industries have concentrated in the South. Moroney and Walker argue that three of the most capital intensive industries in their list of twenty are in reality natural-resource based. These are petroleum and coal, paper and pulp, and chemicals. If these three industries are removed from the list, the positive correlation between capital/labor ratios and concentration in the South disappears. So although there is no support for the Heckscher-Ohlin hypothesis, on the other hand there is no paradox either.

The second step in the test is to argue that the South in reality is not in equilibrium, and that in a dynamic context the comparative advantage of the South in labor intensive industries will be revealed by a higher rate of growth in labor intensive industries than in capital intensive industries. Specifically the second hypothesis is that if the Heckscher-Ohlin model is true, and if the South is not currently in trading equilibrium, there will be an inverse correlation between the capital/labor ratios of their twenty industries and the rates of growth of their location coefficients. In other words, labor intensive industries (low capital/labor ratios) will tend to have large increases in their degree of concentration in the South, at least in comparison with capital intensive industries. This hypothesis is supported by the data that they present.

The work of Moroney and Walker is instructive first because it is a highly imaginative attempt to avoid the empirical pitfalls of international comparisons mentioned above in connection with the Leon-

---

[22] They recognize that lower wages could be due to other causes, e.g., lower quality of labor; but they cite evidence from other studies that tends to show that the wage differences are due to differences in supply within skill categories.

tief paradox. It also shows that insight can be gained by asking indirect questions, e.g., concerning growth rates, when the data do not permit answers to the direct questions suggested by the models. However, not too much weight can be placed on the results of Moroney and Walker. All that can be said is that their results are not inconsistent with the Heckscher-Ohlin hypothesis. It cannot be said that they are inconsistent with other alternative and unspecified hypotheses. This situation is analogous to the statement in logic that it is impossible to prove a negative proposition. We can never be sure that there is not some other unthought-of model which explains the observed facts even better than any of the models we have thought of so far. The realization that this is so is one of the great spurs to continued economic research.

Summary

There are two points to be made concerning the attempts to test the Heckscher-Ohlin model. First, with regard to the Leontief paradox, there are several plausible explanations of the paradox in the United States. It is interesting that the regional test using U.S. regional data which is designed to avoid some of the problems of international comparisons turned out to be a qualified success. But we do not have a good answer to the question, Why are some tests of the model based on the data from other countries successful, while other tests and other countries are not? What factors do the input-output tests on the United States, Canada, and India on the one hand have in common with the input-output tests on Japan and East Germany on the other? And what conditions are different? What conditions might explain the differences in the results in the two sets of countries?

The second point is that the Moroney and Walker test has shown that the Heckscher-Ohlin hypothesis may be applicable to those cases where production functions are the same or closely similar, labor efficiency and the efficiency of other factors of production are the same, and the resource content of trade is relatively unimportant. But the Heckscher-Ohlin framework is incapable of systematically handling variations in these other considerations. This shows the direction in which new theoretical work must go. Either the Heckscher-Ohlin framework must be considerably modified, or qualitatively different conceptual frameworks and models must be developed and ultimately empirically tested.

SOME MISCELLANEOUS EVIDENCE

Often studies undertaken for one purpose may bring to light information relevant to a different kind of problem. Sometimes this "by-product" information will tend either to confirm or contradict other hypotheses. Whether or not this is the case, the result usually is a stimulus to new research either in building new models or seeking new ways to test old ones.

For example, Bela Balassa has made a study of the effect of tariff reduction on trade inside the European Economic Community.[23] The Heckscher-Ohlin model implies that if tariffs are reduced inside a trading area, a dominant or low-cost supplier will expand production and capture a major share of the new international trade within the trading region. Balassa found instead that dominant suppliers did not maintain their share of the market. In most instances for each type of product the percentage increase in the sales of the dominant supplier was less than the percentage increase in general trade in that product. These results of course have important implications for the standard textbook treatment of trade diversion in the context of economic integration.

But also, since the results are not consistent with the Heckscher-Ohlin model, they have broader implications for questions of general trade theory. Balassa argues that the Heckscher-Ohlin model is incapable of explaining his results because of its preoccupation with standard commodities where cost differences cause trade. If trade is in differentiated products, the effect of the tariff reduction is likely to be different than in the case of trade in standard products. Where there is product differentiation, the effect of a tariff reduction might be to increase the degree of specialization of each firm within an industry in producing a particular differentiated product line. With intra-industry specialization no industry, and perhaps no firm, would experience a reduction in total output. The adjustment is all in the form of expanding and contracting brand lines. Balassa points out that to the extent that this is true, the impact of tariff reductions on income distribution and employment within a country would be minimized, and the major impact would be in terms of greater efficiency of exchange and a wider range of consumer choice.

Another study of Balassa of tariff protection also shows results which are inconsistent with one implication of the Heckscher-Ohlin model.[24] In the Heckscher-Ohlin model the opening of trade reduces the real incomes of the scarce factors of production. For Western

[23] Bela Balassa, "Tariff Reductions and Trade in Manufactures Among the Industrialized Countries," *American Economic Review*, 56, No. 3 (June, 1966), 466–473.

[24] Bela Balassa, "Tariff Protection in Industrial Countries: An Evaluation," *Journal of Political Economy*, 73, No. 6 (December, 1965), 573–594; reprinted in American Economic Association, *Readings in International Economics*, Homewood, Ill., Irwin, 1968, pp. 579–604. In a similar study of the U.S. tariff structure George Basevi found some evidence of an inverse relationship between U.S. tariffs and labor intensity in production. However, the results were mixed and inconclusive. See his "The United States Tariff Structure: Estimates of Effective Rates of Protection of United States Industries and Industrial Labor," *Review of Economics and Statistics*, 48, No. 2 (May, 1966), 147–160.

industrialized countries the relatively scarce factor is labor. One would expect then that tariffs would tend to protect the labor intensive industries. However, Balassa finds no tendency for industrialized countries to use their tariff structures to protect labor intensive industries any more than capital intensive industries. In this article, Balassa again suggests that a modification of trade theory incorporating the impact of product differentiation may be necessary to explain his results.

CONCLUSIONS

The conclusions can be divided into two areas, one concerning the role of empirical testing in economic theory, and the other concerning the specific comparisons of the comparative cost and Heckscher-Ohlin models. As for the first we see that confronting our theories with the data by empirical testing sharpens our understanding of the theory. This learning process takes place in two ways. First, we often have to modify the theory to permit empirical testing. This modification may take the form of dropping certain assumptions, or manipulating the model to produce empirically testable hypotheses, or seeking indirect questions. In doing this we are forced to analyze the model thoroughly to find out what are the crucial elements of the model, and what are the superficial elements.

The second benefit from testing arises because our tests can never be completely satisfying and, in fact, are often perplexing and occasionally disastrous. Disasters, puzzles, and paradoxes usually mean back to the drawing board for the theorist. The theorist must develop new models or modify and expand the old ones in the light of what he has learned in the testing process. In the test of the Heckscher-Ohlin model in particular we saw how this works. We saw that further work must be done on models incorporating product differentiation, on redefining factors of production and production functions to take into account natural resource oriented trade, and on incorporating the concept of human capital into production theory.

What about the implied comparison of the comparative cost and Heckscher-Ohlin models? Who won? This may not be a very fruitful question to ask. For one thing, although the tests of the comparative cost model have been moderately successful, the model is not intellectually satisfying. It does not in itself explain the differences in relative productivities which form the basis of trade. In comparison, the Heckscher-Ohlin model is more elegant and has the virtue of connecting the international sector of a country to the central workings of the whole economic system. Whether verified or not, the Heckscher-Ohlin model has been useful in its own right for pedagogical purposes and as a point of departure for more advanced theoretical work. And this will no doubt continue to be the case.

SUPPLEMENTARY READINGS

Bhagwati, Jagdish, "The Pure Theory of International Trade: A Survey," *Economic Journal,* 74, No. 293 (March, 1964), 4–26.

Caves, Richard, *Trade and Economic Structure,* Cambridge, Mass., Harvard University Press, 1960, chap. 10.

Travis, William P., *The Theory of Trade and Protection,* Cambridge, Mass., Harvard University Press, 1964.

Chapter

New Approaches
to International Trade Theory

Any frank appraisal of the current state of international trade theory would show that there is much unfinished business. The most carefully developed theoretical model, the Heckscher-Ohlin factor endowments model, contains some fundamental conceptual problems with regard to the definition of factor inputs and production functions. Furthermore, it has had mixed results, at best, in its empirical tests. The comparative cost theory, while it has perhaps been somewhat more successful in empirical tests, has been found wanting in the number of phenomena it explains. It explains trade but not the assumed productivity differences which are the cause of trade in the model; and it has a very limited ability to deal with the dynamic phenomena of economic growth, technological change, and international factor flows.

Four kinds of approaches can be seen in the continuing search for a better theory and a more complete understanding of the phenomenon of international exchange. While recognizing the distortions inherent in any one- or two-word descriptive phrases, these might be termed the availability approach, the formal approach, the sociopolitical approach, and pragmatic empiricism. These will each be discussed in turn in this chapter.

THE AVAILABILITY APPROACH

The availability approach seeks to explain the pattern of trade by identifying the factors which influence the availability of goods in each country. Availability influences trade through both demand and supply forces. In general a nation would tend to import those commodities which are not readily available domestically and export those which are easily made available in quantities which are greater than domestic demand. At this level the approach is little more than an *ad hoc* set of statements with little scientific substance or economic content. If this approach is to play a meaningful role in international trade theory, it will be because of efforts to identify and quantify those forces which influence availability in a systematic way.

Four influences on availability have been identified.[1] Availability can be affected by the endowments of natural resources, by the extent and significance of product differentiation, by technological progress over time, and by public policy.

The effect of natural resources availability on trade is clear enough. Product differentiation on an international level occurs whenever, for example, U.S. cloth is not a perfect substitute for English cloth in the minds of the consumers of either or both countries. Evidence of the importance of product differentiation can be seen in most of the trade statistics. If a nation simultaneously records both imports and exports in a fairly narrowly defined product class, it is probably because of product differentiation.[2] For product differentiation to play a role in trade, it must be impossible for one nation to supply its consumers with a perfect substitute for the imported good. The United States both exports and imports whiskies because the flavors of bourbon and scotch cannot be duplicated by producers outside of their source countries. Product differentiation is ubiquitous at the domestic level in modern economies, and it will no doubt become an increasingly important characteristic of trade in manufactured goods between nations. Its significance in international trade is the reduction of the role of cost and price differences in explaining trade flows.

Public policy influences trade through availability considerations in a negative way. Tariffs and other restraints on trade are more likely to be imposed by a nation on those goods that are available to it from domestic sources at the same or only slightly higher costs. The lack of available domestic supply is a deterrent to imposing barriers to imports. Thus tariff structures tend to be influenced by domestic availability and in turn are important influences on the pattern of world trade.

Technological change can affect the availability of exportable goods in two ways. First the adoption of new processes that lower

[1] See Irving B. Kravis, " 'Availability' and Other Influences on the Commodity Composition of Trade," *Journal of Political Economy*, 64, No. 2 (April, 1956), 143–155.

[2] An alternative explanation would be a large country where transportation costs are important. The country could be producing for export to adjacent nations in one area while finding it cheaper to import the good in a more distant area than to ship it across the country.

costs seldom occurs simultaneously in all countries. Rather it occurs in one spot and tends to spread, so the argument goes. The first country to adopt new, cheaper means of production enjoys, for a period of time, a cost advantage which may be sufficient to allow it to export that good as long as the cost advantage exists. In a dynamic, ever changing world economy this factor alone may help to explain a substantial part of international trade.

The other way in which technological progress can influence the availability of exportable goods is through the development of new products.[3] Suppose a firm in one country begins to produce and market a new product based on a new process or technological innovation. At first the firm's sales will be solely to domestic purchasers. As productive capacity expands and information spreads, foreign sales and exports will rise. At some time foreign producers will be able to begin production because of licensing, the expiration of patent protection, or by further adaptive innovation. At first foreign production is not likely to be fully competitive with imports from the original innovator; but eventually, through tariff protection or the development of standardized technology, the advantage of the innovating firm will be lost. If new products reach a stage of highly standardized mass production, their technologies may become relatively more suited to use in less-developed countries than when the product was first introduced. If this occurs, small differences in labor costs between developed and less-developed nations may be sufficient to alter the pattern of production and trade even further.

In this model trade is a disequilibrium phenomenon. When technology is completely standardized, there will be no trade arising from this phenomenon. Trade comes with disturbances to this static equilibrium due to changes in technology. But in a modern economy these disturbances (innovations) are frequent enough to be considered the normal state of affairs.

In a recent paper Raymond Vernon has examined the forces which determine the pattern of trade inducing innovations.[4] New product development and innovation may be systematically influenced by economic variables and the economic environments in particular countries. Innovation occurs only when entrepreneurs per-

---

[3] G. C. Hufbauer, *Synthetic Materials and the Theory of International Trade,* Cambridge, Mass., Harvard University Press, 1966. See also M. V. Posner, "International Trade and Technical Change," *Oxford Economic Papers,* N.S. 13 (October, 1961), 323–341.

[4] Raymond Vernon, "International Investment and International Trade in the Product Cycle," *Quarterly Journal of Economics,* 80, No. 2 (May, 1966), 190–207. See also William Gruber, Dileep Mehta, and Raymond Vernon, "The R & D Factor in International Trade and International Investment of United States Industries," and Donald B. Keesing, "The Impact of Research and Development on United States Trade," both in *Journal of Political Economy,* 75, No. 1 (February, 1967), 20–48; and L. T. Wells, Jr., "Test of a Product Cycle Model of International Trade: U.S. Exports of Consumer Durables," *Quarterly Journal of Economics,* 23, No. 1 (February, 1969), 152–162.

ceive the opportunity for profit by innovation. Innovation will be influenced by the physical set of opportunities and the innovator's ability to perceive them. Thus labor-saving production techniques and the development of luxury type or high-income elasticity type goods would tend to occur in labor-scarce, high-wage countries and in high-income countries. Innovation generally would occur where market forces and market orientation are stronger. Development of a new product may be a sufficient basis for trade.

Hufbauer has also attempted some empirical tests of the technological gap phenomenon described here.[5] He based his study on patterns of trade in the synthetic materials such as plastics, fibers, and rubber. He tested the hypothesis that the innovation/technological gap phenomenon could account for observed patterns of trade in these materials, and he found strong support for the hypothesis in the data. His analysis also showed that synthetic materials trade was associated with the ability of nations to protect their domestic markets in order to realize static economies of scale.

While the availability approach, particularly its technological gap version, has scored some initial successes in its empirical tests, its limitations must be made clear. First this approach, if it is a theory at all, is a theory of the one-directional flow of trade in a single good and not a general theory of international exchange. The model from which Hufbauer produced his hypothesis is not capable as it stands of producing other hypotheses or theorems regarding the efficiency of trade, gains from trade, or effects of trade on incomes. However, these criticisms are not meant to inspire a rejection of this approach. Rather what is needed is more theoretical and empirical work along these lines. The technological gap hypothesis is particularly important because it focuses attention on and gives a central role to the most important characteristic of modern economic systems, their sustained growth in incomes based on innovation and rising productivity. Also it might be better seen as a useful supplement to conventional static models rather than as a full replacement.

A FORMAL APPROACH

One might characterize informal approaches such as the availability approach to trade theory as involving observations of events, perception of patterns in these events, construction of models to explain these patterns, and hopefully the eventual generalization of these models into theories with explanatory power over a wider range of phenomena. In contrast, formal approaches, such as the Heckscher-Ohlin model, start with highly abstract but general models from

[5] Hufbauer, *op. cit.*

which can be deduced a variety of theorems and hypotheses. The problem is to build enough concreteness into the model so that the hypotheses can actually be tested.

One very interesting piece of theoretical work in trade breaks new ground by starting with a new set of definitions and postulates. Its author is Peter Kenen.[6] Kenen takes as his point of departure a new definition of capital. The Heckscher-Ohlin model implicitly defines capital in a long-run setting as a homogeneous stock of "waiting." Waiting is embodied in any of a wide variety of physical forms, buildings, factories, machines, and etc. The physical forms that capital takes can be changed, but the supply of capital can only be increased by more waiting (saving). Production is carried out by combining labor with waiting in one of its physical embodiments. There are no natural resources in this model of production, so natural resource endowments cannot be a basis for trade.

The reader may be puzzled as to how waiting can be transformed into a machine and vice versa. In fact this seems to be one of the points that Kenen is making. Kenen assumes that there are two original factors of production, land and labor. However, neither of these original factors of production can be used without some prior improvement by the application of capital. The capital that is applied can be considered to be waiting in the same sense as in the Heckscher-Ohlin model. But in Kenen's model intangible waiting does not enter the production process directly but only through its application to tangible land and labor. For example, a human being represents a combination of animal forces and education, learning, or skills. Education and training are ways to invest in human capital, or to apply capital to the human agent. Machines are the outcome of combining capital or waiting with natural resources or land in the general sense. Production can only take place when improved land is combined with improved labor.

Nations can differ in their production possibilities because of differences in their original endowments or supplies of labor and land, differences in the total amount of capital, and differences in the way the available supply of capital has been divided between improving land and labor. He points out that this may explain the low rate of return on investment in what we usually call physical capital in underdeveloped countries which, paradoxically, accompanies scarcity of capital. It may be that capital has been badly allocated, with the limited supply going primarily to physical capital; this drives

6 Peter B. Kenen, "Nature, Capital and Trade," *Journal of Political Economy*, 73, No. 5 (October, 1965), 437–460.

its rate of return down to a low level. Since physical capital and human capital are highly complementary, this implies that applications of capital to the human agent would have a high rate of return and would also raise the rate of return on physical investment.

Kenen then applies this concept of capital and production to a model of international trade which employs many of the same assumptions that the Heckscher-Ohlin model uses. Specifically, the basic factors of production, unimproved labor and unimproved land, are uniform within countries and between countries, markets are competitive, factors are mobile within countries, demand conditions are alike, and production functions are alike in the two countries. Using these assumptions, Kenen proves that the opening of trade between two nations will lead to the equalization of product prices and the equalization of the prices of the services from improved labor and from improved land. However, the interest rate which is not a factor service price will not necessarily be equalized among nations. Finally, he finds that the terms of trade will be predicted by the net factor ratios in the two countries, where these factors represent the quantities of improved labor and improved land. These net factor ratios depend upon the initial endowments of the unimproved factors, the supply of capital, and, finally, upon how the capital has been allocated between improving the two original factors.

In an interesting empirical application of this framework, Kenen makes an adjustment to Leontief's labor input data to reflect the amount of capital embodied in the labor through the investment of human capital. He finds that the United States tends to export goods requiring skilled labor and import goods requiring relatively unskilled labor. When skills are interpreted as capital embodied as improvements in the human agent, it turns out that Leontief's paradox disappears. Using Kenen's concepts of capital and labor, the United States is capital abundant and does export capital intensive goods.

Kenen's model at this stage of its development is not capable of rigorous empirical testing. The concepts employed in the model require new ways of organizing and processing data before the necessary measurements can be taken. Yet I believe Kenen's work represents a major step forward in developing a more powerful and more universally applicable theory of international trade. His reformulation of the concept of capital allows the trade model to handle international differences in natural resource endowment, climate, and quality of capital stock and skill level without giving up the assumption that production functions are everywhere the same. His work represents a challenge to other economists to refine and improve the theoretical model and to devise measurement techniques which are capable of providing empirical tests of these new models.

SOCIAL AND POLITICAL INFLUENCES ON TRADE PATTERNS

The work to be described in this section is not in the mainstream of economic research. Nevertheless it is significant in its own right, and it serves to bring our own discipline into perspective. Charles Kindleberger has examined an historical situation to show that models based on the purely market-oriented behavior of "rational man" may fail to explain some responses to economic changes.[7] In the two decades between 1870–1890 there was a substantial decline in the price of wheat due to the great technological advances in overland and water transportation. These permitted the opening of large fertile areas in the United States, Canada, and Russia to production of wheat for world markets. Kindleberger analyzed the domestic responses of six European countries to this change in the international trade situation. He asked if we cannot develop models based upon the theory of behavior of groups within nations to predict or, in this case, to explain how different nations respond in different ways to the same external stimulus.

In the United Kingdom there was no active response as the price of wheat fell. Land rents fell, the agricultural labor force declined, the power of the landed gentry as a political force declined, and the process of industrialization was enhanced by lower food prices and the availability of a growing labor force because of migration to urban areas. In Germany and in France, for different reasons and because of different constellations of political power, protective tariff walls were raised to permit continued domestic production of wheat at a higher price. In Italy the political response was slower. The protective tariff was imposed, but later than in France and in Germany, and the evidence suggests that the adjustment was too late. The decade 1880–1890 was a period of substantial emigration from Italy to North and South America.

The Danish adjustment is perhaps the most interesting. Denmark imposed no tariff wall. Rather there was a revolution in the form of agricultural production within Denmark. There was a shift from a position of primarily grain-oriented farming to an agriculture based on dairy products, eggs, and meat. In fact, Denmark became a substantial exporter of these "refined" agricultural commodities.

Kindleberger attempted to explain the different responses to the same market signals in terms of differences in group behavior among countries. His attempt was a tentative one, and he raised the plea for more work along this line. Unfortunately, although this may be a fruitful and interesting line of inquiry, little further work has been done.

[7] Charles P. Kindleberger, "Group Behavior and International Trade," *Journal of Political Economy*, 59, No. 1 (February, 1951), 30–46.

Nevertheless the examination of this historical event does have lessons for our market-oriented theory of trade. For example, the Danish case in particular shows dramatically the interdependence between domestic economic developments and international developments. Demark responded to the fall in the price of wheat in a way which increased GNP and the efficiency of Denmark's utilization of its own factors of production. The fall in the price of wheat probably influenced the price of feed grains, which helped to develop a comparative advantage in refined agricultural production. In addition, this was a period of substantial growth in real income in other nations. This was no doubt very influential in explaining the growth of the Danish export market.

Also this analysis shows that in international trade theory the international flow of factors cannot be entirely ignored. This is something on which we have said virtually nothing to date except to assume that it did not exist. Yet the major response of Italy to this economic change was a substantial flow of labor internationally. Economic historians have long been concerned with both measuring and explaining international migration particularly in the nineteenth century. To summarize their findings these flows have apparently been responsive to economic factors, particularly real incomes in the recipient and sending country. International flows of labor are relatively much less important in the twentieth century. However, the same thing cannot be said of international capital flows. Capital has always been relatively mobile between countries.

PRAGMATIC EMPIRICISM

The aims of the theories of trade which we have outlined up to this point have been by and large quite ambitious. We have looked for theories which were comprehensive and general in the sense that they were capable of dealing with a full range of related phenomena. Also we have looked for theories with long records of successful empirical testing and verification. Since our available set of theories does not measure up to these standards, should we say that our aims have been too high? I do not think so, for two reasons. First, these standards are ones which any field of inquiry aspiring to the status of a science must meet. Also, these standards provide a valuable incentive to further efforts, and there are encouraging signs of progress. The efforts should continue. But it is also true in any discipline that much substantial and scientifically valid progress has been based not on general theorizing but on less exciting work on measurement, description, and recording. In economics this statistical and econometric work is analogous to the refinements of laboratory techniques and testing equipment in the physical sciences. In economics this work might be called "pragmatic empiricism."

The work in this category seldom employs an economic theory more sophisticated than supply and demand analysis. But it does employ sophisticated statistical and econometric techniques. It is helping us to accomplish three things:

1. To increase our knowledge of what is happening or what our world actually looks like. For example two recent studies by Balassa examined for the first time the actual effective tariff rates of the United States, the United Kingdom, and several other countries,[8] and what the effect of the formation of the European Economic Community was on the shares of the market held by the largest firms in each industry.[9] While neither piece of information sounds dramatic, they both have provided incentives for new theoretical investigations, since they have revealed phenomena or economic occurrences which are not adequately accounted for by existing theory.

2. To make progress in solving some of our more severe measurement problems. For example a new piece of work which develops a technique for measuring the skill levels of U.S. labor employed in manufacturing exports may eventually lead to a method for testing Kenen's new model of capital, trade, and growth.[10]

3. To develop predictive models of modest scope. For example, knowledge of the elasticity of supply for imports is a prerequisite for making a prediction of the price and import effects of a change in tariff rates.

From the point of view of effective economic policy, it may be more valuable to be able to predict the effect of trends in prices and incomes on the U.S. balance of trade,[11] or the impact of a proposed devaluation of the dollar on the U.S. balance of payments,[12] or the the welfare gains and losses of a 50 percent across-the-board reduction in tariffs[13] than it is to be able to resolve the Leontief paradox once and for all.

[8] Bela Balassa, "Tariff Protection in Industrial Countries: An Evaluation," *Journal of Political Economy*, 73, No. 6 (December, 1965), 573–594; reprinted in American Economic Association, *Readings in International Economics*, Homewood, Ill., Irwin, 1968, 579–604.

[9] Bela Balassa, "Tariff Reductions and Trade in Manufactures Among the Industrial Countries," *American Economic Review*, 56, No. 3 (June, 1966), 466–473.

[10] Donald B. Keesing, "Labor Skills and International Trade: Evaluating Many Trade Flows with a Single Measuring Device," *Review of Economics and Statistics*, 47, No. 3 (August, 1965), 287–294.

[11] H. S. Houthakker and Stephen P. Magee, "Income and Price Elasticities in World Trade," *Review of Economics and Statistics*, 51, No. 2 (May, 1969), 111–125.

[12] John E. Floyd, "The Overvaluation of The Dollar: A Note on the International Price Mechanism," *American Economic Review*, 55, No. 1 (March, 1965), 95–107.

[13] Bela Balassa and Mordechai E. Kreinin, "Trade Liberalization Under The 'Kennedy Round': The Static Effects," *Review of Economics and Statistics*, 59, No. 2 (May, 1967), 125–137.

As the articles cited here show, we are closer to being able to answer these questions. And most interestingly these questions can be answered with a fair degree of confidence without getting involved in the more perplexing theoretical issues raised earlier in this book. The reason is that these are fairly narrow questions concerning the effects of small movements around present trading positions in response to well-defined and delimited changes in policy variables. Also for the most part they rely for the answers on fairly simple applications of supply and demand analysis and estimates of elasticities. In contrast we ask our theory to be able to explain why things are exactly the way they are and how they got there, and we want a single comprehensive answer for all of it. I will not judge whether or not this is practical. But it is likely to keep us busy for quite awhile.

SUPPLEMENTARY READINGS

Wells, Louis T., "Test of a Product Cycle Model of International Trade: U.S. Exports of Consumer Durables," *Quarterly Journal of Economics,* 83, No. 1 (February, 1969), 152–162.

Orcutt, Guy H., "Measurement of Price Elasticities in International Trade," *Review of Economics and Statistics,* 32, No. 2 (May, 1950), 117–132; reprinted in American Economic Association, *Readings in International Economics,* Homewood, Ill., Irwin, 1968, pp. 528–552.

Chapter

Tariffs, Protection, and the Theory of Trade Policy

Any theory of trade which purports to have relevance to the real world must have room in it for the man-made barriers to trade: tariffs, quotas, and other protectionist devices. The next two chapters deal with some of the major theoretical, empirical, and policy issues concerning tariffs and nontariff barriers to trade for a single nation. Chapter 11 considers aspects of customs unions and tariff discrimination which arise when two or more nations reduce or eliminate tariffs among themselves while maintaining higher tariffs and other barriers to imports from nonmembers.

THE EFFECTS OF TARIFFS

In this section the effects of a tariff imposed on an imported good are examined primarily in a partial equilibrium framework. By this we mean that only the effect of the tariff on the price and quantity of the good (and other directly related variables) is considered. A tariff serves to raise the supply curve of the imported good by making imports more expensive per unit to the domestic consumers. Tariffs can be either specific or ad valorem. An ad valorem tariff is expressed as a fixed percentage of the world price or unit value of the import. A specific tariff is a fixed sum per unit of import. In Figure 9.1 the dashed line, $S_M + t$, shows the effect of the specific tariff on the supply curve of imports, labeled S_M. The geometry of an ad valorem tariff is essentially similar, the only difference being that the fixed percentage rate of tariff causes the supply curve with the tariff to diverge from the supply curve without the tariff, and this divergence is by an increasing amount as the world price increases.

Most of the effects of a tariff can be shown in terms of geometric areas in a supply and demand figure. These areas always represent a dollar quantity because they are found by multiplying prices by quantities in appropriate formulas for areas. The interpretation of any given area depends on how it was formed. For example, the area under a marginal cost curve between two levels of output represents the increase in total cost in moving from one level of output to the next. The area under a demand curve between zero and any given quantity can be interpreted as the maximum amount which a consumer would be willing to pay to receive that amount of the commodity rather than do without it entirely. If this is granted, we can introduce the concept of *consumer surplus.* The consumer surplus is the difference between the maximum amount that consumers would be willing to pay for a given quantity and the actual expenditure for that quantity. The consumer surplus is the area formed by the triangle under the demand curve and above the price line for any price and quantity combination. Under certain limiting assumptions, changes in consumer surplus can be used as a measure of the change in consumer welfare or well-being which results from the imposition of the tariff. The interpretation of consumer surplus raises many conceptual and empirical issues which are beyond the scope of this course. However, the notion is quite valuable at this level of abstraction.[1]

There are eight conceptually separable effects of a tariff:

1. the production effect;
2. the revenue effect;

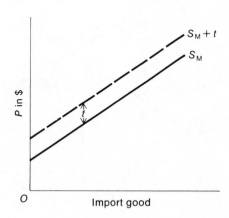

Figure 9.1
The effect of a specific tariff on supply

[1] The concept of consumer surplus is clearly developed for the student who has been introduced to indifference curves in George J. Stigler, *The Theory of Price,* 3rd ed., New York, Macmillan, 1966, p. 78–81.

136

3. the redistribution or transfer effect;
4. the consumption effect;
5. the terms of trade effect;
6. the factor income effect;
7. the employment effect;
8. the balance-of-payments effect.

Some of these can be illustrated with the aid of Figure 9.2. In this figure we temporarily assume that the elasticity of supply of imports is infinite. In other words the nation has such a small impact on the world market for this good that it can import as much as it desires without affecting the price of the import. In this situation, if there is no tariff, the domestic price is determined in the world market. Unless there is complete specialization, there will be some domestic producers in this market, too. The quantities that they would supply at various prices are shown in Figure 9.2 by the domestic supply curve, S_D. If the world price is P_1, this country will produce $O-Q_1$ of the import type good domestically, and import Q_4-Q_1. The total quantity demanded will be $O-Q_4$.

The analysis of a tariff proceeds along lines very similar to the analysis of the incidence of a sales tax or excise tax. If a specific tariff is imposed on the import good, the effect is to shift the supply curve upward to the dashed line labeled $S_M + t$. World producers are still receiving P_1 while domestic consumers pay P_2. The difference, $P_2 - P_1$, is the specific tariff rate.

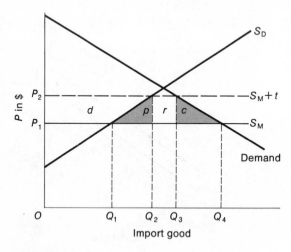

Figure 9.2
The effects of a tariff—infinite supply elasticity for imports

Note: Producers' Gain = d, Government gain = r, Consumers' loss = $d + p + r + c$, Net loss = $p + c$.

The *production effect* is the increase in domestic production from $O–Q_1$ to $O–Q_2$ following the introduction of the tariff. Protection results in the substitution of higher cost domestic sources of output for the lower cost world sources. The area under the domestic supply curve is the opportunity cost in terms of foregone outputs of other goods of increasing output by $Q_1–Q_2$. The shaded area, *p,* is the increase in opportunity costs associated with replacing foreign production with domestic production. This area represents a loss of welfare to domestic consumers.

The *revenue effect* is shown by the rectanglar area between Q_2 and Q_3, and between P_1 and P_2. This represents the dollar value of revenues collected by the customs authorities. The revenue effect is a transfer of income from the consumers of this good to the government. Presumably the government will spend the tariff revenues. The total welfare effects cannot be determined unless we know how the tariff revenues are to be spent. These revenues could be spent in such a way (e.g., transfer payments to low-income families) as to cause shifts in the demand or domestic supply curve. A full analysis of these effects of the tariff would have to take these second-order effects into account.

There is an additional transfer or *redistribution effect* between the consumers, who lose, and the domestic producers of this good, who gain. This redistribution effect is shown by the area *d.* The effect of the tariff is to raise the domestic price and raise the returns to those factors employed in the production of this good. A transfer payment, *d,* is paid by consumers in the form of a higher price on domestic output and is received by the factors of production in the form of a factor return higher than necessary to keep them employed in this industry.

The *consumption effect* is the reduction in consumption from $O–Q_4$ to $O–Q_3$. Associated with this is a loss of consumers' surplus equal to the area $d + p + r + c$.

If we assume that the gains of one group are comparable to the losses of another, we can make a general statement about the welfare effect of this tariff. The components of the consumers' loss, *d* and *r,* are simply transfers to producers and the government, respectively. Their net effect on the country's welfare is zero. The areas *p* and *c* are losses to the country, and to consumers in particular. If the world supply curve of the import good is infinitely elastic, there are no adverse effects in the rest of the world.

Now let us relax the assumption about supply elasticity. If the foreign supply curve is upward sloping, the total supply curve of the imported good is the horizontal sum of the domestic supply curve (S_D in Figure 9.3) and the foreign supply curve (not shown). The total supply curve without the tariff is S_M. In the absence of a tariff the equilibrium price is P_1, consumption is $O-Q_4$, and Q_1-Q_4 is imported. The dashed line, $S_M + t$, shows the impact of the tariff. Domestic production is again increased from $O-Q_1$ to $O-Q_2$. The increased cost of this production is given by the triangular area labeled p as before. The consumption effect and the redistribution effect are exactly as discussed before.

The essential difference between this analysis and the preceding one lies in the effect of the tariff on the world price of this good. The imposition of the tariff causes this country to reduce its imports to Q_2-Q_3. This reduction in import demand in turn causes a drop in the world price of the good from $O-P_1$ to $O-P_2$. The imposition of the tariff forces a reduction in the world price on producers. This is the essence of the *terms of trade effect.* The terms of trade, when the import price is measured net of tariff, are turned in favor of the importing country by the imposition of the tariff. Because of this favorable shift in the terms of trade a country can gain by the imposition of the tariff. The gain comes because part of the burden of the tariff is actually shifted to world producers. As before, the total

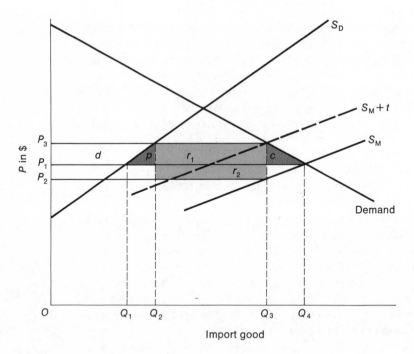

Figure 9.3
The effects of a tariff—imperfectly elastic world supply

Note: Tariff imposing nation: Producers' gain $= d$, Government gain $= r_1 + r_2$, Consumers' loss $= d + p + r_1 + c$, net gain (+) or loss (−) $= r_2 - p - c$. Rest of world: Foreign producers' loss $= r_2$. All nations together: Net loss for all nations $= p + c$.

revenue from the tariff is given by the rectangle with the dimensions P_3-P_2 and Q_2-Q_3. But only the upper portion of this, labeled r_1, is actually paid by consumers. The consumer's price rises only from $O-P_1$ to $O-P_3$. The producer's price falls from $O-P_1$ to $O-P_2$. Consequently the area r_2 below P_1 represents the foreign producer's share of the revenue effect. As before, we must know how the revenues are to be spent in order to predict the final outcome. But there is an additional wrinkle here. The r_1 revenues are merely redistributed within the country from one set of individuals to another. But the r_2 revenues represent claims on foreign goods. These claims can only be made good by increasing imports of the good or some other good.

Now we can deduce the total effect of the tariff on the welfare of this country. The country experiences a welfare loss of $p + c$, and a gain in revenue of r_2. If the elasticity of the supply of imports is less than infinite, r_2 will be positive and may be greater than $p + c$. There may be a net gain to the country. However, since from a global point of view r_2 is not a net gain, the world as a whole loses from the imposition of a tariff. This conclusion, that tariffs will always reduce the size of the world pie even though one nation's slice may be enlarged, is a corollary of the earlier statement on the economic virtues of free trade. If free trade maximizes aggregate world income (never mind how it is distributed), then any interference to trade such as a tariff must reduce world income.

If a country can gain by imposing a tariff, the next logical question is what rate of tariff will maximize this gain; that is, what will the optimum tariff be? We turn to this question in a later section; but first, there are three more effects of the tariff to consider. In discussing these we depart from the narrow partial equilibrium framework used above.

The *factor income effect* is derived from the relationship between trade and factor incomes which was first outlined by Stolper and Samuelson.[2] You will recall that the opening of trade reduced the price and the real income of that factor of production used relatively intensively in the import good. Correspondingly, a reduction in trade, for example, due to a tariff, will normally increase the price and income of this factor of production.[3]

Tariffs can have an *employment effect.* Within the context of a national income model, the imposition of a tariff shifts the marginal propensity to import schedule downward. This has the effect of an autonomous reduction in leakages. Domestic expenditure curves will shift up. There will be an increase in aggregate demand for domestic products. If the nation has unemployed resources, the increased

[2] See Chapter 5, pp. 73–75.
[3] An exception is pointed out at the end of this section.

expenditure will act through a multiplier process to increase national income and employment. If there is full employment, the increase in demand will be dissipated in higher prices and a period of inflation.

However, one would be short-sighted and unneighborly to advocate tariff increases as an antirecessionary policy. It must be recalled that one nation's imports are another's exports. A tariff has foreign employment repercussions as well. Foreign exports would fall leading to a reduction in income levels and employment; and through the foreign nation's marginal import propensity, their imports will fall. Further, they may be tempted to retaliate. This "beggar-my-neighbor" tariff policy is just not cricket, and besides, it could boomerang.

Finally there are direct and indirect *balance-of-payments effects* associated with the tariff. The tariff will reduce expenditures on foreign goods, directly improving the current account of the balance of payments. In this respect the effect of a tariff is equivalent to a devaluation of the currency for use in import transactions.[4] In addition to this direct effect the employment effect just mentioned works to increase money income. Because of the marginal propensity to import, imports will increase. Whether this stimulation to imports will be greater than the initial reduction depends on the size of the multiplier, the marginal propensity to import, and the elasticities of demand and foreign supply for imports.[5] As in the case of beggar-my-neighbor tariffs, tariffs imposed for balance-of-payments purposes will have foreign repercussions which would tend to mitigate any favorable initial effects. Such a policy invites foreign retaliation.

Even though such a policy seems to have little to offer, and in fact is against the rules and guidelines established under the General Agreements on Tariffs and Trade (GATT), it has been utilized by Great Britain in recent times, and it has found at least one noted advocate in the United States. With the tacit approval of her major trading partners, Great Britain imposed a temporary 15 percent surcharge on all imports in October, 1967, in an attempt to forestall what turned out to be the inevitable devaluation of the pound sterling. In the United States, J. K. Galbraith was arguing in 1964 that the gravity of our payments deficit and the high degree of protection against U.S. imports established by the Common Market countries justified an increase in our tariffs.[6]

---

[4] The effect of a devaluation on the balance of payments depends on the elasticities of supply and demand for imports and exports. See any textbook covering the theory of balance-of-payments adjustment for a discussion of the so-called Marshall-Lerner conditions. C. K. Kindleberger, *International Economics*, 4th ed., Homewood, Ill., Irwin, 1968, chap. 15 and appendix F, is good.

[5] Again this effect is similar to the combined price and income effects of a devaluation. These are discussed in Kindleberger, *ibid.*, chap. 17. Kindleberger provides original references.

[6] See John Kenneth Galbraith, "The Balance of Payments: An Administrative View," *Review of Economics and Statistics*, 46, No. 2 (May, 1964), 115–122.

Before leaving this topic there is one other possible effect of tariffs which deserves mention. Chapters 2–6 dealt with models in which factors of production were immobile internationally. The result was differences in costs, comparative advantages, and the flow of goods between nations in international trade. The reverse relationship is also possible. If tariffs impede the flow of goods across international boundries, differences in factor prices will persist; and these differences may stimulate movements of factors of production, particularly capital, from one nation to another. It has been suggested that a major factor in the large flow of American capital into Europe in the early 1960s could be the tariff policies of the European Economic Community. The Common Market was creating a large and potentially profitable market by eliminating tariffs on goods moving in trade between member nations. At the same time a common external tariff structure was being established. The only way American firms could successfully compete for sales within the market was to avoid the tariffs by producing the product in Europe rather than in the United States. This could be done only by sending large amounts of capital to Europe to build new plants or to acquire existing European firms. Therefore, recognizing the increasing international mobility of factors of production, we might add one more effect to the list, the *factor flow effect.*

It is also possible to analyze the effects of a tariff by using offer curves. Country A's offer curve of steel for cloth in the absence of a tariff is shown by $O\text{-}A_f$ in Figure 9.4. Country B's offer curve, $O\text{-}B_f$ intersects it at point X showing that the free trade terms of trade are

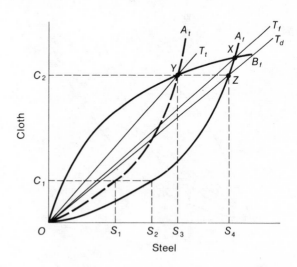

Figure 9.4
The effect of a tariff on the offer curve and the terms of trade

TARIFFS, PROTECTION, AND THE THEORY OF TRADE POLICY

$O-T_f$. Any tariff displaces the offer curve toward the axis representing the imported good. A's offer curve with tariff is $O-A_t$. This displacement can be interpreted as follows. For any given level of imports, say $O-C_1$, consumers in A are willing to offer as much as $O-S_2$ in steel as shown by the free trade offer curve. If the government intervenes by levying a tariff which is collected in steel, the effective offer abroad is only $O-S_1$. The government collects the tariff of S_1-S_2 units of steel from its citizens.

Alternatively the tariff could be assumed to be collected in units of cloth, in which case the offer curve would be considered to be displaced vertically. For either case a fully general analysis must consider the government's disposition of the tariff revenues. It is simplest to assume that the government directly consumes the tariff revenues in such a way as not to affect private incomes, prices, and hence the private offer curve.

The tariff displaced offer curve intersects $O-B_f$ at point Y. The new terms of trade are $O-T_t$. They have shifted in favor of country A as a consequence of the tariff. Whether or not this change in the terms of trade signals an increase in A's welfare is not clear from this analysis. If community indifference curves are introduced and their assumptions accepted, this question can be answered. This is done in the appendix to this chapter. Figure 9.4 can also be used to show that although the world price of cloth has fallen in terms of steel, in country A cloth is more expensive to consumers. Consumers buying $O-C_2$ of cloth must pay $O-S_4$ of steel. The domestic terms of trade line through point Z shows the increase in the relative price of cloth inclusive of the tariff.

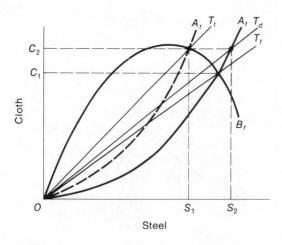

Figure 9.5
A tariff can reduce the domestic price of the imported good

If B's offer curve has a different shape, this result will not hold (see Figure 9.5). The introduction of a tariff on cloth shifts the world terms of trade net of the tariff to $O–T_t$. Cloth imports rise to $O–C_2$. Consumers in country A must pay $O–S_2$ in steel, inclusive of the tariff, but this indicates a reduction in the domestic price of cloth relative to steel. Since the domestic price of cloth has fallen, the production, consumption, redistribution, and factor price effects are the opposite of those described above.[7] This result requires not only that B's offer curve slope down to the right over the relevant range, but also that the tariff be collected in terms of steel rather than cloth and that the government consume the steel in such a way as to leave undisturbed private incomes and prices.

THE OPTIMUM TARIFF

If the imposition of a tariff can prove beneficial to a country, some tariffs must be better than others. The analytical problem is to choose that tariff rate which maximizes the gains from a tariff, that is, to find the optimum tariff. If we consider the import good in a partial equilibrium setting, the selection of the optimum tariff is very similar to the problem of profit maximizing faced by a monopsonist producer operating in an imperfect factor market.

It will be useful to review the principles of monopsony. A monopsonist is the only buyer in a market with many sellers. Because of this he has a kind of market power; that is, the price at which he can buy is influenced by the quantity of his purchases. Because of this he faces an upward sloping supply curve for the factor input which he wishes to purchase. The monopsonist must pay a higher price in order to obtain a larger quantity of the input. Not only must he pay a higher price to the incremental unit, but he must also pass on the higher price to all units of the factor input being purchased. The cost to the monopsonist of one additional unit is greater than the price of that marginal unit. The marginal purchase cost is the increase in total expenditure required to obtain one more unit of the input in the monopsonistic market. For upward sloping supply curves the marginal purchase cost will always be above the supply curve. The monopsonist maximizes profits by choosing that level of purchases which equates the marginal purchase cost with his marginal revenue product. In graphical terms he selects the output where the marginal purchase cost curve intersects his demand curve for the factor.

If a nation faces a less than perfectly elastic supply curve for imports, it can exercise monopsonistic power in the import market by

---

[7] This possibility was first noted by Lloyd A. Metzler, "Tariffs, the Terms of Trade and the Distribution of National Income," *Journal of Political Economy*, 57, No. 1 (February, 1949), 1–29.

144   acting collectively. If it wishes to act like a monopsonist and maximize the gains from trade (as measured by the size of the pie), it
should select that level of imports at which the marginal cost of imports is equal to the domestic price of imports. For simplicity assume
no domestic production of the good. Figure 9.6 shows the demand
for the imported good, the supply curve, and the marginal cost of
imports. This last curve is analogous to the marginal factor cost curve
of the monopsonist. In the absence of any interference in the form of
tariffs or quotas, the imported good would be sold at price $O–P_1$ at the
intersection of the demand curve and the supply curve. An omniscient
"tariff board," which knew the shapes of the curves and knew its
economic theory, could increase the welfare of the nation by reducing imports. Suppose it somehow decreased imports from $O–Q_1$ to
$O–Q_2$. The reduction in expenditure or cost would be given by the
area under the marginal cost of import curve, Q_2DEQ_1. The value to
consumers of the reduction in purchases is given by the area under
the demand curve, Q_2CBQ_1. Consumers lose this by reducing purchases but gain by the amount of the lower expenditure. The net gain
is the shaded area $CDEB$. There will continue to be a net gain from
reducing imports until they have been brought down to the level of
$O–Q_3$. At that point the world price has fallen to $O–P_2$.

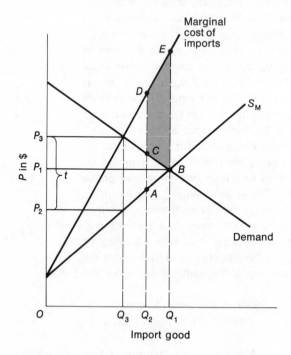

Figure 9.6
Derivation of the optimum tariff

If consumers could buy the good at $O-P_2$, they would want to purchase considerably more than $O-Q_3$. The only way that the tariff board can limit imports to $O-Q_3$ is through some protective device. It could be a tariff, or it could be one of the other nontariff barriers to trade discussed below. But if a tariff is chosen to restrict purchases, it must be large enough to raise the domestic price to $O-P_3$. Therefore the optimum tariff must be equal to P_3-P_2, or t in Figure 9.6. To summarize, the optimum tariff must make the domestic price equal to the marginal cost of imports.

The effects of the optimum tariff are identical to those discussed above. If the supply of imports is perfectly elastic, that is, if S_M is horizontal, the marginal cost of imports curve coincides with the supply curve and the optimum tariff is zero. Otherwise, as long as the supply curve is upward sloping, there is a divergence between the marginal cost of imports and their price. And an optimum tariff rate can be found. It can be shown that the optimum tariff, expressed as an ad valorem tariff rate, varies inversely with the elasticity of the supply curve of imports. This much should be apparent from the discussion above and inspection of Figure 9.6. A mathematical derivation can be used to show further that the optimum tariff rate is equal to the reciprocal of the elasticity of supply of imports.[8]

It is also possible to use offer curves and community indifference curves to derive the optimum tariff. The favorable terms of trade effect has been demonstrated with offer curves in the first section. The terms of trade can actually be pushed too far by a tariff—so that some of the potential gains are dissipated. For the student who has mastered the appendix to Chapter 6, a derivation of the optimum tariff based on community indifference curves is included in the appendix to this chapter.

The practical significance of the optimum tariff analysis must be questioned for at least three reasons. First, as a normative prescription for policy the prerequisites for implementation are not likely to be fulfilled. To find the optimum tariff one must know the community indifference curves of the society; that is, the income distribution question must be settled. Second, the analysis assumes, in effect, that tariff policy is guided by the national interest, that is, the desire to maximize national welfare however it has been defined. But in practice tariffs are imposed on particular goods because of the political power or influence of those who would benefit from them. Tariff legislation typically has about the same kind of effect on national welfare and is handled in Congress in the same manner as the annual public works "pork barrel."

[8] The interested student is referred to Harry Johnson, "Optimum Tariffs and Retaliation," in his *International Trade and Economic Growth*, Cambridge, Mass., Harvard University Press, 1961, esp. pp. 56–59.

The third reason is that the analysis assumes that trading partners will not retaliate with "optimal" tariffs of their own. Obviously this possibility cannot be ruled out. The propositions we have presented concerning the optimum tariff and the gains from a tariff through a terms-of-trade effect have implicitly assumed the absence of retaliatory action by other countries. If the other country retaliates with an optimum tariff of its own, this changes the trading situation of the first country. Normally this means that there is a new, different optimum tariff given the new trading situation. One can see that the outcome is a sequence of optimum tariff, optimum retaliation, counter retaliation, and etc. Under some conditions, but by no means all situations, a nation can be better off by imposing an optimum tariff even in the face of optimum retaliation.[9]

The final point to be made concerning optimum tariff policy is that if a country has monopoly power in its export market, there is an optimum tax policy regarding exports also. The argument is symmetrical with the one just presented concerning monopsony power in import markets. The nation chooses that level of exports which equates the marginal revenue from exports with its marginal opportunity cost of producing exports. It achieves this level of exports by imposing a tax on exports which depends upon the elasticity of foreign demand for the exported good. The tax revenues are analogous to the profits of the monopoly firm in conventional analysis. Once again it must be pointed out that a full analysis of the problem would require a knowledge of how these profits were spent or distributed.

PROTECTION: PRO AND CON

If free trade is good, why are tariff reductions so difficult to negotiate? And why are there so many strong efforts to increase the coverage and effectiveness of nontariff barriers to trade such as quotas? To understand the answer to this question it is necessary to evaluate some of the arguments offered in favor of tariffs and other forms of protection.

Four economic arguments or justifications for protection are logically valid within the fairly narrow contexts in which they can be applied. However, they are applicable under only fairly restrictive conditions. The hoped-for benefits to be expected from protection according to each of these arguments are not likely to be realized in most situations where tariffs are actually likely to be employed.

We have already met the first three of these "valid" arguments, the *terms of trade* or optimum tariff argument, the *balance-of-pay-*

[9] The question of optimum retaliation is considered and analyzed thoroughly by Harry Johnson, in *ibid*, pp. 31–61. Also see the appendix to this chapter.

ments argument, and the *beggar-my-neighbor* employment argument.   147
To employ the terms of trade argument in justification of a tariff
successfully, one must show that the nation is a major importer of
the good and thus can influence the world price of the good. And
one must show that tariff retaliation is not likely. Further one must
show that the elasticity of foreign supply can actually be measured
so that the optimum tariff rate can be calculated. As for the employment and balance-of-payments arguments, their applicability is
limited to those cases where indirect or feedback effects are likely
to be small and retaliation is not likely. The power of these two
arguments is considerably reduced by the availability of alternative
policy instruments for achieving full employment and balance-of-
payments equilibrium.

The fourth valid argument has a long intellectual history. It was
employed by Alexander Hamilton, among others, in the *Report on
Manufactures*. This is the *infant industry argument.* It is said that
newly established firms and industries require protection in their
early stages so that they may grow and prosper and eventually take
their place in the ranks of efficient and competitive industries. Logically the argument implies that the necessity or justification for
protection is temporary, and that the protection should be removed
as soon as the industries have reached a viable level of maturity.
There is no doubt that protection can aid infant industries. It can
be of benefit to most industries. It is necessary for the argument to
be able to show both that the industry will achieve self-sufficiency
with protection and that it could not achieve self-sufficiency in the
absence of protection.

Consider a product for which each firm's long-run average cost
curve is as shown in Figure 9.7. Also consider a small, relatively

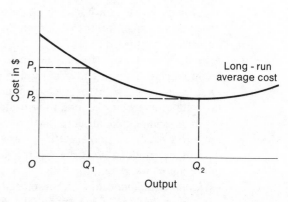

Figure 9.7
A long-run cost curve with economies of scale

undeveloped country, which has no domestic production of the good and is importing Q_1 per year at the world price of P_2. A firm established to produce the good for domestic markets only would have to charge a price of P_1 in order to cover its costs of producing for the domestic market. The firm could stay in business supplying its domestic market only if a tariff provided sufficient protection so that it could sell at a price above the world price, or a subsidy was available to cover the losses incurred by selling at P_2. The infant industry argument has to explain why the firm could not start out producing at its most efficient point, Q_2, and sell the excess on the world market. And it must show that the firm which starts at Q_1 under protection can grow to Q_2 and eventually become competitive.

The key to the argument lies in the concepts of *dynamic scale economies* and *external economies.* If there were dynamic scale economies, the long-run average cost curve of Figure 9.7 would portray not alternatives facing a firm at any point in time, but the time path of the firm's positions as it grew over time. If there are costs of entry which are related to the scale of the plant to be built, if capital generated from retained earnings is cheaper than borrowed capital, and if learning by doing is an important aspect of the efficiency and cost structure of the plant, then no firm could start from scratch producing Q_2 at a low cost of P_2. Firms would have to start small and grow and learn and cut costs as they went.

If there are external economies, a firm finds that, as it increases its output over time, its cost curves shift down because suppliers can provide materials at lower cost, transport and utility services are used more intensively, lower prices per unit can be charged, etc. These are economies that are not visible to the firm contemplating starting at Q_2 but are realized only in the process of growth.

In summary there is substance to the infant industry argument. The difficulties lie in identifying those industries which are likely to experience significant dynamic scale economies and external economies and in ensuring that the infant industry argument is not simply a rationale for the continued protection of inefficient static industries. Also the shield of protection tends to reduce the incentive for the technological change and cost cutting which are part of growing up. As a result the list of protected industries which have announced their maturity and renounced their protection is notoriously short.

It is sometimes argued that certain industries should be protected in order to preserve firms, equipment, and skills which are essential to national security. To rely on imports of national security materials in peacetime is risky, it is said, since foreign sources of essential equipment may be foreclosed in time of war. This is essentially a noneconomic argument. The evaluation of national security and defense needs must be based on considerations beyond economics. But this is not to say that the economist has no contribution to make to the discussion.[10]

The economist can make three kinds of suggestions. First, he may be able to estimate the size and composition of the resource and materials needs for various levels of combat and mobilization by using such techniques as input-output analysis. He may find that industries listed for protection for national security reasons are not really essential to the types and durations of expected conflicts, particularly in the age of the bomb and limited warfare. Second, he may be able to estimate the opportunity cost of protecting an inefficient industry through tariffs. Then policy makers can weigh the estimated national security benefits against the costs of achieving them. Finally, the economist may be able to suggest alternative ways of achieving the same ends, for example through stockpiling or planning for conversion of other related industries. In any event the national security argument should not be accepted in the case of any industry without a careful critical evaluation of the role of the industry in national security, the costs of protection, and the alternatives.

Much of this discussion has very little connection with the pages of the Congressional Record or conversations on tariffs in the corridors of Congress. In the political realm, which is where the issues of protection are settled, the battles are over shares of the pie. It is the distribution question of Chapter 6 once again. While free trade will enlarge the pie, we know that as things stand some parties will wind up with a smaller piece if all protectionist devices were to be dismantled.

Most arguments over tariffs and protection revolve around the fear of unemployment, elimination of profit, and loss of capital in industries which are already under pressures due to lack of technological advance, shifts in tastes and preferences, and/or foreign competition.[11] The head of a labor union seeing layoffs, a possible mill closing, and the inability to match the wage gains of workers in economically healthier industries will use any possible argument to support his plea for protection. So will the mill owner and even the mayor of the one-industry town who sees a declining population and shrinking tax base. They all favor protection; but what they really want to protect is their slice of the pie. Any effective antiprotectionist policy must find ways of dealing with this problem, both as a matter of practical politics and, I think, as a matter of justice. There are

[10] For one thing, management of the defense establishment entails choices among priorities and problems of allocation of scarce resources. And economists have found many ways to make useful contributions to defense management. See, for example, Stephen Enke, *Defense Management,* Englewood Cliffs, N.J., Prentice-Hall, 1967.

[11] For an alternately amusing and despairing survey of the pro-protection arguments and trade issues in general see Leland B. Yeager and David Tuerck, *Trade Policy and the Price System,* Scranton, Penn., International Text Book Company, 1966.

150   some possibilities, and these will be discussed in the final section of
the next chapter.

For supplementary readings, see the end of Chapter 10.

APPENDIX
TO CHAPTER 9

OFFER CURVES AND THE OPTIMUM TARIFF

Once it is assumed that the trade indifference map can be derived,
the determination of the optimum tariff is straightforward. In Figure
9.8 two countries, A and B, export steel and cloth, respectively. At
the free trade equilibrium country A is on TIC_{A1}. Unless this trade indifference curve happens also to be tangent to B's offer curve (which
could happen only if B's offer curve were a straight line from the
origin), a portion of B's offer curve lies above and to the left of TIC_{A1}.
Country A would rather move to the left along B's offer curve into
more preferred territory. It can do so by displacing its offer curve with
a tariff. The optimum tariff is the one which displaces A's offer curve
so that it intersects $O–B_f$ at the latter's tangency with TIC_{A2}. In other

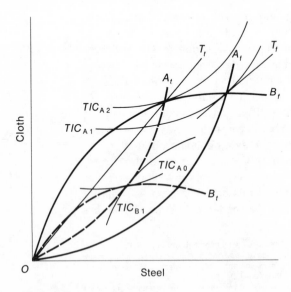

Figure 9.8
An optimum tariff and retaliation

words the optimum tariff point for A is at a tangency between B's offer curve and one of A's trade indifference curves.

The argument works both ways. Given A's new tariff-displaced offer curve, $O-A_t$, B can find an optimum retaliatory tariff which will place it on its highest attainable trade indifference curve, TIC_{B1}. Whether the retaliation and counterretaliation will continue until all trade is halted by prohibitive tariffs depends on the shapes of the offer curves and trade indifference maps. It is possible that the position after B's retaliation could prove to be a stable equilibrium if A's trade indifference curve through that point was also tangent to B's new offer curve. If not, the battle would continue.

Chapter

Some Aspects of Protection and Trade Policy

MEASURING TARIFF BARRIERS: THE EFFECTIVE RATE OF PROTECTION

The protective effect of a tariff is to increase the amount of domestic production where domestic production takes place at a cost above the world price. A measure of the magnitude of protection offered to domestic producers is the disparity between domestic and foreign costs. Where domestic production utilizes no imported raw materials or intermediate goods, the degree of protection is signalled by the *nominal* or actual tariff rate on the imported good. But where domestic production relies in part on imported materials, the *effective rate of protection* may be larger or smaller than the nominal rate. In order to determine the effective rate of protection (EPR) we must further examine the production process.

Our theories of trade and the underlying production theory have assumed that only final products were traded between nations and that all production took place in vertically integrated firms which purchased only the basic factors of production and produced only final products. This is obviously not a realistic assumption. More importantly it will be shown that a theory of the effects of protection based upon such an assumption will produce seriously misleading conclusions.

Let us assume that what we have called a production process consists of a sequence of *activities*. Each activity absorbs basic factor inputs and the outputs of other activities. For example coal mining uses capital, labor, gasoline, electricity, and steam shovels. Coal passes through several activities between the ground and its use as a final product. It is mined, cleaned, sorted, and transported. Also coal can become a final product, e.g., for home heating, or an input into another activity, e.g., electrical power generation.

Each activity increases the value of the product. The *value added* by each activity is the difference between the value of the output and the value or cost of the material inputs to the activity. This means that value added is also equal to the sum of the payments made to basic factor inputs for their services in the activity. For example if the value of an output is $100 and the cost of its material inputs was $30, this means that the sum of the payments for labor, capital, land, and profits must have been $70; and value added was $70.

Now consider a domestic radio industry. Let us suppose that domestic production consists solely of assembly of parts imported from other nations, and that the assembly activity requires only labor and parts in the proportion of 1 to 4. In other words 20 percent of the final cost of the assembled radio can be traced to the domestic labor input. Let there also be an imported radio which competes in domestic markets with the domestic assembled model; but it must pay a 10 percent tariff.

The effective rate of protection tells us how much more expensive the domestic activity, assembly, can be in comparison with the foreign activity and not be priced out of the market. The degree of protection afforded to domestic radio assemblers is considerably higher than 10 percent. In fact domestic assemblers could be 50 percent more costly (or less productive) and still meet the foreign competition. Thus the effective rate of protection is 50 percent, not 10 percent.

To see this, examine Table 10.1 where it is assumed that the price of the foreign radio is $10: $2 for assembly and $8 for parts. The tariff raises the price to $11. Domestic producers can also obtain parts for $8 and can sell radios at $11, which means that they can afford to pay up to 50 percent more or $3 for assembly. The two crucial factors in determining the degree of divergence between

Table 10.1
The components of cost for imported and domestic radios

Imported radio		Import competing domestic radio	
Parts	$8	Parts	$8
Assembly activity	$2	Assembly activity	$3
Tariff	$1		—
Price	$11	Price	$11

nominal and effective tariff rates are the share of domestic value added in the total cost of the product and the rate of tariff, if any, on the imported material inputs. They are related in the following way:[1]

$$EPR = \frac{t_d - a_f(t_f)}{1 - a_f} \qquad (10.1)$$

where t_d = nominal tariff rate on the imported product
t_f = tariff rate on the imported material inputs
a_f = value added by the foreign activity as a percentage of total value of the good before tariffs

When the values from the hypothetical example are plugged into (10.1), we obtain:

$$EPR = \frac{0.1 - 0.8(0.0)}{.2} = 0.5 \qquad (10.2)$$

Expression (10.1) shows that the higher the nominal tariff, the higher will be the EPR as well. But a higher tariff on imported materials *lowers* the EPR. Suppose that in Table 10.1 there was a 10 percent tariff on imported parts, too. Parts would cost the domestic industry $8.80 and leave $2.20 for the protected assembly activity. The effective rate of protection on assembly then becomes only 10 percent. Any tariff on imported materials raises costs for domestic activities using these materials, and results in a lower EPR for them. Also one can deduce from expression (10.1) that the more important the domestic activity is as a percentage of total cost, the lower will be the EPR. In fact as the domestic share approaches 100 percent the EPR approaches the nominal tariff rate, t_d.

Expression (10.1) shows the possibility of a negative EPR. This would be equivalent to a tax on the domestic producers in that it

[1] This expression can be derived with the aid of the following additional variables:
V_d = domestic value added per unit in the absence of a tariff;
V_d' = domestic value added per unit with a tariff;
P_d = domestic price in the absence of a tariff.
P_d' = domestic price with a tariff.
Domestic value added per unit is the domestic price less that part of the price attributable to foreign production, or:
$V_d = P_d(1 - a_f)$
With a tariff, the domestic price is:
$P_d' = P_d(1 + t_d)$
If there is a tariff on the imported materials (parts), costs are higher and the deduction from unit price to determine value added per unit must be larger by $(1 + t_f)$:
$V_d' = P_d(1 + t_d) - P_d(a_f)(1 + t_f)$
The EPR is defined as the percentage increase in domestic value added per unit allowed by the existence of a tariff, or:

$$EPR = \frac{V_d' - V_d}{V_d} = \frac{t_d - a_f(t_f)}{1 - a_f}$$

See W. M. Corden, "The Structure of a Tariff System and the Effects of Protective Rate," *Journal of Political Economy*, 74, No. 3 (June, 1966), 212–237.

would require them to have a higher level of productivity than their foreign competitors in order to meet their competition. EPRs for domestic activities can be negative if there are high tariffs on the materials inputs and relatively low tariffs on the good in question. Two recent empirical studies of patterns of effective tariff rates in several developed nations have both shown occasional negative EPRs.[2] Negative EPRs would result from a desire to protect domestic raw material suppliers more than domestic manufacturers. This tendency can be seen in Basevi's study of 1958–1960 tariff rates in the United States. The most substantial negative effective tariff rates are in fertilizer production, rice milling, poultry dressing, and paper mills.[3] These activities could produce at lower cost if they were permitted to import their raw material requirements duty free rather than buy from protected domestic farmers and timber owners.

The negative EPRs cited here represent rather special cases. Both studies found that, for most activities, the EPRs were above, and often substantially above, the nominal rates. Actually this is consistent with an already observed tendency for the tariff structures of developed nations to display "escalation" or rising nominal tariff rates for goods requiring a higher degree of processing. Whenever the nominal tariff rate on an activity is greater than the nominal rate on its imported inputs, the effective rate of protection will be above the nominal rate. This is a widely noted characteristic of the tariff structures of developed nations. Raw materials imports enter under very low or zero nominal tariffs, while intermediate goods and final goods enter only under increasingly higher tariffs. One result is that developed nations often display surprisingly high effective tariff rates on manufactured goods. Balassa and Basevi both found EPRs of over 100 percent for some activities. Weighted averages of tariffs for the five economic units in Balassa's study were almost twice the nominal rates and ranged from 12.5–29.5 percent. The U.S. average in 1962 was 20 percent. Another result of high EPRs is to encourage less-developed nations to export unprocessed raw materials and to discourage the export of processed and manufactured products.

Before turning to the questions of nontariff barriers to trade and trade policy, one further aspect of measuring tariff barriers has to be cleared up. This is a question of aggregation. Given that effective tariff rates have been calculated for all goods for a country, can this information be reduced to a meaningful single number which ex-

[2] Giorgio Basevi, "The United States Tariff Structure: Estimates of Effective Rates of Protection of United States Industries and Industrial Labor," *Review of Economics and Statistics,* 48, No. 2 (May, 1966), 147–160, and Bela Balassa, "Tariff Protection in Industrial Countries: An Evaluation," *Journal of Political Economy,* 73, No. 6 (December, 1965), 573–594. Balassa's study covered the United States, the United Kingdom, the six-member European Economic Community, Sweden, and Japan.
[3] Basevi, *ibid.,* pp. 155–156.

presses the *average* rate of tariff? Averages can be calculated in several ways. Simple unweighted averages of all tariff rates can be struck. Or the tariffs can be weighted by some system which would give greater importance in the average to those tariffs which played a larger role in the economy of the nation. The problem is to select a meaningful set of weights. It is a variation of the index number problem discussed in Chapter 6.

The only thing that can be said in favor of unweighted averages is that they are simple. They give equal weight to all goods, no matter what their importance in trade or in the domestic economy. Another simple weighting system is to utilize the actual value of imports for each good. But this introduces an undesirable kind of distortion. A prohibitively high tariff which reduced imports of a good to zero would receive no weight in this average, even though its consumption and protective effects on the economy would likely be substantial. A highly protective tariff structure might be made to appear quite low by this choice of weights.

The correct or ideal set of weights would be the hypothetical "no tariff" values of imports for each good for that country. However, these would be extremely difficult to calculate given present levels of knowledge about the shapes of demand and supply curves for individual goods. One directly observable set of potential weights would, under some conditions, approximate the ideal. This is the total value of world trade in each good or commodity. If there is no systematic tendency on the part of all countries to protect certain activities, there would be no correlations among tariff structures. Under these conditions a good which might be highly protected by one nation might be admitted duty free by another. The two nations would "average out" in their effects on the total value of trade in that good. In addition, if all nations' consumption patterns were similar, this set of weights would approximate the ideal. While neither of these conditions is in fact satisfied, this weighting system either is more practical or has fewer obvious flaws than any of the others.

NONTARIFF BARRIERS TO TRADE

Domestic producers can be protected in a variety of ways not related to the imposition of tariffs. These so-called nontariff barriers to trade are becoming increasingly important in economic analysis and policy for two reasons. The first is the strength of the trend toward lower tariffs and, therefore, freer trade. The most recent evidence of this is the successful conclusion of the Kennedy Round of multilateral tariff negotiations in June, 1967, which resulted in an average reduction in tariff rates of about 35 percent. In view of the momentum established by the Kennedy Round, political leaders are not likely to respond to requests for greater protection by increasing tariff rates. They are more likely to respond by seeking more subtle, gentle forms of protection which do not rely on changes in tariff rates. The second reason is that after the Kennedy Round nontariff trade barriers have become more visible and relatively more important as factors which inhibit the free flow of goods and services among nations.

There are several types of nontariff trade barriers. The most obvious is the quota or absolute restriction on imports beyond a certain level. The effect of a quota on the price at which domestic production can be sold is similar to the effect of a tariff. The excess demand beyond the amount of the quota can be supplied by domestic producers at a price above the world price. The effective rate of protection to domestic industry varies inversely with the size of the quota. Smaller quotas lead to higher domestic prices and higher effective protection.

The redistributive, production, and consumption effects of a quota are similar to those of a tariff. Figure 10.1 shows an example where imports would be Q_1–Q_4 in the absence of a quota or tariff and the price would be P_1. If a quota equal to Q_2–Q_3 were imposed, the price would rise to P_2, and the production, consumption, and redistributive effects would be as shown. The main difference between the quota and the equivalent tariff lies in the distribution of what would be the revenue effect in the case of a tariff, that is, the rectangle with the question mark. If world producers could gain access to the domestic market at P_2, but in an amount limited by quota, they would reap the benefit of the higher domestic price. Whether the

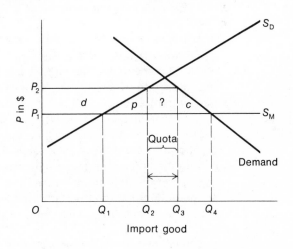

Figure 10.1
The effects of a quota

higher price more than compensates the foreign suppliers for the smaller quantities sold cannot be known without reference to their cost curves.

However, the higher revenue per unit of imports need not benefit foreign suppliers. The distribution of this benefit depends in large measure on how the quota is administered. If rights to import up to the amount of the quota are granted on a first-come, first-served or some other arbitrary basis, the foreign suppliers who obtain importing rights will be able to capture the added revenue for themselves. However, if the government put the quota rights up to auction, their price would be bid up to the point that would exhaust the benefit of the higher domestic price (unless foreign suppliers colluded to keep the bidding down). The government would obtain the revenue benefits, and the revenue effect of the quota would be identical to that of an equivalent tariff. If the quotas were granted to domestic importers, they receive the benefit if they can purchase the quota amounts at the old world price, P_1. But if the foreign suppliers have monopoly power, they can still capture some of the benefit by bargaining with the importers over price.

Where ad valorem tariff rates are employed, any given tariff rate can be made more effective as a protectionist device by raising the basis for valuation. One device for accomplishing this is to value imports for tariff purposes at the domestic price rather than the lower world price. The most notable instance of this practice is the so-called American Selling Price (ASP) system for imposing tariffs on certain benzenoid chemicals. Where domestic valuations are used the true tariff rate can be calculated as follows:

$$\text{True tariff} = \text{nominal tariff} \left(\frac{\text{domestic price}}{\text{world price}} \right) \tag{10.3}$$

In the case of the ASP system, American domestic prices average about twice world prices. And while nominal tariff rates average about 25 percent, the true tariff rate is closer to 50 percent.[4] It is this true tariff rate which should be used in the calculation of effective rates of protection.

Another instance of using valuation practices to increase the degree of protection offered by a given ad valorem rate is the U.S. practice of taxing the alcohol content of imported liquors and requiring that liquors of below 100 proof (50 percent alcohol) be taxed as if they were 100 proof. Since most imported whiskeys are bottled at about 86 proof, the true tariff rate is about 16 percent higher than the nominal rate. This would tend to protect domestic whiskey pro-

[4] Harry Johnson and H. G. Grubel, "National Tariff Rates and United States Valuation Practices: Two Case Studies," *Review of Economics and Statistics*, 49, No. 2 (May, 1967), 139–140.

ducers. However, it also encourages foreign producers to ship whiskey to the United States in bulk at 100 proof, and have it bottled there. So this tariff practice provides protection to the U.S. bottling industry as well. In fact, Johnson and Grubel estimate the effective rate of protection on domestic bottling to be about 43 percent.[5]

Several nations have protected domestic industry through the establishment of regulations governing procurement of materials by their governments. For example, in the United States the federal government must award contracts to U.S. companies so long as their bid is no more than 12 percent higher than the lowest foreign bid. This is equivalent to a tariff rate of 12 percent. In defense contracts, the allowable differential is 50 percent. Other nations also follow this practice. Recently the Pennsylvania State Legislature was asked to pass a similar measure applying to the purchase of materials by contractors on state and local government construction work. The steel industry would have been a major beneficiary.

A whole host of minor administrative and regulatory practices can make it more difficult for foreign sellers to market their goods successfully. Safety requirements, quality standards, and labelling regulations can be set arbitrarily to exclude foreign products or to place them in a disadvantageous competitive position. In the United States mink from Japan must be labelled "weasel." Excessive requirements for paper work, forms, and licenses can make importing unnecessarily difficult and therefore costly.

Usually tariffs and nontariff barriers to trade are used to protect domestic firms in the markets in which they sell their products. But firms also enter markets as buyers of raw materials and factor inputs. Similar practices can be employed to protect firms as buyers.

For example, the United States once imposed quantitative restrictions on *exports* of shoe leather to protect its domestic shoe industry. And it was once proposed that exports of softwood logs to Japan from the Pacific Northwest be limited to keep raw materials prices down for paper and lumber mills in that area. It is fairly simple to explain why this type of trade restriction is not nearly as common as restrictions on imports. When imports are restricted consumers lose. But very few consumers are hurt enough to make a fuss, organize politically, retain lobbyists, and do all the other things that special interest groups do. Thus the firm or industry seeking protection from imports is at an advantage and likely to be without effective opposition as it seeks protection. If exports are restricted to protect firms using these as inputs, the suppliers are going to be hurt. And it is far more likely that they will be able to block any attempt to restrict their trade.

[5] *Ibid.*, pp. 140–141.

　　　　There is no simple phrase to describe accurately the last item on the list of nontariff trade barriers. This is because the phenomenon in question is somewhat complicated and can affect the extent and direction of trade in several ways. The root of the problem is differences among nations in the structure of their tax systems and specifically in the degree to which they rely on indirect taxation as a source of revenue. Indirect taxes are those taxes on business which are shiftable or which can be passed on to the purchasers of the goods. Direct taxes on the other hand are basically taxes on the incomes of the owners of the factors of production. The taxes on corporate and personal income are at least in part direct taxes. Indirect taxes include sales and excise taxes and taxes on business-owned property. Actually, these definitions misleadingly imply a dichotomy which is at best difficult to see in practice. In some circumstances part of a sales or excise tax will not be passed on to the consumer; and both theory and empirical evidence suggest that part of the corporate income tax has been shifted on to the consumer.

　　　　The way in which indirect taxation affects trade can be shown by an illustration. Assume a simple model of the economy with no intermediate goods. Suppose country A levies sales and excise taxes on a good to the amount of 10 percent of the cost or value of the good. If these taxes are fully shifted to the consumer, the price will be 10 percent above the factor cost. Suppose that country B also produces this good at the same factor cost but levies no indirect taxes on its production. Assuming no transportation costs, country B's product will sell at a lower price in country A. There is a negative rate of effective protection in A on this good.

　　　　Country A can rectify the situation by imposing what is known as a border tax on B's product. The tax should be equal in amount to the indirect taxes A levies on its own production. A 10 percent border tax on imports of this good from B is legally and economically different from a tariff provided it is equivalent to A's internal indirect taxes. Indirect taxation also can place A's product at a competitive disadvantage in export markets. As a recognition of this, nations can rebate the indirect taxes paid on those goods leaving the country as exports.

　　　　Indirect taxation introduces a disparity between factor costs or opportunity costs and prices. Unless corrected, this will lead to a distortion of the patterns of trade. If the maximum gains from free trade are to be realized, trade must follow comparative advantage and true cost ratios, and the distorting effects of indirect taxation on prices must be eliminated. Border taxes and export rebates do not accomplish this. While they compensate for competitive disadvantages caused by differences in taxes, the distortions to resource allocation caused by indirect taxation remain. Economists generally argue against indirect taxes for this reason. They are not neutral in the sense that they do distort the allocation of resources and leave the nation inside its production possibilities curve.

The nations of western Europe rely much more heavily on indirect taxes than does the United States. In recognition of the problems raised by this system of taxes, border taxes and export rebates are important parts of the trade policies of these nations. The U.S. federal tax system is based largely on direct taxes on corporate and personal income. However states and localities impose sales, excise, and property taxes at varying rates. This poses a difficult policy question for the United States. As border taxes and rebates become more widely adopted, U.S. products become increasingly disadvantaged in world markets. An element of indirect taxation is already included in the price of the U.S. product at the border of the other nation, where it is hit with yet a further tax. At the federal level it would be extremely difficult to compensate for this in the usual manner with a rebate, since the federal government has not collected the taxes. Indirect tax rates are highly variable from place to place. It would be very difficult administratively to keep track of these taxes and rebate them on exports. An alternative has been proposed: to have the federal government subsidize exports in an amount equivalent to what would have been rebated. There also have been proposals to have the United States impose a uniform border tax set to equal the average indirect tax paid on goods produced in this country.

The major difficulty with any system of border taxes and rebates is the uncertainty regarding the degree of shifting of all kinds of taxes. If nominally indirect taxes are actually only partly shifted, border taxes based on the nominal tax rates will overprotect domestic industry. Export rebates will subsidize exports. But if nominally direct taxes such as the corporate income tax are actually partly shifted, domestic industry will be at a disadvantage both at home competing against imports and in export markets because border taxes and rebates are justified by the actual forward shifting of the tax.

TRADE POLICY: PROTECTION VS. DOMESTIC ADJUSTMENT

Despite the general presumption that free trade will make all nations better off or maximize world welfare in some sense, there is considerable political opposition to further reductions to tariffs, and there are strong efforts to strengthen nontariff trade barriers. Both kinds of reactions to moves toward freer trade are quite understandable. As was pointed out before, the opposition to freer trade revolves around

162   questions of how the national pie is to be sliced. Loss of protection for an industry or firm can be costly and painful to both the labor and the capital employed in the activity.

In the past it has been necessary (politically, at least) in this country to include "safeguards" in any legislation designed to lead toward lower tariffs. Four kinds of safeguards have found their way into U.S. trade legislation at various times in the past.

From 1948 to 1962 the acts empowering the President to negotiate reductions in tariffs included a "peril point" clause. This clause required that the Tariff Commission determine in advance of any negotiations the maximum possible decrease in any tariff rate which could be granted without causing "serious injury" to domestic producers. While the President was not bound to stay above the peril point, there was a procedure for congressional review of any reductions which went beyond the Commission's recommendations. While this provision, and the ones below, may sound reasonable, one can point out the tremendous burden of interpretation, judgment, and foresight placed on the Commission since "serious" and "injury" are not clearly defined economically, and the judgment must be made in advance of the actual reduction.

"Escape clauses" provide for the increase of tariffs if it has been found that prior reductions in tariffs have caused injury. The escape clause currently found in U.S. law defines injury rather carefully so as to make it difficult for firms to establish the necessity for restoring tariff cuts. Idle capacity, losses, and/or unemployment must be shown, and it must be shown that these were *in major part* the result of tariff reductions.

Antidumping clauses can be applied to those situations where a foreign producer is selling "below cost." One practical difficulty here is in determining cost. Usually, when dumping can be shown, the remedy is an antidumping tariff. The major conceptual problem is in identifying the several different kinds of economic behavior which might come under the legal heading of dumping but which have considerably different effects and implications for policy. This question is dealt with in the appendix to the chapter.

A fourth possible safeguard is the authorization to negotiate orderly marketing arrangements with other nations. This is a polite way of saying that, after consultation with other nations, quotas can be established.

Current U.S. trade law, as embodied primarily in the Trade Expansion Act of 1962, incorporates all of these features except the peril point clause. However, in a radical departure from past policy, this act also provides a whole new range of alternatives to be employed when and if tariff reductions do cause harm to domestic interests. These new features come under the heading of adjustment assistance. The underlying theory is straightforward. In Chapter 6, while trying to determine under what assumptions we could say that trade is unambiguously good, the principle of compensation was discussed. Under that principle, an economic situation is deemed an improvement if it would enable the gainers to make payments to all of the losers sufficient to buy them off, that is, to compensate them for their losses. A multilateral reduction in tariffs such as that achieved by the Kennedy Round is likely to be able to pass that test in every country, since if all nations are reducing tariffs, adverse movements of the terms of trade for any one nation are not likely to be serious. Thus the way to make everybody happy with the tariff reductions is to provide a mechanism whereby the compensations can actually be paid.

The Trade Expansion Act of 1962 incorporates several ways of making such "compensating payments." First eligibility has to be established. And the elegibility requirements are stringent. As in the case of the escape clause, it must be shown that the tariff reductions were a major cause of idle facilities, lack of profits, or unemployment. If this can be established, then adjustment assistance is available both for labor and for business (or capital). Firms can obtain technical assistance in developing new products or in lowering costs. They can obtain low-interest loans or loan guarantees for new equipment, modernization, or conversion to a new activity where market conditions are better. Also, eligible firms obtain more favorable treatment of losses for tax purposes. Laborers are able to obtain extra unemployment compensation and relocation allowances for moving to areas where the prospects of employment are better. Most importantly, workers are eligible for retraining programs to learn more marketable skills.

This appoach to the problem of injury from tariff reduction seems to be very promising. Experience to date is limited. So far no industries or firms have been able to establish eligibility under the Trade Expansion Act.[6] Thus it may be that the eligibility requirements are too stringent. As long as escape clause tariff increases were the only kind of action allowable after a finding of injury, it made sense to try to keep the eligibility provisions as tight as possible. But when meaningful assistance is available, eligibility requirements perhaps should be eased somewhat.

---

[6] A subsequent treaty with Canada establishing free trade in automobiles and auto parts contains similar adjustment provisions. However, the eligibility requirements were much less stringent. From 1965 to 1968 (the end of the adjustment period) 14 of 21 cases submitted were found eligible and close to $4 million was dispensed to U.S. workers for retraining, relocation, and general assistance. See James E. Jonish, "Adjustment Assistance Experience Under the U.S.-Canadian Automotive Agreement," *Seminar Discussion Paper No. 13*, Research Seminar in International Economics, University of Michigan, 1969.

CONCLUSIONS

Tariffs and nontariff barriers to trade can lead to protection of domestic activities in the sense that higher cost and less efficient domestic activities are sheltered from foreign competition and domestically produced goods are more costly. It is of great interest to know the degree of protection actually afforded to each activity in a country. Both average levels of protection and the structures of protective rates are of interest. However, protection is a complicated phenomenon, and estimates are very difficult to make. The effective rates of protection depend on the structure of domestic production and the extent of reliance on intermediate goods and raw materials from other nations as well as on nominal tariff rates. This part of the theory of protection has been worked out, and estimates have been made for several nations.

Effective protection can also be afforded by quotas, valuation practices, miscellaneous regulations, and the structure of taxes in the country in question and the rest of the world. These other aspects of protection have been identified, but they have not yet been integrated into the theory of protection.

SUPPLEMENTARY READINGS

Snider, Delbert A., *Introduction to International Economics,* 4th ed., Homewood, Ill., Irwin, 1967, chaps. 9, 10.

Kindleberger, Charles, *International Economics,* 4th ed., Homewood, Ill., Irwin, 1968, chaps 7–9.

de Scitovsky, Tibor, "A Reconsideration of the Theory of Tariffs," *Review of Economic Studies,* 9 (Summer, 1942), 89–110; reprinted in American Economic Association, *Readings in the Theory of International Trade,* Philadelphia, Blakiston, 1950, 358–389.

Metzler, Lloyd A., "Tariffs, the Terms of Trade, and the Distribution of Income," *Journal of Political Economy,* 57, No. 1 (February, 1949), 1–29; reprinted in American Economic Association, *Readings in International Economics,* Homewood, Ill., Irwin, 1968, 24–57.

Johnson, Harry G., "The Cost of Protection and the Scientific Tariff," *Journal of Political Economy,* 68, No. 4 (August, 1960), 327–345.

Balassa, Bela, and Kreinin, Mordechai E., "Trade Liberalization Under the 'Kennedy Round': The Static Effects," *Review of Economics and Statistics,* 49, No. 2 (May, 1967), 125–137.

DUMPING AND DISCRIMINATION

The terminology and usage in this area can best be described as confused. There are important differences among the layman's usage, the legal definitions, and the economist's models. The illegal practice which is called "dumping" in U.S. law usually turns out to be what economists call price discrimination. Furthermore the economist is likely to say that this practice tends to benefit the country which outlaws it at the expense of the nation whose firms break the law by doing it.

Let us begin with the economist's definition of price discrimination. Discrimination occurs when one seller, with market power, simultaneously sells his product in two different markets at two different prices. This can be done only under certain conditions. But it can be shown that the seller can maximize his profits by doing it, if the opportunity presents itself.

First, the seller must be able to separate the two markets to prevent the transfer or resale of goods from one market to the other. Price discrimination seems to be fairly common in the provision of personal services such as medical treatment since, once the service has been rendered, it cannot be resold by the recipient. Second, the two markets must have different demand conditions in the sense that at any price the demand curves in the two markets have different demand elasticities. Assuming the first condition is met, Figure 10.2 portrays the second condition.

The diagram shows the demand curves and marginal revenue curves for two different groups of buyers. If the seller cannot separate the two groups, so that he must charge the same price to all, the demand curve that he faces is the horizontal sum of D_1 and D_2, $\overline{D}$. To maximize profits he finds the marginal revenue curve associated with $\overline{D}$, and finds that output which will equate his marginal cost (MC) with marginal revenue ($\overline{MR}$). The quantity sold is $O-Q_\mathrm{M}$ and the price to both groups is $O-P_\mathrm{M}$.

At this price the quantities sold to each group can be found by reference to D_1 and D_2. At this price the marginal revenue associated with $O-Q_2$ is greater than that for $O-Q_1$. This means that if the monopolist were to reduce his sales to Group 1 by one unit he would lose relatively little revenue in comparison with the revenue to be gained by increasing his sales to Group 2. If he could do this, the difference would be clear gain to him since total output and costs would not have changed. The only way that he could effect this reallocation of sales from the low marginal revenue market to the high *MR* market is by cutting price to Group 2 and raising price to Group 1. But this is impossible unless the two markets are separated so that Group 2 people cannot resell their extra units to Group 1 people at a profit. If market separation is possible, the seller would readjust his sales between the two markets so as to equate the two marginal revenues. MR_1 would equal MR_2 would equal $\overline{MR}$. But this means that the price in market 1 would be higher than in market 2 (see) Figure 10.3). The price will be lower in the market with the more elastic demand curve, in this case, D_2.

We conclude that the seller who can discriminate will always charge two different prices, and that the price will be lower in the market with a more elastic demand. Of what relevance is this to international trade? The firm that has market power at home may have competition in the world market or in third-country markets. Once goods are shipped to other countries, transportation costs probably provide an effective barrier to reshipment back to the seller's home market for resale. Hence he is likely to find his markets separated and to find that demand in the world market is more elastic than his home market. His expected response to this would be to cut prices in the world market and adopt a two-price structure, that is, to discriminate.

From the point of view of other countries, discrimination should be fine, since they have the opportunity to buy goods at a lower price

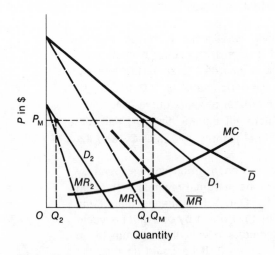

Figure 10.2
The seller's demand curves in two markets with
no discrimination

than they might otherwise get. From the point of view of the discriminating monopolist's country, things are not so good, since they are being charged the higher price and experiencing the malallocation of resources which accompanies market power. The U.S. trade laws define dumping as a foreign producer selling in U.S. markets at a price below average cost. In other words what the economist calls monopolistic discrimination, which can benefit the receiving country, the U.S. law calls dumping and decrees illegal.

Two other kinds of pricing behavior might also fit under the legal definition of dumping. These are both properly called dumping by economists as well, and both may have adverse effects on the buyer country, although each case must be considered separately. The first is known as sporadic or distress dumping. If a firm has accumulated excessive inventories which it wants to withhold from its domestic market to prevent a disruption of the market, or which it has held so long that it considers the opportunity cost of selling them to be very low, it might dump these on a foreign market at whatever price it can get. Whether this should be considered bad for the country getting dumped on depends on how you value "orderly markets" relative to the opportunity to pick up a bargain. Consumers would tend to benefit, while producers in the importing country may experience short run losses.

The second kind of dumping is predatory in nature and has the aim of driving competitors from the foreign market. If the predatory dumper is successful, he then raises the price to the monopoly level

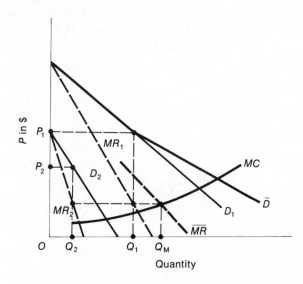

Figure 10.3
A price discriminator maximizing profits

and reaps the profit. But this assumes that there will be no attempts to return to the market by competitors once the price has been increased by the dumper. Predatory dumping must be on a massive scale to be successful; if attempted it would provide opportunities for bargain shopping. But against this must be weighed the chance that it would be successful and result in eventual monopoly power and higher prices.

If successful predatory dumping is unlikely in the United States, and if price discrimination and sporadic dumping are both likely to benefit consumers through lower prices, it might seem that the U.S. antidumping legislation does more harm than good. However, the established procedures make it very difficult to bring successful action against an alleged case of dumping. Upon complaint from a domestic producer, the U.S. Treasury must determine whether dumping is taking place, that is, whether the foreign firm is in fact selling at less than cost in the United States. This may be difficult to prove except in the most extreme cases. If the Treasury finds dumping, the case moves to the Tariff Commission, which attempts to determine whether or not the dumping has in fact harmed domestic industry. If there is no finding of harm, the case is dropped. If harm is found, the Tariff Commission can recommend to the President that special antidumping tariffs be invoked against the offending firm or nation. The procedure is difficult, both in terms of the time required to bring a case to conclusion and in the burden of proof. While there have been some surprising findings of dumping and harm in recent times, the most likely outcome is to find no harm. For example, between 1963 and 1965 the Commission found no harm in sixteen of its twenty-one cases.[7] This suggests that the Tariff Commission is much more broadminded about low prices than many U.S. businessmen.

[7] Reported in Yeager and Tuerck, *Trade Policy and the Price System*, Scranton, Penn., International Text Book Company, 1966, pp. 149–154.

Chapter

Economic Integration

INTRODUCTION

Economic integration is a general term which covers several kinds of arrangements by which two or more countries can agree to draw their economies closer together. All of the arrangements have one common feature, the use of tariffs to discriminate against goods produced by countries not party to the agreement. All tariffs discriminate against foreign products. The key feature of the various arrangements for integration is that tariffs are used to discriminate *among* different countries. This kind of discrimination is achieved by according preferential treatment to the goods produced by the other member countries.

There are several degrees or levels of economic integration. In all cases the member nations cut all tariffs on intra-union trade to zero. Anything less than the full elimination of tariffs on intra-union trade would fail to qualify the union under certain provisions of the General Agreements on Tariffs and Trade (GATT). Under the "most favored nation" clause of the agreement, tariff reductions granted to one nation must be extended to all nations. The exception is tariff reductions granted to a fellow member in an economic union. In order to escape the provisions of the most favored nation clause, which is meant to rule out tariff discrimination among nations, members of unions must plan to reduce their tariffs eventually to zero.

The simplest form of economic union is a *free trade area.* In a free trade area member countries levy no tariffs on goods from other members while maintaining their existing separate tariff systems for imports from outside. In a *customs union* member nations go one step further in agreeing to establish a common system of tariffs against outside goods while eliminating tariffs on intra-union trade. Thus, a customs union implies that some or all of the union members will have to make changes in their external tariffs to bring them into correspondence with the agreed upon common tariff structure. The problems of reaching agreement on the common tariff structure should not be underestimated. They are particularly acute when two member nations have quite different tariff levels on a particular good or have quite different average levels of tariffs.

On the other hand, free trade areas are not without their problems as well. If the member nations have common borders, it may be possible to import goods through the low tariff country, and transship them to other member countries, thereby avoiding payment of the higher tariffs that country would have imposed. This can be prevented, or at least made more difficult, by systems of certificates of origin and customs checks at the borders between members. But this is costly and troublesome, and by making trade more difficult it tends to dissipate some of the advantages of more liberal trade among member nations.

A *common market* carries integration beyond the markets for goods and services and into the markets for factors of production by eliminating legal and administrative barriers to the free flow of labor and capital among member countries. Even in a common market barriers due to differences in language and custom may remain, but overt legal discrimination against factor inputs from other countries is ended.

To go beyond a common market in integration, countries must coordinate their monetary and fiscal policies, harmonize their tax systems, eliminate disparities in their regulation of business and commerce and in their legal systems, and take all of those other steps which in the end mean effectively a merger of the several nations into one. In fact it is argued by some that a common market is an unstable kind of halfway house between economic separatism and the full integration of the member nations into a single economic and political entity.

Methodology

A major theme in this book has been the role of economic theory and analysis in increasing our understanding of observed economic phenomena. One of the important aims of economic analysis is to develop models which after testing can be accepted as being "not false." These models enable theorists to make generalizations about the world they study and predictions about what further observations should reveal. So far in this book we have been equally concerned with the description and details of the models themselves and with the extent of their success in providing empirically valid generalizations. In this chapter this "methodological purity" is lost, and a word about why this must be so is in order.

The theory of economic integration consists largely of a set of models which have been developed independently of either the Heckscher-Ohlin or comparative cost models of trade. This theory takes existing patterns of trade as given without being concerned with explaining them. It describes them in a set of price-quantity relationships which are in principle observable. The analysis of the models is based on general economic tools, such as supply and demand theory, which are generally accepted as having been tested and verified through wide use.

It is probably fair to say that the theory of integration has not produced any useful generalizations or explanations of observed phenomena or even any testable hypotheses about the behavior of economic variables. This is due to several factors. First, with regard to the major concern of all economic theories, the effects of economic forces on prices and quantities, the models of integration have shown that it all depends. It depends on the initial situations of trade flows, preunion tariffs, and relative values of elasticities of offer curves. Such elasticities are very difficult to define empirically let alone to measure accurately. The outcome also depends on the level and structure of external tariffs chosen by the new union; and this depends in a large part on political factors, bargaining, and negotiations. Thus each economic union must be considered to be a special case. Second, it has not been possible to deduce hypotheses about what kinds of economic union are likely to be observed. Who will actually get together and form customs unions seems to depend far more on historical, political, and social factors than on purely economic forces.

Finally, the principal interest in economic integration has stemmed from the question, "Is it good?" Policy makers have wanted to know whether or not a proposed union would make their country better off or worse off. Hence the major thrust of analysis has been toward the effect of customs unions on economic welfare. While logically this kind of normative analysis must be based on empirically valid theory, because of the difficulties mentioned above economists have generally been content to rely on the formal models and expend their efforts on working out all the possibilities. As it turns out, the principal generalization about welfare has also been, "It all depends."

Because of this generally unsatisfactory state of the theory, in this chapter we have to content ourselves with a general description of the forces that a priori reasoning suggests are at work when a customs union is formed. The kinds of models used will be described, but their full implications will not be worked out because this can get rather complicated and because it has not proved to be very useful. In other words a kind of benefit-cost calculus suggests that the marginal cost of additional effort in manipulating these models and describing their equilibria far exceeds the reward in terms of better understanding of the economic world.

A word should be said at this point about the plan of the chapter. The next section will consist of a static analysis of economic integration. That is to say, comparisons will be made of the situations of those countries both involved in and influenced by the move to integration before and after the move is taken. Both the before and after situations are described in terms of static equilibria in which conditions such as factor endowments, technology, demand, and population are assumed to remain unchanged throughout the period of the analysis. The concluding section deals with the expected effects of economic integration in a dynamic context where factor endowments and technology in particular may change.

THE STATIC EFFECTS OF INTEGRATION

The Question of Criteria

The economic analysis of integration is concerned fundamentally with two things. The first is the effect of union on the pattern and volume of trade. This is a question of positive economic analysis. The answers depend on the changes in relative prices brought about by the realignment of tariff patterns between the union and outside countries. The second concern is with the effects of economic union on welfare. The question, briefly put, is, "Is economic integration a good thing?" The answer depends on the criterion we select for distinguishing good from bad.

In earlier chapters there were two kinds of economic criteria employed to evaluate the predicted outcomes of trade in various situations. These were: the efficiency criterion, which focuses on the total size of the economic pie; and the distribution criterion, which emphasizes the way the pie is sliced or the shares going to different groups.[1] Let us review some of the earlier normative statements made regarding the consequences of trade. First, free trade maximizes economic efficiency from a global point of view. Also, in comparison with the situation of no trade, in terms of the efficiency criterion, each country is better off entering into trade rather than

---

[1] As was mentioned in Chapter 1, the rate of economic growth is another possible criterion. The possible influence of integration on the rate of growth will be discussed in the final section of this chapter.

doing without trade entirely (autarky). However, even though the pie is larger for all countries, it is possible, even likely, that some groups within each country will be hurt by the opening of trade. Once this is recognized, it is clear that the efficiency criterion may not adequately encompass all the relevant effects of an economic change. The incidence of that change or the way the resulting changes in income are distributed may also be important.[2]

Our normative evaluation of economic integration could also be based on a global efficiency criterion. In other words integration could be judged as good or bad according to whether the aggregate of world income was larger or smaller as the result of it. But just as we were concerned with the distribution of the gains from free trade among groups within a country, here we might also be concerned with the way in which the gains, if any, are distributed among nations.

Economic integration may or may not increase the size of the world pie. It is more likely that economic integration will increase the size of the slices of that pie going to the countries which formed the economic union. However, the gains of member countries may come at the expense of losses to nonmember countries. Once this is realized, we have a question of evaluating income distributions in an international dimension. Of course it is likely that policy makers from member countries will be willing to overlook adverse distributional consequences for nonmember countries. It is also relevant to examine the distribution of the gains, if any, among countries within the union. In summary, we could take a global point of view in which the distribution of income among countries or among groups within countries would not matter. But we could also permit distributional considerations to enter the analysis by looking at the division of income between member and nonmember countries as well as the division of income within a union among union members. In any event, it must always be made clear from what point of view we are approaching the question of the evaluation of economic integration. Also it must be remembered that any statement such as "nonmember countries lose because of integration" either ignores the distributional consequences within those countries or makes some implicit value judgments concerning an income distribution criterion.

In the early analysis of integration, the first question posed by economists focused on the efficiency criterion or the effect of integration on total world income. It was long thought that the answer to this question was quite simple. The line of reasoning went like this: (1) If there is free trade, world income is maximized; (2) Economic union is a step toward free trade since it brings an increase in the

[2] The student should review the discussion of the distribution question and welfare criteria in Chapter 6, pp. 81–84.

number of countries which maintain no tariff barriers between themselves; (3) Any move which increases the scope of free trade must also increase world efficiency.

More careful analysis based on model building and the rigorous application of logic has shown that the second statement is false, and therefore the third does not necessarily follow. The second statement is false, for while the area within which free trade takes place is larger, the area within which higher cost firms enjoy the protection of an external tariff is also larger. A customs union contains elements of both greater free trade and greater protection. Credit for the first discovery of this point goes to Jacob Viner.[3]

Subsequent writers have extended and developed Viner's analysis to build a logically correct theory of economic integration, elements of which will be outlined below. In addition, in determining why the second statement above is false a new principle of general analytical importance was developed, known as the theory of second best.[4] The second-best principle can be explained as follows. If certain mathematical conditions are met, the optimum of an economic system can be described mathematically by a set of equations known as the marginal conditions. If one of these marginal conditions cannot be satisfied for some reason, the optimum or maximum cannot be achieved. The general theory of second best states that in that situation, that is, if one variable is held at a value such that it does not satisfy the optimum condition, the best possible outcome given that constraint will involve the failure to satisfy at least one of the other original optimum conditions as well. In other words, if one of the variables cannot be adjusted to the optimum value, bringing all other variables to their optimum values may not be the next best thing.

The application of this principle to the theory of integration is straightforward. In terms of the efficiency criterion, the optimum conditions can be stated in terms of the tariff levels on all goods for all countries. A global or worldwide efficiency optimum is achieved when all tariff values are set at zero. If one country sets one tariff on one good at a nonzero value, the next best thing for world efficiency or income may require that at least one other tariff also be set above zero. To put it another way, given that the member nations in a customs union have set tariffs at some positive level for goods imported from nonmember countries, the maximum conditions for *world* income may require that the member countries set nonzero

[3] See Jacob Viner, *The Customs Union Issue*, New York, Carnegie Endowment for Peace, 1953.

[4] For the original statement of this see Richard Lipsey and Kelvin Lancaster, "The General Theory of Second Best," *Review of Economic Studies*, XXIV, No. 63 (1956–1957), 11–32.

tariffs on trade within the union. Nonzero tariffs on nonmember trade is a deviation from the optimum conditions. Therefore to achieve the next best or second-best optimum, member nations may also have to deviate from the other optimum conditions. That is to say, they may also have to introduce tariffs on trade within the union.

The general theory of second best says that a customs union is not necessarily the next best thing to worldwide free trade from a global point of view. It says that in general there will be a set of nonzero internal tariffs, which will move the world closer to the free trade optimum. While it is true that a customs union may not be the next best thing to free trade, this does not mean that it is necessarily worse than the position with trade restricted by tariffs before integration. A customs union is not second best but this does not mean that it is ninth best or worst. It may be better or worse than the alternative of no union. To find out requires an analysis of the particulars, to which we now turn.

Trade Creation vs. Trade Diversion

The question of the efficiency of an economic union hinges on the relative magnitudes of two effects: trade creation, which is good from a global point of view, and trade diversion, which is not. One or the other or both may occur in a given situation. When both occur, the two effects must be measured and compared before normative judgments based on the efficiency criterion can be made.

To illustrate the two opposing forces in the simplest possible case, let us examine a world of three countries, the home country (H), its partner in the union (P), and a third country representing the excluded rest of the world (R). To simplify things further, we will examine the effects on only one good, Pepsi, leaving a full general equilibrium analysis to the next section. Assume for the moment that in all three countries production of Pepsi takes place at constant cost, but that the cost levels are different for each country.

Here it should be pointed out that the only interesting case for analysis is where R is the low-cost producer of Pepsi. If H is the low-cost producer, it supplies itself under all conceivable situations. If P is the low-cost producer it supplies H both before and after union, unless H's tariff before the union is prohibitive. But either case can be handled with the less complex theory of Chapter 9, since discrimination against third countries (R) is not relevant. Also P's costs must be below H's or else H would have no incentive to form a union with P, at least in terms of this one good.

The hypothetical cost data for this example are shown in Table 11.1. Before the union, H levies a $.60 per unit tariff on Pepsi from both the partner and the rest of the world. Since R is the low-cost

176

Table 11.1
Costs and tariffs for three countries: trade diversion

	Home country (H)	Partner (P)	Rest of world (R)
Cost	2.00	1.50	1.25
Tariff in H before union	—	.60	.60
Price in H including tariff	2.00	2.10	1.85
Tariff in H after union	—	—	.60
Price in H including tariff	2.00	1.50	1.85

supplier, all imports come from R. If a union is formed, imports from P into H are duty free, while imports from R continue to pay the tariff. Much depends on the level of the external tariff selected by H and P. As long as the tariff is greater than $.25, goods from P will now have an advantage over those from R in H's markets. In the example the external tariff is assumed to continue at $.60. The result is that P displaces R as the supplier of Pepsi for the union. This is *trade diversion*. Trade has been diverted by discriminatory tariffs from a low-cost external source to a higher cost source within the new union. The tariff in H is simply a transfer from consumers who pay to the government which collects it. Therefore, the true cost of imports to the nation, that is, the amount paid to other countries, rises from $1.25 to $1.50. Trade diversion is a loss to H, equal to $.25 per unit purchased. Production under constant cost in P and R means that these countries can shift resources into and out of this good at no sacrifice in efficiency. Since there is no efficiency cost in these two countries, H's trade diversion loss is also a loss to the world as a whole.

If the external tariff were cut below $.25, R would continue to supply H after the union is formed and in addition would now supply P. In that case the tariff would not be discriminatory in practice, and nothing would have been accomplished that either H or P could not have done by acting unilaterally. A reduction in the union's external tariff which enabled R to supply the union despite the discriminatory tariff would be a step toward free trade and an unambiguous improvement. This case is of no interest in this chapter and will not be considered further.

Suppose instead that before the union, H's tariff had been $.80. This tariff would be prohibitive, and H would have imported nothing. In this case formation of the union would have resulted in P's Pepsi being imported by H. This is *trade creation*. Trade creation is the replacement of higher cost domestic production by lower cost sources of supply within the new union. As before, H's gain is the world's gain since neither P nor R loses.

In this highly simplified example we can have either trade creation or trade diversion but not both at the same time. This is because an important part of the economic world has been left out of the model, namely demand. In both of the above examples the price of Pepsi to consumers in H is reduced as a consumption of Pepsi to increase. This increase in quantity demanded can give rise to trade creation, even if trade has been diverted from R to P. In the example of Table 11.1, any increase in the quantity imported by H as a consequence of the fall in price for domestic consumers to $1.50 is trade creation, and it is a gain from the global efficiency point of view.

Trade creation in a single good can be demonstrated in Figure 11.1. In this new example demand is explicitly treated by the introduction of H's demand curve for Pepsi. Also production in H is assumed to take place under increasing costs, even though, for simplification, constant costs are assumed in P and R. Again R is the low-cost supplier. A tariff of t is imposed on imports from both P and R. R's supply curve is labeled $S_R + t$, while P's supply curve inclusive of the tariff is omitted as being irrelevant.

Before the union is formed, R supplies Q_1–Q_2 to H, and H's domestic producers supply O–Q_1.[5] Assume that after the union is formed the external tariff remains at t. Since no tariff is imposed on

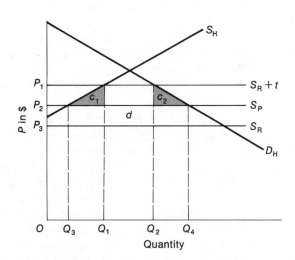

Figure 11.1
Trade diversion and trade creation in a single good

[5] As in the earlier example, if the tariff is prohibitive and no imports come from R, union causes only trade creation. This relatively trivial case is not treated below.

178 imports from P, P becomes the supplier. The price to H's consumers drops from $O–P_1$ to $O–P_2$. As a consequence, H's producers cut back production from $O–Q_1$ to $O–Q_3$. The difference is made up by P's production, which is at a lower cost. This is trade creation. It is a gain to H. The amount of the gain is shown by the small triangle to the left labeled c_1 in Figure 11.1. It is the reduction in the cost of obtaining $Q_3–Q_1$, which is made possible by shifting to a foreign source. A second effect of the lowering of price in H is the increase in total consumption to $O–Q_4$. Again, this increase is supplied by production in P, and is trade creation. The net gain from increased consumption is labeled c_2 in the figure. This is part of the increase in consumer surplus which is associated with the lower tariff payments and payments to factors of production. The trade creation effect equal to the area $c_1 + c_2$ is a gain from H's point of view. Production is shifted to a lower cost source (c_1) and consumers gain by having more H at a lower price (c_2).

There is also a loss to H due to trade diversion. While the total volume of trade has increased, indicating trade creation, part of this trade ($Q_1–Q_2$) has been diverted from the low-cost source, R, to a higher cost source, P. The increase in the cost of obtaining $Q_1–Q_2$ of imports is shown in Figure 11.1 by the area labeled d. This is a loss to H, and to the world as a whole. Again because of the assumed constant costs (horizontal supply curve) in P and R, these countries neither gain nor lose by the change. H's gain (or loss) is the world's.

It is evident by inspection that in this example H's trade diversion losses outweigh the trade creation gains since d is greater than $c_1 + c_2$. This would not always be the case. The trade creation will be larger the more elastic are the supply and demand curves in H and the higher is the preunion tariff relative to the supply price in P. The trade diversion losses will be lower the smaller is the difference in costs between P and R. Also, trade creation would be zero if the elasticities of supply and demand in H were both equal to zero. In fact this is what was implicitly assumed in the example of Table 11.1.

Our ability to make relatively unambigous statements about the welfare gains or losses of the various nations has been the direct result of two simplifying assumptions. The first is the treatment of only one good in a partial equilibrium framework. This simplification will be dropped in the next section. The second assumption has been that the supply elasticities in P and R are infinite. As long as this is true, the welfare gains and losses of P and R have been zero, and the gain or loss to H has also been a gain or loss to the world as a whole. If this assumption is dropped, the analysis becomes more complicated. However, some statements can be made about tendencies.

First, provided that R was a supplier to H before the union, the quantity exported by R will fall due to trade diversion, whether or not there is a net gain in welfare for H. This fall in quantity will be accompanied by a fall in price in R and a loss of economic welfare in that country.

For H in addition to the trade creation and trade diversion effects, there is a terms of trade effect with R. Since the price of R's exports fall, to the extent that H continues to import any of the good from R after the union, H gains. This increases the likelihood that H will gain but decreases the likelihood that the net change in welfare for the world as a whole will be positive.

As P's production of the good expands, its price will rise. This is a gain to P. However, since the good is being exported to H, P's gain comes at H's expense. Therefore, if there is a gain to the union as a whole, P shares in it if its supply curve for the good is upward sloping. Even if H is a loser, P stands to gain from the higher price for its good. Also the rising supply price in P will tend to retard intra-union trade and reduce the total gain.

Beyond this the relative strengths of trade creation, trade diversion, and terms of trade effects and their distribution among countries depend on too many factors to make further generalization feasible.

The General Equilibrium of a Customs Union

While the partial equilibrium models of the preceding section may be useful for illuminating important phenomena associated with international discrimination, they are incomplete and potentially misleading. For example we learned that formation of the union is likely to lead to a reduction in the imports of the good from the third country, R. If balanced trade is to be maintained, then R's imports from the union must decrease also. What is the impact of this adjustment on prices, the terms of trade, or welfare? Rather than attempt to sort out these effects separately, we turn to an analysis based on offer curves.

In this model we will assume three countries, H, P, and R, as before, and two goods, ham and Pepsi. Relative to P, H is assumed to have a comparative advantage in ham, while P's advantage lies in Pepsi. R's comparative advantage is also assumed to lie with Pepsi, so that before the formation of the union H imports Pepsi from R. The remaining assumptions are that all nations' economies are competitive, transport costs are zero, and, as in Chapter 4, production in all countries takes place under generalized increasing costs. The model closely corresponds to the examples used in the preceding section. The exceptions are that another good, ham, has been introduced, balanced trade as an equilibrium condition is treated explicitly, and all supply curves slope upward to the right.

Three countries can be treated in a two-dimensional offer curve diagram by aggregating the trade information of any pair of the countries into an *excess offer curve.* Because it is H's and P's combined trade with R which is of interest, H's + P's offer curves are combined as shown in Figure 11.2. If the world price ratio is $O-T_1$, H and P are in balanced trade with each other. But if the price ratio is $O-T_2$, P wishes to trade at point A, offering $O-P_1$ for $O-H_1$, while H wishes to import $O-P_2$. Assuming that P's offer is "accepted," there is still an excess demand for Pepsi and an excess supply of ham. The excess constitutes an offer to trade to the rest of the world at that price. The excess offering at $O-T_2$ is plotted at point C. The offerings at other price ratios can be plotted to obtain $O-E_P$, the excess offer curves of H and P combined. There is also an excess offer curve for P at prices above $O-T_1$, but since the union's comparative advantage is in ham, this is not relevant to the present analysis.

By adding the offer curve of R to the diagram, the world equilibrium of trade in the absence of discrimination by a customs union can be found. It is at the intersection of R's offer curve and the excess offer curve of H and P. This is shown in Figure 11.3. The individual offer curves of H and P are retained in the diagram to show the pattern of trade between H and P as well as between them and R. To explain the pattern of trade in Pepsi, point A shows that R

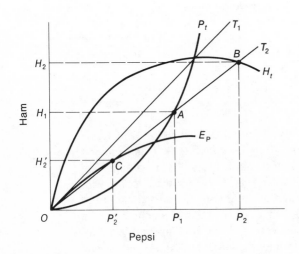

Figure 11.2
The excess offer curve of H and P

exports O–P_1, which by the construction of the excess offer curve is
equal to P_2–P_3. Point B shows that P exports O–P_2. And point C shows
that H imports O–P_3, which is necessarily equal to the combined exports of R and P. In exchange, H exports O–H_3 of ham. Of this O–H_2
goes to P, and O–H_1 ($= H_2$–H_3) goes to R.

Now suppose that H and P form a customs union. The world
trading equilibrium with discrimination can be readily found with the
apparatus already developed. Figure 11.4 shows the preunion excess

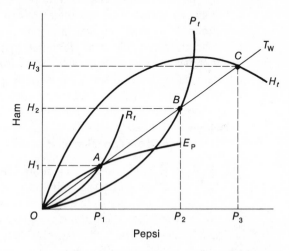

Figure 11.3
World equilibrium of trade without a customs union

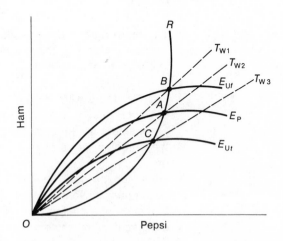

Figure 11.4
World equilibrium of trade with a customs union

offer curve of H and P, $O-E_P$, R's offer curve, and the preunion equilibrium at point A. This reproduces the situation shown in Figure 11.3. With the customs union, H and P eliminate tariffs on trade between themselves. Therefore, a new free trade excess offer curve must be derived from their individual free trade offer curve, $O-P_f$ and $O-H_f$ (not shown in this figure). The free trade excess offer curve is $O-E_{Uf}$. If the union establishes an external tariff wall, the excess offer curve must be displaced downward to reflect this tariff. The union's excess offer curve with external tariff is $O-E_{Ut}$. The intersection of this curve with R's offer curve at point C is the new equilibrium. As shown here the effect of the union is to lower R's exports (trade diversion), imports, and terms of trade. However, this is not a necessary result. It all depends on the level of the external tariff, that is, the degrees to which the union discriminates against R's exports of Pepsi. If no external tariff wall were formed by the union, the no discrimination equilibrium would be at point B. Any result between this and the complete elimination of trade with R by a prohibitive tariff is possible.

Now for some conclusions:

1. Within the union, H's welfare may either increase or decrease. H's terms of trade with P will normally change unfavorably as it shifts from the world low-cost supplier to P (trade diversion); but trade creation gains may offset this loss. Also H's terms of trade with R are likely to be improved.
2. Correspondingly, the welfare of P will probably improve, since its terms of trade with H are likely to be improved by the trade diversion. But under some circumstance P may lose because of the union.
3. As for the union considered as a group, one cannot be sure. The more normal case would be for its welfare to increase. But the division of the possible gains between the partners might be quite uneven.
4. R will probably lose as a consequence of the union since its terms of trade with the union are likely to move unfavorably. But even this is uncertain since under some circumstances, for example, an external tariff which is below the average of the preunion tariffs of H and P, R's terms of trade could improve.
5. What about world welfare? This is the problem of second best again. Universal free trade maximizes world welfare. But formation of a customs union contains elements of both freer trade and more protection or discrimination. The lower the external tariff wall and the larger the union relative to the rest of the world, the more likely it is that world welfare will in-

crease. But the question of how these gains, if any, are divided among countries remains. And it is likely that despite any gain in world welfare, nonmember countries may be worse off. One must ask whether the question of world welfare has been worth the effort that economists have put into it. It can be argued that national welfare is a meaningful concept since it is possible that compensating payments (a redistributional policy) may be instituted to assure that at least no one is worse off—and some will be better off. But compensating payments among nations seem pretty unlikely.

6. All of the above statements concerning the welfare changes of a country refer only to the size of the national pie, not the way it is divided. Since the theory of integration does not specify an underlying theory of production, the welfare changes of groups and individuals within a nation cannot be determined. Therefore any statement about the welfare change of a nation either implies a strong value judgment concerning the distribution of the welfare changes, or it assumes that compensating payments will be made to assure that no individual is made worse off because of the change.

7. Referring to Figure 11.4, as the external tariff of the union increases, for example from point *B,* the welfare of the union as a whole will increase relative to its level at point *B,* reach a maximum, then decrease. In other words, from the union's point of view there is an optimum external tariff. The analysis of Chapter 9 applies.

8. More detailed analysis could reveal at least a hundred more conclusions of varying degrees of generality.[6]

Measuring the Effects of Integration

The question of the welfare effects of integration is of interest not only because, like Mount Everest, it is there, but because of the planned and already accomplished formation of free trade areas, customs unions, and common markets among important groups of nations. Policy makers would like to know in advance whether their particular proposal is likely to increase or decrease their economic welfare. Prospective nonmembers will be concerned with possible adverse effects on them. And all concerned will be impatient with "It all depends" as an answer.

The desire for *ex ante* studies of the effects of proposed unions has led to some interesting empirical work. The problems in such

---

[6] See Jaroslav Vanek, *General Equilibrium of International Discrimination,* Cambridge, Mass., Harvard University Press, 1965, which includes a helpful summary tabulation of the 107 theorems proved in the text.

studies are truly large, and the published studies have not gone without criticism. Yet their results may be suggestive of the orders of magnitudes involved. The approach generally is to build a model of the international sectors of the nations involved and to estimate statistically the parameters of this model. The degrees of complexity of the model and the extent to which it accurately reproduces the actual economy depend largely on the resources, time, and money available to the investigator. For example statistical estimates of the elasticities of demand and supply of particular goods might be made. In a more sophisticated model interrelationships among commodities and markets could be estimated in a general equilibrium framework. Then after assuming that the economic structure represented by the model will not change significantly over the time span of the proposed integration or be changed by the integration itself, the model's equations can be solved to yield the effects of assumed changes in tariffs, etc. Because of the pitfalls in this approach, not too much weight can be attached to any one study. However, it is suggestive that two estimates of the static welfare gains to be expected from various moves toward integration in Western Europe predict increases in national income of one percent or less.[7]

In trying to assess the effect of an actual step toward integration after the fact, the investigator faces the problem of comparing what is with what might have been. His problem is to construct a reasonable, plausible "might have been" from available information which is necessarily limited to what is and what was. Another way to look at it is that the investigator must find a way to break down his observations of what is into what would have happened anyway and what was caused by the integration; then a way must be found to differentiate between the trade diversion and trade creation aspects of the latter. Two major economic forces make this approach difficult. The first is simply the rapid growth of incomes in Western nations. Higher incomes mean higher levels of trade. The analyst must be able to separate the income-induced growth in trade from that induced by integration. The second force is technological changes and innovation (and, similarly, changes in tastes) which tend to alter the structure and commodity composition of trade over time. The major steps toward economic integration in Europe after 1958 have coincided with rapid technological change and income growth, both of which seriously complicate the job of sorting out the effects of integration.

In a major study of the effects of the European Common Market, Bela Balassa has focused on changes in the relationship between

[7] See P. J. Verdoorn, "Two Notes on Tariff Reductions," *Social Aspects of European Economic Cooperation*, Geneva, International Labor Office, 1956; and Harry G. Johnson, "The Gains from Freer Trade with Europe: An Estimate," *Manchester School*, 26 (September, 1958).

income and trade flows as a means of isolating the trade creation and trade diversion phenomena from the mass of interrelated observations.[8] Specifically he assumed that the true income elasticities of demand for goods would not be affected by the formation of the Common Market or the other extraneous economic forces at work between the preunion period of 1953–1959 and the post-integration period of 1959–1965. Therefore any changes in the *measured* income elasticities of demand could be tentatively attributed to the formation of the Common Market. Furthermore, according to Balassa, trade diversion and trade creation could be specifically identified. If the measured relationship between income and imports from outside the union was lower in the second period, this would indicate that trade had been diverted to member countries. Trade creation would be signalled by an upward shift in the measured relationship between income and imports from all areas.

In aggregate Balassa found little or no trade diversion but some evidence of trade creation. Working with individual commodity groups both trade creation and trade diversion were shown in the data. As for the magnitude of the effects Balassa makes a rough estimate that the cumulative gain in national income is in the order of one-tenth of one percent.[9]

THE DYNAMIC EFFECTS

A number of writers through the years have asserted that the static efficiency effects of economic union are not the only ones and perhaps not the most significant. These writers assert generally that economic integration can have an important effect on the rate of economic growth of member nations. Since available evidence suggests that the static effects are rather small relative to national income, and since the static effects are "one shot" improvements while higher growth rates compound over time, the arguments bear investigation. Unfortunately, the arguments are not always clearly stated and are occasionally contradictory. Furthermore some of the arguments do not involve clearly dynamic forces, even though they are ruled out of consideration as static effects by the assumptions made there.

One such argument says that the increased size of the domestic market, now including other member countries, will enable producers to exploit economies of large-scale production. In addition, expanded

[8] Bela Balassa, "Trade Creation and Trade Diversion in the European Common Market," *Economic Journal,* 77, No. 305 (March, 1967), 1–21.

[9] See also J. Wemelsfelder, "The Short-Term Effect of the Lowering of Import Duties in Germany," *Economic Journal,* 70, No. 277 (March, 1960), 94–104. Wemelsfelder estimated the welfare gains in Germany, due to substantially lowered tariffs in 1956 and 1957, to be on the order of one-fifth of one percent.

186   output may yield external economies. Clearly this argument is related to the infant industry argument discussed in Chapter 9.[10]
Examination of the economies of Switzerland or Sweden, for example, shows that it is not at all clear that small domestic markets
need result in inefficient, small-scale production. Also this argument
is not dynamic in nature. Ultimately a higher growth rate for an economy can only be supported by an increase in the rate of growth
of factor inputs over time, especially capital, and/or an increase in
the rate of technological improvement. Scale effects, if present,
would have the same general effect as the other improvements in
efficiency, a once and for all lowering of costs. However, it should
be pointed out that the scale effects argument (as well as the infant
industry argument) may be much more appropriate for the less-
developed countries.

Another possible dynamic effect is the increase in competitive
pressure on stagnant industries or firms. If tariffs walls have served
to shelter monopolistic firms from price or product competition from
abroad, their market power will be broken or at least weakened by
the removal of barriers to intra-union trade. A correct statement of
this case would point out that the elimination of market power brings
about a closing of the gap between marginal cost and price which
would have the same significance for economic efficiency as the
removal of tariff barriers. For the competitive effect to be truly
dynamic in nature, it must be shown to spur firms to sustained higher
rates of investment and/or devoting more resources to research
leading to technological change.

A related but somewhat contradictory argument holds that larger
firms do in fact spend relatively more on research and development,
and integration which encouraged the growth of firms (economies
of scale?) would result in higher rates of technological change and
growth. The basis for this argument is the fact that in the United
States, firms in highly concentrated or oligopolistic industries do
spend relatively more on R & D. But what has yet to be shown is that
this larger expenditure has resulted in faster technological change
rather than simply more product differentiation or model changes.

It is occasionally asserted that economic integration will stimulate investment. But a causal link between investment and integration, beyond the points discussed here, has not yet been provided.
There is some evidence that U.S. firms in particular greatly increased
their investment in Western European facilities after the formation of
the Common Market. This may have reflected a desire to establish
production behind the tariff wall as a way of avoiding the external
tariffs, in which case it will not have an impact on long-term growth

[10] See pp. 147–148.

rates. In effect this is a capital shift accompanying trade diversion. Alternatively, this flow may reflect the belated recognition of opportunities in a market which was already booming before the Common Market was formed.

As a final observation, if it can be shown that integration does increase the long-term rate of growth of member countries, the benefits of this will not be confined to the union alone. Higher growth rates in the union mean more rapidly growing demand for imports, and this will stimulate incomes and growth in the rest of the world. In the long run it is possible that more rapid worldwide growth, if it is achieved, would more than compensate nonmember countries for their static efficiency losses due to trade diversion.

SUPPLEMENTARY READINGS

Kindleberger, Charles, *International Economics,* 4th ed., Homewood, Ill., Irwin, 1968, chaps. 11, 13.

Clement, M. O., Pfister, Richard L., and Rothwell, Kenneth J., *Theoretical Issues in International Economics,* Boston, Houghton Mifflin, 1967, chap. 4.

Balassa, Bela, *The Theory of Economic Integration,* Homewood, Ill., Irwin, 1961.

Lipsey, Richard G., "The Theory of Customs Unions: A General Survey," *Economic Journal,* 70, No. 279 (September, 1960), 496–513, reprinted in American Economic Association, *Readings in International Economics,* Homewood, Ill., Irwin, 1968, pp. 261–278.

Meade, J. E., *The Theory of Customs Unions,* Amsterdam, North Holland, 1955.

Chapter

The Analysis
of Trade and Growth

In this and the final chapter we shift from the timeless, unchanging world of comparative static analysis to the dynamic world of technological improvement, investment, and population growth. We want to know how trade and growth interact over time. Without too much oversimplification, we can say that there are two kinds of questions to be asked. First, what are the effects of economic growth on trade? And second, how does the pattern and extent of trade affect the rate of economic growth and development? In this chapter the analytical tools and models are laid out. In the final chapter we use these theoretical tools and the available empirical evidence to examine issues such as the effect of growth on balance-of-payments equilibrium, the trends in terms of trade, and the role of trade in economic development.

AN INTRODUCTION TO GROWTH THEORY

Until this point in the book, we have assumed that the supplies of productive resources used as inputs in the economy were given and unchanging. The assumption is justified not because it is realistic, but because it is a useful simplification. It enables us to focus attention on certain aspects of the economic system without the complications caused by conditions which are irrelevant to the questions being asked. It is as if we took a photograph of a moving or growing economy in order to analyze in detail the features that our stop action photo reveals. The Heckscher-Ohlin and comparative cost models are stop action photos of growing economies which show us the patterns of trade at that moment, and what determined them. More importantly, they deal with equilibrium positions and the forces which tend to move the economy toward those equilibria.

The equilibrium of a static model can be viewed as a target. The equilibrium position and the target shift with changes in the under-lying conditions of the static model. In a growing economy this target is moving continously, if not always at the same speed. The value of static analysis is that it permits us to assume that the growing economy at any point in time is right on the target, or at least very close and moving in. In the models of growing economies studied in this chapter, we assume that at all times the static equilibrium conditions of a single price, balanced trade, and etc., are fulfilled, and that at any point in time the pattern of trade is determined by the relative factor endowments, technology, and demand of that particular time.

If it is assumed that the economic system is in equilibrium at all times, and if growth is defined as a continuous increase in the level of output, then growth can come only from two sources. Either the quantities of inputs being used must grow over time, or the productivity of these inputs must be increasing as a result of steady technological improvements. Assume that output depends on the quantities of capital and labor services used as inputs, and that this relationship can be expressed as a production function as in Chapter 4. Furthermore, assume that this production function displays constant returns to scale and diminishing marginal returns to increases in one input, the other being held constant. With this simple model we can illustrate several important facts about growth.

Taking each of the inputs in turn, the rate of growth of the labor input is limited in the long run by the rate of population increase. Actually it is likely to be less as years spent in education and training increase, retirement ages decline, and the average work week declines. If the existing capital stock is already fully employed, an increase in the inputs of capital services requires net investment in new capital equipment. Investment or new capital formation requires that individuals spend less on consumer goods, that is, save, so that resources can be shifted to the production of capital goods. The savings ratio, or the proportion of total income saved, is the critical variable here. An increase in the savings ratio, if other things are equal, will increase the rate of new capital formation and the rate of growth.

Assume for the moment that there is no technological change. In this case the rate of growth of output is a weighted average of the rates of increase of the labor and capital inputs, where the weights depend on the production function and the relative importance of

190   the two inputs in the production process.[1] If there is no new capital formation, but population and therefore the labor input is growing, the growth of output will be less than the growth of the labor input. If the growth of the labor input is due to population growth rather than the same number of people working more, we can be sure that per capita incomes are falling. Another way to express this point is that because there are more workers using a fixed stock of capital, the marginal productivity of labor and labor's wage are declining due to diminishing marginal returns. To prevent this decline in per capita real incomes, the capital input must grow at the same rate as the labor force, so that capital per worker does not decline over time.

Suppose that the capital input is growing faster than the labor input. Then per capita incomes will be rising, since the rate of growth of income will be greater than the growth of the labor input. But this cannot continue forever. Capital per worker will be rising, and this will result in a diminishing marginal productivity of capital and a diminishing incentive to invest. If other things are equal, the result would be a declining rate of growth of capital until capital and labor were growing at the same rate and per capita incomes were constant. Of course this unhappy state of affairs has been held off, at least in the developed nations, by continuous technological change which has raised the productivity of capital and labor. Technological improvement is the third input in the production function which has helped to maintain the incentives to invest, forestalled the appearance of diminishing returns, and resulted in the rapid and more or less continuous increase in per capita incomes in Western nations over the last two hundred years.

So far we have discussed growth in terms of the rate of increase of some homogeneous good called output. In this way the problem of aggregating and measuring the outputs of many commodities and services into a single figure has been avoided. The problem of the allocation of inputs, and particularly increments in inputs, among different goods is ignored. Also the questions of tastes and preferences and demands for different goods, and how these might change with changes in income and relative prices, have been ignored. Because of these simplifications, these simple models cannot shed

---

[1] This is rather vague. We can be more precise by using some fairly simple mathematics. Assume that the production function is of the form: $Y = K^a L^b$. Then for any very small changes in the inputs, the change in output is: $dY = dK \cdot MPP_k + dL \cdot MPP_l$ where the "d" symbolizes very small changes in the variables. Since by the calculus it can be shown that $MPP_k = aY/K$ and $MPP_l = bY/L$, we can convert the above expression into percentage terms and make the appropriate substitutions to obtain: $dY/Y = (dK/K)a + (dL/L)b$. Under the assumptions about returns to scale made in the text, $a + b = 1$. This expression says that the percentage rate of growth of income cannot exceed the rate of growth of the most rapidly growing input nor fall below the rate of growth of the slowest input.

any light on the relationship between growth and international trade.

Models of trade and growth must deal with at least two commodities. Suppose again that there is no technological change and that all growth is due to increases in factor inputs. How will this growth be divided among the two goods? This depends on the relationships between income and demand for the two goods. If incomes are rising, the output of the good with the higher income elasticity of demand will rise faster. Adding technological change to the model complicates things because the increases in productivity can take place at different rates in the two industries, causing changes in relative prices as well. In other words growth can affect the composition of output on both the demand side, through incomes, and on the supply side. In either case growth will affect the level and pattern of trade. In the next section we examine these effects using, for simplicity, a comparative static framework. In other words stop action photos are taken at two points in time and compared so that the changes due to growth during that period can be identified.

An important distinction should be made between movements *along* a given supply curve due to changes in price and *shifts* of that supply curve. It is only the latter which can properly be called growth (assuming, of course, that the shift is to the right). If a supply curve is not vertical but slopes upward to the right, changes in price will lead to changes in the quantities supplied. When movements along a supply curve occur, they must have been caused by a shift in the demand curve yielding a different price. These shifts can occur for a variety of reasons, but they do not represent economic growth. Growth is essentially a supply phenomenon. Growth is, in part, the steady rightward march of the supply curves for factor inputs, as well as the steady increase in the unit productivity of inputs. In dealing with economic growth in the remainder of this chapter, we will continue to use the earlier assumption that factor supply curves are perfectly inelastic. In other words, our stop action photos would show vertical supply curves, while our movies would show their continuous movement to the right.

THE EFFECTS OF GROWTH ON TRADE

As we pointed out above, growth, whether caused by increases in factor endowments or by changes in technology, can affect trade in a variety of ways. There are several channels through which growth can make its effects felt; and when the interaction through trade of two growing nations is taken into account, there are manifold possible outcomes. We would like to know how growth affects the net barter terms of trade, that is, the relative prices of imports and exports. With this information we might be able to hazard some tenta-

192   tive statements about how trade affects the economic welfare of a
growing nation. As a practical matter, since the model tells us how
the terms of trade must change in order to maintain balanced trade,
the predicted change in the terms of trade can also indicate possible
emerging balance-of-payments problems. Also of interest is the rate
of growth of trade relative to total output. In other words, is growth
tending to make the nation relatively more or less self-sufficient?

The first step is to identify the channels through which growth
operates to affect trade. Here we are establishing a terminology and
developing analytical tools. The framework is that of the Heckscher-
Ohlin two-factor, two-good model. First we will deal with one country
under the assumption that it faces a perfectly elastic foreign offer
curve. In other words, the nation is so small that the amounts it
exports and imports have no effects on world prices and the terms
of trade. After the tools are developed, it will be possible to predict
the net effect of trade on the relative quantities of exports and imports. With this information it will be possible to drop the assumption
of a perfectly elastic foreign offer curve and to predict changes in the
terms of trade. All of this analysis proceeds under the artificial
assumption that the other nation is not itself growing. The last step
is to undertake some generalizations about the pattern of trade and
the terms of trade when both countries are growing, although not
necessarily at the same rate.

Changing Factor Supplies

First consider the effects of growth on production. Let us assume
temporarily that there is no technological change but that growth
occurs through increases in factor inputs. Figure 12.1 shows the
production possibilities curve for one country at a point in time.
The equilibrium of production is at point P_1. The consumption equilibrium would be on the terms of trade line $T-T$ to the left of point
P_1. It is not shown here. An increase in either or both factor endowments would shift the production possibilities curve outward, the
exact shape of the new curve depending on the relative sizes of the
factor increases. If the terms of trade do not change, the new production point will be at the point of tangency between the production
possibilities curve and $T'-T'$. The figure shows one possible outcome
in which the production of importables and exportables have increased by the same percentage. This is termed *neutral growth*. As
long as the new production points fall on the extension of the straight
line $O-P_1$, the effect of growth on production is neutral.

If the new production point had fallen between P_2 and A, the
production of exportables would have increased more in percentage
terms than the production of importables. If other things are equal,

this will increase trade relative to production, since relatively more exportable goods are available for trade and imports would have to rise to maintain the same proportionate consumption of the importable good. For these reasons this outcome is called *protrade biased* growth. If the production point had fallen to the right of *A*, production of the importable good would have decreased in absolute amount. This would be very favorable to trade; hence this kind of growth is termed *ultra protrade biased* growth.

Points to the left of P_2 would indicate *antitrade biased* growth since the faster rate of growth in production of importable goods would tend to result in domestic production being substituted for imports. In a symmetrical manner, if the production of exportables declines absolutely, the result is *ultra antitrade biased* growth.

Under what conditions of factor supply growth will these several types of growth occur? First we can show that if only one factor is growing, growth will be ultra biased. It will be ultra antitrade biased if the scarce factor is growing and the abundant one is constant. Growth will be ultra protrade biased if the abundant factor is growing and increasing the nation's comparative advantage.

Figure 12.2 shows the Edgeworth-Bowley box for a labor rich nation. The solid lines mark the initial factor endowment. The isoquant X_1 shows the initial outputs of the labor abundant exportable good; M_1 shows the output of the importable good. If growth in labor occurs, the box will take on the new dimensions shown by the dashed line extension. The importable good isoquants are now referred to

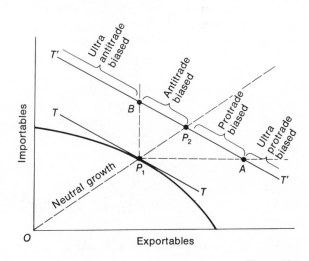

Figure 12.1
The effect of production growth on trade

194 point O'_M. Recall that in order to separate the effects of growth from those of changes in relative prices on trade, it was assumed that the terms of trade remain constant. Because of the nature of the production function, there is a unique relationship between product and factor prices.[2] Therefore, factor prices and the ratios in which factors are combined in the production of both goods do not change. As a consequence, the new production equilibrium for the exportable good must fall somewhere on the ray O_x–X, and the production point for the importable good must be on O'_m–M', which is parallel to O_m–M. The only point satisfying both conditions is the intersection of the two at point B, showing that after growth output must consist of M_2 of the importable good and X_2 of the exportable good. The output of the exportable good has clearly increased, while that of the importable good has decreased.

Figure 12.3 shows the effect of growth in only one factor on the production possibilities curve. It is everywhere outside the old curve, but the shift favors the output of the good using the growing factor intensively. The equilibrium output, if relative prices do not change, is below and to the right of the original output point, showing ultra protrade biased growth. If the growth had occurred in the scarce factor, capital, the opposite result would have occurred. As the student should be able to demonstrate, growth of capital alone would result in a decrease in the production of exportables and ultra antitrade biased growth.

Next we can show where the boundary between ultra biased growth and simple biased growth lies. We ask at what rate capital

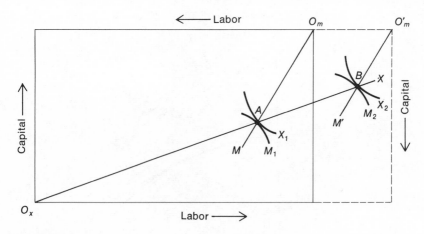

Figure 12.2
Production equilibrium with growth in one factor

[2] See Chapter 5, pp. 68–70.

and labor must grow to cause an increase in the production of one good with no change in output of the other. If the increments to capital and labor are in the same proportion to each other as labor and capital are combined in the production of the exportable, then output of the exportable will expand with no growth in the other good.[3] As before, in Figure 12.4 the original factor endowment is shown by the solid lines of the Edgeworth-Bowley box. This special case of growth is shown by the expansion of the Edgeworth-Bowley box along the line O_m–O'_m, which is parallel to O_x–X. As before, since

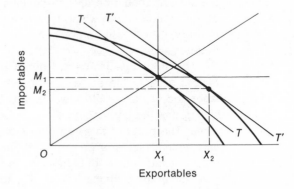

Figure 12.3
Production equilibrium and the terms of trade with growth in one factor

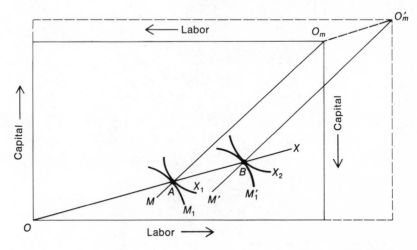

Figure 12.4
Factor growth in the proportions employed in the exportables industry

[3] Specifically the condition for growth of the export good is $\Delta K/\Delta L = K_x/L_x$.

product and factor prices do not change, the new output point must lie on the rays O_x-X and O'_m-M' (which is parallel to O_m-M). Point B must be the new equilibrium. It shows an expansion of X. That M has not changed can be shown by the fact that $O_m-A-B-O'_m$ is a parallelogram by construction. Therefore O_m-A and O'_m-B have the same distance from the origin and the same capital/labor ratio. Therefore output of the importable good has not changed. This proves that the boundary between ultra protrade biased growth and simple protrade biased growth occurs where the factors grow in the same proportion as they are combined in the production of the export good. Similarly, the student should be able to demonstrate that when growth occurs at the proportions in which factors are combined in the importables industry, growth will border between antitrade biased and ultra antitrade biased.

The third special case, neutral growth, occurs when the two factors grow in the same proportions as the overall endowment of labor and capital. In other words, $\Delta K/\Delta L = K/L$. This is the same as saying that the percentage growth rates of labor and capital are the same. The proof of this is a little more complicated than the others and depends on the geometry of similar triangles. In Figure 12.5, proportionate growth of both inputs is shown by extending the aggregate factor proportions line O_x-O_m to the northeast. Proportionate growth is shown by the following formula.

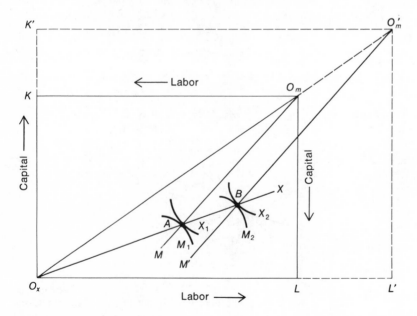

Figure 12.5
Both factors growing at the same rate

$$\frac{K-K'}{O_x-K} = \frac{O_m-O'_m}{O_x-O_m} = \frac{L-L'}{O_x-L}$$

From O'_m draw a new ray for the importable good parallel to O_m–A. Its intersection with O_x–X at point B shows the new production equilibrium. By construction, the triangles O_x–A–O_m and O_x–B–O'_m are similar. Therefore the percentage increase in the output of the exportable, A–B/O_x–A, is equal to O_m–O'_m/O_x–O_m and as shown above is equal also to the percentage increases in both inputs. The construction can be repeated by expressing the growth of inputs as a movement of O_x to the southwest in order to prove the similar result for the growth of importables.

The results of these three special cases can be generalized to show the range of possibilities. In Figure 12.6 growth is represented by expansion of the Edgeworth-Bowley box to the northeast. Five alternative growth paths for inputs are shown. Assuming that this labor abundant nation exports its labor intensive good, the effects of alternative growth paths on trade can easily be demonstrated. Neutral growth of the inputs along the extension of O_x–O_m results in neutral growth in output. If labor grows faster than capital, the growth path will be somewhere to the right, indicating either a protrade or ultra protrade bias. The boundary between protrade and ultra protrade bias is indicated by the growth path where $\Delta K/\Delta L = K_x/L_x$. Any

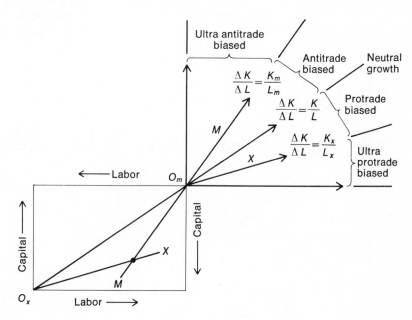

Figure 12.6
Factor growth and trade bias—a classification

movement to the southeast from O_m would be ultra protrade biased but might not be growth since one factor would be decreasing in absolute amount. Similarly, if capital, the scarce factor, grows faster than labor, growth will be antitrade or ultra antitrade biased, and the boundary between the two is where $\Delta K/\Delta L = K_m/L_m$.

Changing Technology

Technological change which increases the productivity of inputs acts to conserve inputs since the same output can be produced with fewer inputs. Also technological change can be viewed as an increase in total resource availability since, if the same output could be produced with fewer inputs, continuing to use the same level of inputs should result in higher outputs. With this basic symmetry between resource growth and productivity changes in mind, we can examine the effects of technological change on trade assuming that the actual endowment of resources remains unchanged.

Technological change can occur in one industry or both, at different rates in the two industries, and can save mostly capital, or mostly labor, or both proportionately. Figure 12.7 shows biased technological change in one industry. The isoquant for a given level of output is shifted toward the origin. In addition, at *unchanged factor prices* the capital/labor ratio is changed. When technological change is biased toward one input, it is said to save that factor. The isoquants shift in such a way that at unchanged factor prices less of that factor input is used relative to the other input. Figure 12.7 shows *capital saving* technological change, since the capital/labor ratio

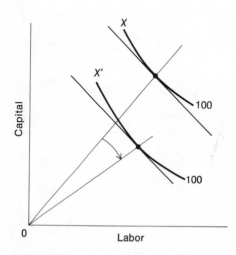

Figure 12.7
Capital saving technological change

decreases. When capital and labor are saved in the same proportions in which they are used, this is called *neutral technological change.* It is equivalent to an equal proportionate growth of inputs in this industry.

The net effect of technological change on output and trade depends on the type (whether labor or capital saving or neutral) and magnitude of technological change in each industry. In a two-good, two-factor model there are fifteen possible combinations of zero, neutral, labor-saving, and capital-saving technological change. For five of these combinations, unambiguous statements can be made about the net effects. For the rest the results depend on the *relative* rates at which change takes place.

The simplest case is one of neutral technological change at the same rate in both industries. Recalling the functional equivalence of technological change and factor growth, we can see that the result is neutral growth. Neutral technological change saves both factors in the same proportions in which they are being used. With equal rates of progress this is equivalent to equal proportionate increases in the supplies of both factors for both industries, a case which was analyzed above.

When there is neutral progress in one industry and no progress in the other, the output of that industry will grow, while the other will remain unchanged. This is the borderline case between ordinary and ultra bias. Neutral growth in one industry is equivalent to an increase in factor supplies in the proportion at which they are being employed in that industry, as in Figure 12.4. If the export industry experiences neutral progress, the result is protrade bordering on ultra protrade biased growth. Similarly, when the importable goods industry experiences neutral progress, growth is antitrade biased.

When progress in the exportable good industry is biased toward the abundant factor, and there is no technological change in the importable goods industry, the result is ultra protrade biased growth. The shift from neutral growth to growth which saves the abundant factor pushes the case over the boundary between ordinary and ultra biased growth. Similarly, when there is growth in the importable goods industry which saves the scarce factor, and no progress in the other industry, growth will be ultra antitrade biased.

The Effects of Growth on Consumption

The effect of economic growth, from whatever source, is to push out the production possibilities curve. If we continue to assume that the terms of trade will not change, this growth can be represented by a series of outward parallel shifts of the consumption possibilities or relative price line as shown in Figure 12.8. Point *A* marks the initial

200 equilibrium. The changes in the composition of consumption in the economy in response to these shifts can be classified according to their effect on trade. If the consumption of importables and exportables increases at the same percentage rate, or proportionately, the effect will be *neutral* on trade. In Figure 12.8 this would be shown by movement along the ray from the origin through point *A*. If the consumption of importables increases at a faster rate than the consumption of exportables, the effect will be favorable to the expansion of trade; that is, it will be *protrade biased.*

If the protrade bias is so strong that consumption of the exportable good actually declines, this is termed *ultra protrade biased* growth. This may seem like an unusual result but it is one which cannot be ruled out a priori. If all persons' incomes changed the same amount, ultra bias of either sort could only occur if one good were an inferior good, that is, a good which people consumed less of as their incomes rose. But overall growth in the economy does not rule out the possibility that some people's incomes may be falling due to adverse factor price changes. If these people had a high income elasticity of demand for the exportable good, they would be cutting down substantially in their consumption of that good. If those whose incomes were rising had a high income elasticity of demand for the importable good, they would be spending a high proportion of their income gains on the importable good. The result could be ultra protrade biased growth in consumption.

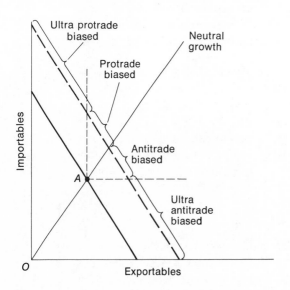

Figure 12.8
The effect of income growth on consumption and trade

The net effects of consumption and production changes on exports relative to imports determines the size of trade relative to total production and ultimately the effect of growth on the terms of trade. When at constant terms of trade, exports (or imports) increase in proportion to total output, *neutral growth* has occurred. If growth results in a more than proportionate increase in exports (or imports) at constant terms of trade, growth is *protrade* biased. But if exports (or imports) increase less than proportionately or decrease at constant terms of trade, growth is *antitrade biased*.

The consumption and production effects can be combined graphically to show the net effects of growth on trade. Consider first the case where both consumption and production effects are trade neutral when considered separately. Points P and C in Figure 12.9 show the production and consumption equilibria before growth. Neutral growth in both sectors results in expansion along the rays $O–P$ and $O–C$. At constant terms of trade, the new equilibria are at P_1 and C_1. The distance $P_1–C_1$ is a measure of the new volume of trade. As can be seen from similar triangles, the volume of trade, production, and consumption have all increased by the same proportion or percentage, showing neutral overall growth.

If the new measure of trade is longer than $P_1–C_1$, e.g., $P_1–C_2$, then growth has been overall protrade biased. Ultra protrade bias occurs if the line is longer than $P_2–C_2$. On the other hand, if the line is less than $P_1–C_1$, antitrade bias is said to have occurred; and if the volume of trade is actually less than $P–C$, the growth has been ultra antitrade biased.

Neutral growth is not neutral in its effect on the terms of trade.

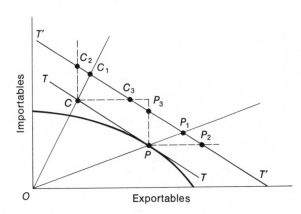

Figure 12.9
The net effect of growth on trade

Neutral growth represents a combined increase in the supply of exports and increase in the demand for imports. The impact of neutral growth will be to turn the terms of trade against the country, assuming now that the offer curve of the other nation is less than perfectly elastic and that the other country is not itself growing. As Figure 12.10 shows, in neutral growth the increase in the production of importable goods (ΔM_P) is less than the increase in their consumption in moving from point C_1 to C_2. This results in an increase in the quantity demanded of imports and turns the terms of trade against the nation. The same prediction can be obtained by examining the changes in the production and consumption of exportables.

Figure 12.11 shows two instances of antitrade biased growth, either of which will serve to prevent an adverse movement of the terms of trade. First assume neutral growth in consumption, that is, expansion along $O–C$. In order for the volume of trade to remain constant, production must expand along a line parallel to $O–C$; that is, it must be antitrade biased. This expansion path is labeled $P_1–P'$. The distance $P'_2–C_2$ is equal to $P_1–C_1$, showing that the terms of trade will not decline. Similarly, with neutral growth in production, consumption must be antitrade biased as in $C_4–C'$ in order to maintain a constant volume of trade. In short, if the terms of trade are to remain unchanged, given a foreign offer curve which is less than perfectly elastic, growth must border on being ultra antitrade biased in its overall effect.

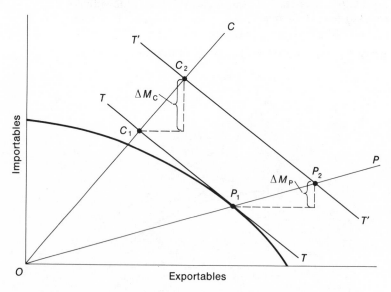

Figure 12.10
Neutral growth with an adverse terms of trade effect

We have outlined the general principles governing growth and terms of trade effects and provided some examples. Beyond this point, statements about the effects of growth on the volume of trade or the terms of trade are difficult unless the specifics of the case are known. The results depend on interrelationships among growth rates for various factor inputs, rates and types of productivity change, income elasticities of demand, and changes in income distribution associated with growth. Furthermore, no country grows in a "vacuum." In a two-country model, both countries are likely to be experiencing some kind of growth. One of the most important influences on one country's terms of trade is sure to be the effect of growth in its partner country on the offer curve that it faces.

If the terms of trade between two countries are to remain constant, growth in each country must be such that in each case the increase in the imports of one country which would occur with constant terms of trade just equals the increase in exports of the other. This could happen under a variety of circumstances; but it seems likely that the exact coincidence of factors necessary to produce this result would not be too common.

In a two-country (or multicountry) model the important variables for a full analysis of interdependencies are the *relative* rates of growth of factor inputs and technological change and the *relative* income elasticities of demand for all goods. Relative price elasticities

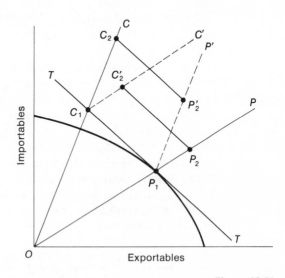

Figure 12.11
Alternative growth and trade paths

of demand will be important only in determining *how large* a change in terms of trade is required to restore equilibrium. Without developing a full two-country general equilibrium analysis, which would be beyond the scope of this book, we can attempt some tentative statements about general tendencies in a two-country model.[4]

In the Heckscher-Ohlin model it was assumed that the same technology was available in all countries. A corollary assumption would be that technological change proceeded at the same rate and took the same form in all countries.[5] Even were this so the effects would not be neutral for growth and trade. The impact on output and trade of technical progress in an industry in a country will depend on the relative importance of that industry in the economy and on the proportions in which the factors were originally being used. In other words, equal technological progress in all countries will not necessarily be neutral in impact.

Turning to growth in factor supplies, if the abundant factor is the faster growing one in each country, both countries will experience protrade biased growth, if other things are equal. Both would tend to experience a falling terms of trade. But since they trade with each other, this cannot happen to both countries simultaneously. One country's growth will tend to offset the adverse effects of the other. The direction of change of the terms of trade will depend on relative rates of growth, but in any case it will be slower than it would be if only one country were growing. Whatever the change in the terms of trade, both countries will be becoming more specialized in production and more dependent on trade. If the scarce factor in each country is the faster growing one, both countries experience antitrade biased growth, which tends to be offsetting, in its terms of trade effect; but both countries become less specialized and less dependent on trade.

On the demand side, suppose that two countries have the same income elasticity of demand for good A. Assume also that the same is true for good B, but that the elasticity coefficient for good A is higher. If the country exporting good A has the slower growth rate, it will tend to experience rising terms of trade. This is because the other country's demand for its exports of A will be rising faster than its demand for imports. On the other hand, if the exporter of A is the faster growing nation, its terms of trade will tend to deteriorate since foreign growth in demand will not keep up with its capacity to export.

A final generalization concerns equal rates of growth in all countries. If the income elasticity of demand for the importable good in a

[4] Harry G. Johnson has provided a thorough analysis of these factors in *International Trade and Economic Growth*, London, Allen & Unwin, 1958, chaps. 3 and 4.
[5] This assumption is appropriate only in the very long run. For a different view of technological change and growth recall the product cycle model of trade in Chapter 8.

country exceeds the foreign income elasticity of demand for its exportable good, the combined consumption effects will be protrade biased and this nation's terms of trade will turn against it.

The Terms of Trade and Welfare

In an earlier chapter we discussed several measures of the terms of trade and their value in measuring welfare changes. We also discussed some of the problems of evaluating economic welfare when changes in the distribution of income were involved.[6] Here we must keep in mind these limitations on the terms of trade, and remember that our models of this chapter have dealt only with the net barter terms of trade. We must also recall that growth and changes in trade patterns (due to growth and to changes in the terms of trade) affect the distribution of income as well. If we keep these reservations in mind, some tentative statements about welfare are possible.

Growth means an increase in production. At least in the absence of trade we are tempted to say that growth is good if we know that production or output per person is increasing. We have no difficulty in making judgments if we know that all persons are sharing in this increase. When one nation trades with another, it is not its output which matters for welfare analysis but its consumption. And this depends partly on its output and partly on what that output will buy from other nations. Ignoring income distribution problems within the nation, the terms of trade are an indicator of how much of the benefits of growth a nation is able to capture for itself, and how much is passed on to its trading partners.

Figure 12.12 illustrates one of the three possible outcomes. The others can easily be inferred from it. The solid production possibilities curve and terms of trade line represent the initial equilibrium position with production at P_1 and consumption at C_1. The production possibilities curve with growth is the dashed line. If the terms of trade do not change, production is at P_2 and consumption is at C_2. C_2 represents an improvement in welfare in the limited sense that it represents more of both goods. If the terms of trade move against this country, the production equilibrium would be to the left of P_2, say at P_2'. The corresponding consumption point would be C_2'. This still represents an improvement over C_1, but in this case the nation has "shared" some of the benefits of growth through deteriorating terms of trade.

If growth were sufficiently antitrade biased to improve the terms of trade, the new consumption point would be above and to the right of C_2, showing that the nation's gains from growth stemmed partly from physical improvements and partly from an improved bargaining

[6] See Chapter 6, pp. 81–84.

position. It is also possible that the terms of trade could turn so adversely against this nation that it would actually lose through growth. If P'_2 shifted far enough to the left, the resulting consumption possibilities curve would lie below and to the left of C_1, showing that the nation loses through "immiserizing growth."[7] Actually, a nation could avoid such an absolute loss by an appropriate tariff policy. Since immiserizing growth could only occur with very inelastic demand curves for its exports and supply curves for its imports, it could exploit this inelasticity by imposing optimum tariffs and taxes on exports.[8]

These, then, are the elements of the theory of trade and growth, or at least a theory of the ways in which growth can affect the patterns of trade, the terms of trade, and the distribution of the gains from growth. In the next chapter the tools are put to work on some interesting and important questions.

For supplementary readings, see the end of Chapter 13.

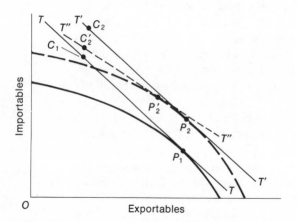

Figure 12.12
Growth, the terms of trade, and consumption

[7] See J. Bhagwati, "Immiserizing Growth: A Geometrical Note," *Review of Economic Studies*, June, 1958, pp. 201–205.

[8] This assertion requires some qualification. The ability to impose an optimum tariff rests on market power. Inelastic demand for one's exports does not necessarily mean market power and the ability to improve the terms of trade with a tax on exports. The presence of *potential* entrants into the world market can effectively limit market power on the export side.

Chapter

Trade in a Growing World Economy

THE EFFECTS OF GROWTH ON TRADE

Growth and the Balance of Payments

The models and the tools developed in the previous chapter provide a way of making predictions about the movement of the terms of trade over time. We can determine whether the terms of trade will have to improve or deteriorate in order to maintain a balanced trading equilibrium. While the model is essentially long run in nature, it has short-run policy implications in those cases where the terms of trade are not quickly self-adjusting, or where the equilibrating mechanisms in the economic system work poorly or not at all.

We must ask how in the real world changes in the terms of trade occur? First, it must be pointed out that the terms of trade measures which regulate actual trade flows are defined and measured in monetary units. Therefore, changes in the observed terms of trade require changes in one of the two monetary variables involved, either changes in the levels of domestic prices (through inflation or deflation) or changes in exchange rates (through devaluation or revaluation).[1] For the most part today exchange rates are fixed by policy and held unchanged except in cases of fundamental disequilibrium in trade (or capital flows). Price levels are largely determined by (if not controlled by) national monetary and fiscal policies. In the real world, the terms of trade can change in a possibly disequilibrating way

---

[1] It might be helpful here to review the numerical example provided in the second section of Chapter 2.

independently of underlying real trade forces. But more importantly for our purposes, underlying trade forces, namely growth, can require equilibrating terms of trade changes which will not occur automatically except in a world of freely fluctuating exchange rates or the pure classical gold standard.

To get down to specifics, suppose our model predicts that growth will turn the terms of trade against a nation. If relative inflation rates or devaluations do not bring this about, the nation will experience a deficit on its trade account and, if other things are equal, a balance-of-payments deficit.[2] Then the model will have been useful in predicting an impending policy problem and perhaps shedding light on its fundamental causes.

One important prediction of the model was that if one nation's income elasticity of demand for imports was higher than the elasticity of the rest of the world's demand for its exports, it would experience deteriorating terms of trade unless its growth rate were sufficiently below the rest of the world's to offset this effect. In the short run, if growth rates were equal, this nation would experience increasing balance-of-payments difficulties until or unless price level and/or exchange rate changes were employed to effect the required change in the terms of trade.

Some have argued that this situation is a common characteristic of the less-developed nations. They have a high income elasticity of demand for manufactured imports, while developed nations have a low elasticity of demand for raw material imports from these nations. This argument will be evaluated in the next section. Suffice to note that there are two empirical points at issue, whether the elasticities are as assumed by those who make the argument, and whether the less-developed nations have as a group experienced a decline in the terms of trade which cannot be better explained by other factors.

In an important article, Houthakker and Magee have started from the other end by first measuring income elasticities of demand for fifteen developed nations, and then making use of the model to show that persistent balance-of-payments problems of three nations can be explained in terms of the model and their measurements.[3] For example, they found that the income elasticity of demand for Japan's exports was nearly three times higher than the income elasticity of its demand for imports. This means that, if all else is equal, Japan could grow three times as fast as its trading partners without running into a balance-of-payments problem because of growth. In fact, Japan has had a persistently strong balance of trade for several years

[2] Other items in the balance of payments, particularly capital flows, are ignored.
[3] H. S. Houthakker and Stephen P. Magee, "Income and Price Elasticities in World Trade," *Review of Economics and Statistics,* 51, No. 2 (May, 1969), 111–125.

despite a rate of increase of price levels which has been on the high side. On the other hand, the United States and the United Kingdom both have significantly higher elasticities of demand for imports than for exports. The United Kingdom has had persistent balance-of-payments problems since World War II, and the United States has seen its balance of trade decline dramatically over the past ten years, from around $6 billion in 1960 to about $2 billion in 1969. It would be too simple to explain complicated real world phenomena in terms of a single factor, as this book should make clear. Houthakker and Magee do not claim to have discovered "the cause" of these persistent disequilibria. They do say that the theory suggests that differences in income elasticities can be a factor, and that they have uncovered large differences in this variable among nations.

Growth and the Terms of Trade of the Less-Developed Nations

Considerable interest is attached to the question of whether there is anything inherent in the nature of trade between developed nations and the less-developed countries (LDCs) as a group which would result in the secular deterioration of the LDCs terms of trade. Some economists have argued that there is, on the basis of both historical evidence and economic theory.[4] To the extent that the terms of trade move against LDCs, their share in the gains from growth is reduced. One could readily view the debate and controversy over this subject as a conflict over the international distribution of income with the have-not LDCs using their historical and theoretical arguments to support their advocacy of a redistribution of world income.

From the point of this text, the controversy is of interest principally because of the issues in economic theory and empirical testing of hypotheses. We will first consider the a priori or theoretical reasons for expecting a decline in LDCs terms of trade and evaluate them in terms of the model of trade and growth. Then we will look at the evidence. Our model consists of a group of developed countries which produce manufactured goods for their own use and export and import raw materials and foodstuffs. The LDCs are low-income countries importing manufactured capital equipment as well as con-

---

[4] This argument is often associated with the name of Dr. Raul Prebisch, who first presented it in the United Nations, Department of Economic Affairs, *The Economic Development of Latin America and Its Principal Problems*, 1950. See also, United Nations Conference on Trade and Development, *Towards a New Trade Policy for Development*, a Report by the Secretary-General of the Conference, New York, United Nations, 1964. For discussion of the issues, see Gottfried Haberler, "Terms of Trade and Economic Development," in H. Ellis, ed., *Economic Development of Latin America*, St. Martin's Press, New York, 1961, and M. June Flanders, "Prebisch on Protectionism: An Evaluation," *Economic Journal*, 74, No. 294 (June, 1964), 305–326.

sumers' goods and exporting primary materials. Note that the model assumes that LDCs and primary goods producers are synonymous. This identification is often made but not universally valid. We all return to this point below.

There are three principal theoretical arguments in support of the secular deterioration hypothesis. The first states that demand conditions are antitrade biased in developed countries and protrade biased in the LDCs. As a consequence, rising demand for imports on the part of LDCs coupled with relatively declining import demand from the developed countries should lead to deteriorating terms of trade for the LDCs, assuming no offsetting forces on the supply side. Demand is biased in two ways. First, Engel's law, which is an empirically valid generalization, states that as a family's income rises, it spends a lower *percentage* of its income on food, if other things are equal. In other words, the income elasticity of demand for food is less than one. Secularly rising incomes should be accompanied by a rate of increase in food consumption which is less than the overall growth rate. Also, the income elasticity of demand for manufactured goods is greater than one. Therefore, income growth in both groups of countries would tend to increase food consumption and trade in foodstuffs less than proportionately, while consumption and trade in manufactured goods would rise more than proportionately. The result would be deteriorating terms of trade for the LDCs.

This argument can hold only for those countries which fit the descriptions outlined above. Where developed countries, such as the United States, Canada, or Australia, are major exporters of foods, the effect is reversed. Also, LDC and food exporter are not synonymous. Of course, some LDCs are food-deficit nations themselves, and more importantly some LDCs—for example, South Korea and Taiwan—do considerable export business in low skill, labor intensive manufactured goods such as plastics and the classical transistor radio.

The second argument applies to those LDCs which export raw materials to the developed countries. To the extent that technological change makes it possible to produce the same manufactured output with less raw material inputs, it is antitrade biased. The secular deterioration hypothesis asserts that this is in fact the case. Again, the result would be that the terms of trade would move against the suppliers of raw materials, if other things are equal. However, it is not clear that the necessary antitrade bias is a valid generalization. While it is no doubt often true on a case-by-case basis for specific goods and processes, it is also true that technology results in new products and processes and hence creates demands for raw materials in new uses, and even new kinds of raw materials. To generalize from a specific example could involve a fallacy of composition.

The third argument takes an interesting twist. It starts with the premise that when technological change occurs in the production of export goods in developed countries, the money price of exports does not fall. Rather, because of the administered pricing behavior of oligopolists in the developed countries and because of the power of unions, the benefits of productivity increases are realized in the form of higher wages and profits while prices remain constant. In contrast, so the argument goes, competition in world markets among the LDCs results in their productivity increases being passed on in the form of lower export prices.[5] Thus with export prices in the developed countries holding constant, the terms of trade turn against the LDCs.

There is a flaw in the argument as stated. Although the terms of trade is an equilibrium concept, the argument has not been carried through to its logical conclusion to determine the impact of the processes described on the trading equilibrium. To see this, consider two developed nations trading with each other with constant domestic price levels, rising wages and profits, and constant terms of trade. Now let country A decide to alter the way its productivity gains are distributed by choosing a policy which holds money wages constant. The money prices of goods (including exports) will fall in A. And the terms of trade, when expressed in money terms, will turn against A. But since all goods are cheaper in A, A's exports will rise and its imports fall. B will start to run a balance-of-payments deficit. B must either lower its domestic price level or devalue its currency to restore balanced trade. In either case, after equilibrium is restored the terms of trade will not have changed. In other words, the phenomenon described in the preceding paragraph could not occur without causing offsetting changes in exchange rates or money price levels which would leave the real terms of trade unchanged.

Validity can be restored to this argument in a way which brings out an essential feature of the economies of the LDCs. Assume rising money prices in the developed nation and falling prices in the LDC. The adjustment described above would have the developed nation buying its manufactured goods (and food) from the now cheaper LDC source, while the LDC would also find it cheaper to substitute domestically produced manufactured goods for imports. This presumes an ability on the part of the LDCs to shift resources into manufacturing, utilizing a similar technology. But an important aspect of underdevelopment is the inability to use modern technology effectively. To the extent that the quality of labor and other factors is lower, or that markets and other information gather-

---

[5] Where all prices are measured in terms of the developed countries' currencies. This proviso is necessary to eliminate the effect of high rates of inflation of domestic price levels common in many LDC's.

ing and disseminating systems are not fully developed, or that cultural values and institutions work to thwart economic incentives, then resource reallocations in response to changes in prices or to comparative advantage will be slow or nonexistent. If it is true that developed countries do exercise the kind of market power described here, to the extent that the LDCs are unable to shift resources out of the declining industries and into rising price industries, the argument has validity. This argument also does not depend on the assumption that LDCs export primary products.

There is another argument to be introduced which tends to weaken the impact of the preceding paragraphs. This argument rests on differential effects of increases in factor supply. However, because of problems in defining factors, it cannot support too great a burden. Ignoring the United States and Australia, suppose that developed countries were rich in capital and scarce in land, while the opposite were true for LDCs. In both types of country, capital would be growing faster than land. Growth would be protrade biased for the developed countries and antitrade biased for the LDCs. And the terms of trade would shift in favor of the latter. When this possibility is combined with the possible opposite tendencies due to income growth and technological change, no simple generalizations or comprehensive predictions about the direction of change of the terms of trade are possible. Once again it all depends. Each particular country's case must be considered separately.

In earlier chapters we have argued that investigators should not rest when they have deduced conclusions from an abstract model. The test of the model and its conclusions is its correspondence with observation. We have found that we are unable to justify the prediction of a general tendency for terms of trade to turn against LDCs. Rather there should be some cases going both ways. What have previous investigators found?

In the original empirical work on this subject, Prebisch claimed to have found a general deterioration in LDCs terms of trade.[6] But his data cannot in fact bear the weight of the argument. The problem is that export and import price indexes for a substantial number of LDCs and covering a sufficiently long time period were not available. Prebisch instead used the terms of trade data for the United Kingdom, covering 1870–1938. He argued that if the U.K. terms of trade improved, and they did, those of the LDCs trading with it must in general have fallen. However, there is an alternative explanation for the observed movement of the U.K. terms of trade which is consistent with constant or rising terms of trade for the U.K.'s trading partners. The U.K.'s import price index values imports at c.i.f. (cost plus insur-

---

[6] See Prebisch, *op. cit.*

ance and freight). Since ocean freight rates declined markedly during the period covered, due to improvements in shipping technology, the "f" component of c.i.f. could have fallen enough to improve the U.K.'s terms of trade, even while export prices in the LDCs were constant or rising. Whether this actually happened is not known, but the tendency was certainly real and substantial. Certainly, if the empirical case rests on this evidence alone, the case is weak.

Other attempts to settle this issue have confronted major data gathering and conceptual problems. For example, it is very difficult to construct an index which adequately takes into consideration the improvements in the quality and productivity of manufactured goods and the introduction of new products over time. More recent studies have tended to come to conflicting conclusions, or no conclusions at all. For example, Morgan constructed terms of trade indexes for India, Japan, New Zealand, South Africa, and Brazil, as well as for the United Kingdom and the United States. He concluded that "the data . . . suggest that emphasis ought to be placed on the heterogeneity of price experience."[7] Morgan's data generally covered the latter part of the nineteenth century and the first half of the twentieth. Kindleberger concluded that there was no evidence that the terms of trade of primary products had deteriorated relative to manufactured goods. However, he did believe that there was a discernible trend against the LDCs and in favor of the developed countries, independent of the type of goods traded.[8] This tends to support the third "structural" argument discussed above. Kindleberger's evidence on this is only suggestive and the prevailing opinion is that the case has not yet been made for deteriorating terms of trade, either for the LDCs as a group, or for primary products as a class, and either empirically or on a priori grounds.

The Volume of Trade Relative to Income

The question here is whether economic growth has resulted in a more than proportionate growth in trade. Or has trade diminished in relative importance as growing nations become relatively more self-sufficient? In other words, on net, has growth been protrade biased or antitrade biased? The question has policy relevance for at least two reasons. First, financial and monetary institutions must be developed and maintained to facilitate the international exchange of goods and services. And the long-run relationship between growth and the volume of trade to be facilitated can be a factor in planning

[7] Theodore Morgan, "The Long-Run Terms of Trade Between Agriculture and Manufacturing," *Economic Development and Cultural Change*, 8, No. 1 (Oct., 1959), 21.

[8] Charles P. Kindleberger, *The Terms of Trade: A European Case Study*, New York, Wiley, 1956.

for the future reform or expansion of the international monetary system.

Second, past and future trends in the world volume of trade can be a factor in establishing development strategies for LDCs, where one of the issues is whether to channel resources to export development or to import substitution. This is not to say that if investigation shows that growth tended to be protrade biased in the past, these countries should try to make trade grow rapidly now. History will not necessarily repeat itself. And association does not prove causality. We leave to the next section the question of the effect of trade on growth rates. Here we deal with the question within the more limited framework established in the previous chapter where the causality runs from growth to trade. In other words, given observed growth rates, what does our model predict would happen to the flows of trade relative to income levels?

Our model and a priori reasoning suggest that four kinds of tendencies would be at work.[9] On the demand side it has been argued that modern consumption trends are antitrade biased since the income elasticity of demand for nontraded services is greater than that for goods which enter international trade. On the supply side, the principal factor thought to be affecting trade through growth is the nature of technological change. We learned that if technological change tends to favor or "save" the scarce factor, it will be antitrade biased, if other things are equal. Suppose that technological change is sensitive to incentives. In other words, suppose that resources tend to be directed toward solving those problems which have the highest potential payoff, and the rates of discovery and innovation depend on the amounts of resources devoted to research. This would lead to technological change with a consistent bias toward saving the scarce factor in all countries. This, of course, is inconsistent with the traditional Heckscher-Ohlin assumption of a universal technology available to all. But in a dynamic setting, the two can be reconciled. New discoveries will tend to be adopted first in their "home" countries. There is also a premium for imitating successful innovators. But this also tends to favor antitrade biased imitations of successful imitators since the premium or reward for imitation of a given discovery is highest in countries with similar factor endowments. The new technology is eventually learned by all, but the speed and pattern of its dispersal is sensitive to relative factor scarcities.

A third factor which will be consistently protrade biased for all countries is the effect of technology in lowering transportation costs.

---

[9] The following discussion is based on Richard N. Cooper, "Growth and Trade: Some Hypotheses About Long-Term Trends," *Journal of Economic History*, 24, No. 4 (Dec., 1964), 609–628.

The fourth factor, trade policy, worked against trade as tariff barriers rose from the end of the nineteenth century to World War II. Subsequently, tariff barriers in general have been lowered, favoring the growth of trade relative to income.

The model suggests conflicting forces, with demand and biased innovation retarding trade, trade policy working with these forces until after World War II, and declining transportation costs working in the opposite direction throughout the period. What is the evidence? Cooper has reviewed several earlier studies and provided additional evidence of his own.[10] He argued that historical U.S. trade data do not support the hypothesis of diminishing importance of trade; and that international comparisons over time and across countries at a point in time provide some support for the rising importance of trade hypothesis. For example, a comparison of countries in 1955 showed that, at least above a certain per capita income level, countries with higher incomes tended to have higher ratios of trade to income. This finding does not support the demand hypothesis concerning nontraded services.

Cooper's own evidence was gathered from an examination of changes in U.S. regional comparative advantage and interregional trade over time. He found that while regional comparative advantages were diminishing between 1840 and 1960, interregional trade was increasing as a percentage of GNP. This led Cooper to speculate on possible influences and relationships between trade and growth which are not captured in the conventional model of Chapter 12. For one thing, innovation can be in the form of new products as well as new processes for making the same old stuff. Product innovation will tend to be protrade biased. High-income countries tend to support firms with larger R&D expenditures; and if R&D expenditure and innovation are proportional to the size of the industry, large economies will tend to have relatively more innovation and therefore trade.[11] Second, if economies of scale are important, firms will tend to specialize and grow to realize these economies. If technological change makes the optimum size of firm or plant grow more rapidly than income, trade based on economies of scale will grow more rapidly than income, too. The third possible influence is demand-related. Cooper hypothesized a high-income elasticity of demand for differentiated products, variety, and trade-related services such as transportation and tourism.

It must be recognized that these possible hypotheses are *ex post* rationalizations and have not received independent tests. But it

[10] *Ibid.*, 614–623.
[11] This is closely related to the Hufbauer-Vernon product cycle model. See Chapter 8, pp. 125–127.

216 is interesting that they are closely related to some of the approaches to trade theory discussed in Chapter 8, and that they all involve breaking out of the conventional Heckscher-Ohlin framework and directly confronting the problems of dynamic changes in technology and tastes.

THE EFFECTS OF TRADE ON GROWTH
IN THE LESS-DEVELOPED COUNTRIES

Does trade play a leading or a major supportive role in economic growth? Or does trade inhibit growth? Or as Meier has put it, ". . . the overriding question [is] whether there is a conflict between the gains from trade and the gains from growth—whether the process of development is facilitated or handicapped through international trade."[12] The distinction between the gains from trade and the gains from growth is important and worth reviewing. The gains from trade refer to the difference between national income with trade and the hypothetical national income with no trade under the same conditions of factor endowments and technology. Their size is determined by the relative factor endowments and demand conditions in both countries as they shape each nation's offer curve. The gain from growth is the increase in actual national income from one period to the next as a consequence of increases in factor supplies and technological change. The question is whether trade will hinder or help a growing nation to convert its increases in factor supplies and technology into increases in income.

This section is limited to the LDCs because continued economic growth in the developed countries is not a problem in the conventional sense. Rather we face the question of what form our growth should take in view of increasing congestion and the deterioration of our environment. But the LDCs do not yet have the luxury of this problem. For them the question of how to increase physical output per person is very real, in some cases desperately so.

Once we have posed a question, the next step, normally, would be to build a model to see what could be learned from it. We are at a bit of a loss here because of the lack of readily applicable models of the growth process which describe how growth begins or explains why one country grows and another does not. However, we can describe a process of successful growth through trade, or what has been called *export-led growth,* and then try to find out what conditions appear to be prerequisites for its occurrence. Consider an

[12] Gerald M. Meier, *International Trade and Economic Development,* New York, Harper & Row, 1968, p. 8.

underdeveloped country with little capital or skilled labor. The only kind of good it can have a comparative advantage in is some kind of raw material or primary product, under these assumptions. If there is a strong and rising demand for this good in the developed center, the stage is set for export-led growth.

Before exports can occur, investments must be made to develop and exploit the source of supply. Foreign countries bring in their knowledge and their capital to develop the resource. Foreign investment makes up for the lack of domestic capital in the LDC. The development of the mines, railroads, port facilities, and other necessary capital investments might have no further impact on the domestic economy. The result could be a "dual economy" with a stagnant domestic sector and a foreign-owned resource exploiting enclave. If export-led growth is to occur, the investment in the export sector must stimulate further investments in the remainder of the economy or provide spillover benefits to the domestic sector. Investments can be stimulated through backward and forward linkages with suppliers to the export sectors or to producers attracted to the area to take advantage of proximity to the source of supply. Spillovers arise if the development of the export sector requires investments in *social overhead capital* such as roads, education, and power systems. Three things could thwart the growth process. On the domestic side, if income were very unequally distributed, with the income generated by the export sector being divided between the foreign investors and a leisure-oriented ruling class, further domestic capital formation would be unlikely. Also, if the domestic sector were so traditional or lacking in an entrepreneurial tradition as to be unresponsive to the incentives and opportunities offered by the export sector, there would be no further domestic growth. Also, if export demand were to fall, the stimulus for growth would be lacking.

To summarize, for successful export-led growth to occur, export demand must be strong, there must be linkages and spillovers into the domestic economy from the foreign investment, and the domestic economy must be responsive and able to mobilize resources from traditional uses and redirect them into growth-oriented activities.

It is generally agreed that the export of primary products was an "engine of growth" during the nineteenth century, particularly for the United States, Canada, Australia, New Zealand, and Argentina, and must play an important role in explaining the economic growth of these countries. But there is not yet agreement as to whether this historical experience has any relevance to the less-developed countries today. Haberler has argued that trade can still provide important dynamic benefits such as inducing foreign capital investments, facilitating the transmission of new technology (embodied in exports to the LDCs) and skills, and the bracing effects of competition in world and domestic markets.[13]

The opposite view has been argued by Nurkse, among others.[14] Nurkse asserts that the engine of growth has been considerably slowed down, if not halted, because it is low on its fuel, the strong and growing demand for the primary product exports of the LDCs. According to Nurkse, demand for primary products has lagged behind the growth and export of manufactured goods in the twentieth century. In the nineteenth century, protrade biased growth in the United Kingdom first, and later Western Europe, meant rapidly expanding demand for primary exports. In effect, Nurkse is arguing that growth in the developed countries has become much less protrade biased, at least in terms of primary products, and that as a result further growth at the center is not pulling along the peripheral LDCs. The reasons he presents are familiar: low-income elasticity of demand for agricultural products, innovation which economizes on natural resource inputs into production, and the growth of synthetics based on petrochemicals, among others.

In a review and commentary on both Haberler's and Nurkse's work, Cairncross has argued that the data do not support Nurkse's contention of lagging demand. The decline in primary products trade has not been as universal as implied by Nurkse and, where it has occurred, it can be explained by factors other than the demand conditions cited above. Actually, the nineteenth century was an extraordinary period with the rapid industrialization of Western Europe and the United States, and a rapid shift to rich newly discovered sources of primary materials. Furthermore, these sources were in a much better position to benefit from trade than today's LDCs because of quite different internal conditions.[15]

To summarize, the nineteenth century saw rapid industrialization in Western Europe. Trade in primary products extended the benefits of industrialization to the regions of recent settlement and resulted in their sharing the benefits of growth and the associated high levels of material well-being. Continued growth at the center has not led to the same kind of dramatic extension of its benefits to the remaining LDCs during the twentieth century. This may be due to lagging demand for primary products, as Nurkse contends, or it may have its roots in the different characteristics of the present LDCs. In any event, we should not look to trade to play a dominant role in reducing the disparities of incomes among nations in this century, except

[13] Gottfried Haberler, *International Trade—Economic Development*, National Bank of Egypt, 50th Anniversary Commemoration Lectures, 1959, reprinted in James Theberge, *Economics of Trade and Development*, New York, Wiley, 1968.

[14] Ragnar Nurkse, *Problems in Capital Formation in Underdeveloped Countries and Patterns of Trade and Development*, New York, Oxford University Press, 1967, pp. 163–226.

[15] A. Cairncross, *Factors in Economic Development*, London, Allen & Unwin, 1962.

perhaps for some major oil-producing nations where conditions for export-led growth are favorable or where the extraordinary wealth could be used consciously to create the necessary conditions.

SUMMARY

In this book we have attempted to present the main elements of the modern theory of international trade and to describe how this body of theory has been developed and tested empirically. We have applied the theory in the areas of trade policy, economic integration, and economic growth to test its explanatory power and its usefulness in policy analysis. It is time to summarize briefly what we know about the power and limitations of this body of theory. The power of the Heckscher-Ohlin model lies in its elegant simplicity, its representation of many complex economic relationships in terms of a few easily understood generalizations. The same framework can be used to analyze problems of tariff policy, integration, and growth.

The framework enables the analyst to focus on the few important relationships involved in each of these cases. But in almost every case, specific answers are difficult to come by because they depend on the relative values of difficult-to-observe variables. For example, has innovation in fact been antitrade biased in developed countries? How does one measure relative factor endowments when education and natural resources are of recognized importance? Another major limitation of the modern body of theory is its capacity to deal systematically with the dynamic forces of innovation and new resource and product discovery. This limitation is apparent in the discussions of the dynamic effects of economic integration and the effect of trade on growth and development.

The development of economic theory might be described as an unending race as our knowledge and understanding try to keep up with newly emerging questions. The questions may arise simply because of our curiosity and desire to explain the world to ourselves. But more often the questions are there because of problems which require action. And we cannot or should not act until we understand and can predict the consequences of our actions. For example, the widespread interest in the theory of economic integration after 1955 was obviously stimulated by the fact that integration was going to occur, if as much for political reasons as economic. The growing awareness of and concern for the disparities in income levels among countries stimulated the field of economic development and consideration of the possible role of international trade in either causing or helping to close these income gaps. As long as substantial disparities in levels of development persist, we can count on continued interest and effort in this area of theory.

We can also count on continued efforts to strengthen the weak areas of the existing theory, especially in the areas of dynamics and the definitions and measurements of factor endowments and technology. Other areas for continued work include the international flow of factors of production, both capital and human beings (the brain drain), nontariff barriers to trade, and trade with nonmarket economies (so-called state trading). As for new areas, guesses or predictions can prove embarrassing. But one possibility seems to me to be particularly likely to come to the fore. This is the international or global dimension of the environmental quality/resource/population problem. There are many possible international ramifications of this complex set of issues, too many to spell out here. But one pertinent example is illustrative of the range of problems. Continued high rates of use of persistent pesticides such as DDT can be expected to raise residual pesticide levels in the oceans. The possible long-run effects of this are not clear; but they could include impairment of the ocean's vital function as a source of oxygen for the oxygen-consuming continents. Some of the possible outcomes could be irreversible and catastrophic. A worldwide ban on the use of DDT would fall most heavily on the LDCs, for it is they who are most dependent on DDT (which is inexpensive and easy to apply) for increasing productivity in agriculture. What would be the cost to the LDCs of such a ban? If such a ban were imposed, how would the LDCs be compensated for the burden they are being asked to bear? How would this affect the structure of comparative advantage and trade flows, and the rates of growth and development in both the LDCs and the rest of the world? These are intriguing and challenging and important questions.

SUPPLEMENTARY READINGS

Kindleberger, Charles, *International Economics,* 4th ed., Homewood, Ill., Irwin, 1968, chaps. 4, 5.

Meier, Gerald M., *The International Economics of Development,* New York, Harper & Row, 1968.

Hicks, John R., "National Economic Development in the International Setting," in *Essay in World Economics,* Oxford, England, Clarendon, 1959.
1959.

Chenery, Hollis B., "Comparative Advantage and Development Policy," *American Economic Review,* 51, No. 1 (March, 1961).

Johnson, Harry G., *Comparative Cost and Commercial Policy Theory for a Developing World Economy,* Wicksell Lectures, 1968, Stockholm, Almquist and Wiksell, 1969.

Myint, Hla, "The Gains from International Trade and the Backward Countries," *The Review of Economic Statistics,* 22, No. 58 (1954–1955).

Index

382
Freeman, A. Myrick
International trade.